THIRD THURSDAY
COMMUNITY POTLUCK
COOKBOOK

THIRD THURSDAY
COMMUNITY POTLUCK
COOKBOOK

RECIPES AND STORIES TO CELEBRATE
THE BOUNTY OF THE MOMENT

NANCY VIENNEAU

NELSON
BOOKS

An Imprint of Thomas Nelson

Published in Nashville, Tennessee, by Nelson Books, an imprint of Thomas Nelson. Nelson Books and Thomas Nelson are registered trademarks of HarperCollins Christian Publishing, Inc.

Photography by Mark Boughton
Candid photos courtesy of Teresa Blackburn
Photos on pages 67, 126, 144, and 247 from Shutterstock.com

Food and Prop Styling by Teresa Blackburn

Special thanks to Chilewich and Pat McNellis for the modern placemats.

Thomas Nelson, Inc., titles may be purchased in bulk for educational, business, fund-raising, or sales promotional use. For information, please e-mail SpecialMarkets@ThomasNelson.com.

Library of Congress Cataloging-in-Publication Data

Vienneau, Nancy, 1954–
  The third thursday community potluck cookbook : recipes and stories to celebrate the bounty of the moment / Nancy Vienneau, Nancy Vienneau.
     pages cm
  Includes index.
  ISBN 978-1-4016-0517-9 (hardback)
  1. Cooking, American. 2. Seasonal cooking. I. Title.
  TX715.V6234 2014
  641.5'64—dc23   2013046633

Printed in the United States of America

14 15 16 17 18 QG 6 5 4 3 2 1

Gigi, my potluck partner-in-crime, who had the inspiration

Bill, who encouraged my writing all the way

Heather, who caught the vision

Teresa, who knew forty years ago in our printmaking studio
we'd be working on this cookbook together?

And all the Third Thursday potluckers, come and gone and still abiding

....

In fondest memory of John Egerton, our friend, whose generous spirit
always sought to bring more people, food, and stories to the table.

Contents

....

A Potluck Like No Other

WELCOME TO THIRD THURSDAY.

What good things might we find spread out upon the harvest table this time?

We've had crusty homemade pretzels with stout mustard and farmstead pimento cheese on sesame-onion crackers. Chicken grilled in a barbecue sauce made from just-picked garden raspberries. Savory pork shoulder braised with plump figs. Local burgers with real-deal ketchup. Fancy-Pants Shepherd's Pie.

We've dipped our spoons into bowls of warm potato salad flecked with Benton's bacon, fresh asparagus tips dressed in lush herbed Green Goddess aioli, and brilliant red beet-cider quinoa. We've devoured butternut squash–leek lasagna, tomato-mozzarella strata, and Cuban grilled corn with lime. We've sipped iced watermelon-lemongrass refreshers; autumn tonics heady with rum, star anise, pear juice, and pomegranates; and tangy cilantro lemonade.

We mustn't forget desserts. Sumptuous desserts! How about fresh-churned strawberry ice cream with strawberry-filled Victoria sponge cake? Or a chocolate-cayenne tart? Glazed lemon-rosemary cookies? Cherry-peach clafoutis? Or a passion fruit Pavlova?

At our Third Thursday Community Potluck, we never know what kinds of tasty dishes will find their way to the feast. But as we head into our sixth year of monthly gatherings, we've come to trust that they will be extraordinary. As Rhonda, one of our dedicated potluckers, says, "What happens here is not your usual potluck."

It's a potluck like no other.

YOUR THIRD THURSDAY HOSTS

I'm Nancy Vienneau, a chef, "recovering" caterer, and food writer living in Nashville, Tennessee. My cohost, Gigi Gaskins, is a hat maker who developed an urban farm on once-blighted lots in our city's Wedgewood neighborhood. Both food activists, we met at a local summit on food security. There, we learned that we were also neighbors, living just blocks from each other. We soon became friends.

We started talking about community-minded things and decided it would be cool to host a once-a-month potluck gathering of folks, to get a cross-section of friends and acquaintances to meet, share food, and talk about what they're growing, cooking, eating, and advocating.

A CASUAL GATHERING OF GOOD FOOD

There's nothing formal about our potluck. No assigned dishes. No RSVP. We wanted to lightly structure it and allow for those creative sparks that happen in a more spontaneous space. There's an element of surrender in that, but it always works out.

The constant is this: we hold the potluck on the third Thursday of each month, at 6:30 p.m. We alternate the site between our homes, although we've met at other venues, such as Gigi's lovely urban garden oasis. Beyond that, guests can bring friends and whatever food and beverage strikes their fancy.

We should note that this differs from a supper club or a neighborhood dinner. Together, Gigi and I know a lot of different people from all around town who do not know each other. More than eighty receive our e-mail invitation; anywhere from twenty-five to thirty attend each time.

The connection is a love of cooking and sharing good food—emphasis on sharing. At the potluck you could meet a food stylist, community gardener, writer, caterer, or food journal publisher, but also a nurse, real estate broker, architect, musician, philosophy student, and organic soap maker. It's always different, just like the food!

People bring seasonal dishes, using produce from their gardens, CSAs, or farmers' markets, and they bring their best efforts. In forming plans for our contributions, Gigi and I take into account what's ready to harvest.

For the launch of our first Third Thursday in June 2009, twenty-eight people came bearing splendid covered dishes and casseroles, cakes, salads, and sangria! So fun! And, remarkably, there were no overlaps or cop-outs. No umpteen bowls of potato salad. No limp bags of baby carrots and tubs of commercial onion dip.

That convivial feast was heavy on fresh, local veggies, with a tantalizing balance of desserts. And in the months to follow, it continued to blossom into a fluid, creative, and much-anticipated gathering. People sampled new dishes and made new friends. A few discovered nascent cooking talents. We've seen a couple of marriages, three births, a divorce, numerous career changes, grad school enrollments, and independent businesses launched.

Our Third Thursday has formed its own community.

Each month we never know what people or food or feeling the potluck will bring.

Each month we celebrate the bounty of the moment.

In that celebratory spirit, we'd like to share our favorite recipes, month by month. Consider it a potlucker's best. And we've assembled some potluck tips. We hope it will inspire you to start your own Third Thursday.

First Solstice

OUR BEGINNING, ON THE CUSP OF SUMMER. WHEN FRESHLY DUG POTATOES STILL HAVE A DUSTING OF fine silt, and sweet onions bulge out of the earth. Cucumbers, wrinkled and small, dangle on a crisscross of trellised vines. Arugula, rangy and potent, begins to bolt.

Beginnings, by nature, are uncertain. In preparing for our first community potluck, our thoughts occasionally gravitated to worry: *Will we have enough food? Will people like it? Will anybody come?* Those concerns were natural, but ran contrary to the joy and purpose of the gathering.

Beginnings also brim with promise.

Better to launch the event, we decided, keeping these three things in mind. Call them Potluck Axioms: Use what you've got. Draw on what you know. And—the most important—let it go, confident that you're putting your best out there. It's potluck!

After Gigi and I sent out our first Third Thursday invitations, we sat down together to strategize.

We had the practical aspects covered. Between the two of us, we had plenty of dinner plates and forks. Gigi had purchased bundles of green linen napkins—price greatly reduced—from a big box store. We'd assembled a hodgepodge of glassware, Mason jars included.

What to cook?

It came down to those potluck axioms.

Gigi's experimental crop of fennel was thriving. There were numerous bulbs with lacy feather-headed fronds ready to harvest. I had snatched an armful of plums from my backyard tree (before squirrels and birds could enjoy them all), and they were in a kitchen basket, plump and ripening.

One vegetable and one fruit triggered the inspiration for two dishes: a shaved fennel salad, layered with orange slices, awash in lemon basil-citrus vinaigrette, and chicken brined in Asian spices, roasted with my clutch of plums.

A salad, a main . . . anything else?

Gigi wanted to serve a stellar dessert, and her Pavlova is the stuff of dreams. So was her preferred fruit to adorn the dish: passion fruit—lush and tropical, and nowhere to be found in the month of June. But, in the end, sliced fresh strawberries floated just as beautifully on that cloud of cream mounded on crisp shells of meringue.

As we set up the buffet for the first potluck, we laughed. If no one else showed up, we'd have a fine dinner of our salad, roast chicken, and Pavlova. But at 6:30 p.m., there was a knock at the door. Gigi's cousin Bryan was the first to arrive, bearing a bowl of spiced couscous. In followed Teresa and Liz carrying a pitcher of chilled melon soup and a salad with cucumbers, mangos, and jicama. Paulette brought herbed dumplings. A friend of a friend showed up with poached salmon. New faces, new foods! Our eyes widened. The table was becoming crowded with assorted covered dishes. The room filled with the happy clamor of people sharing food and stories.

Third Thursday was off and running.

JUNE: FIRST SOLSTICE

Garden Margarita

Cooling Cantaloupe Soup

Plumgood Roast Chicken

Layered Orange-Fennel Salad with Orange Vinaigrette

Teresa's Cucumber Salad with a Caribbean Twist

Oven-Poached Side of Salmon with Yogurt-Dill Sauce

Smoked Gouda and Spring Pea Risotto

Vidalia Onion Pie with Cornbread Crust

Warm German-Style Potato Salad with Benton's Bacon

Italian Cheese Dumplings with 3-Herb and Arugula Pesto Sauce

Chocolate Truffle Ring with Raspberry Whipped Cream

Fresh Dill-Feta Quick Bread

Gigi's Pavlova

You can't really say you are drinking a salad in a glass, but cucumber does add a really refreshing note to this cocktail while tempering the habanero sting.

GARDEN MARGARITA

SIMPLE SYRUP

1/2 cup water

2 habaneros, diced

1/4 teaspoon sea salt

3 black peppercorns

1/2 cup agave nectar

❯ In a small saucepan add the water, diced habaneros, salt, and peppercorns. Stir in the agave nectar. Place over medium-high heat. Bring to a simmer, and let it simmer for 1 minute. Remove from stove and allow to cool. When cool, strain and discard the habanero pieces and peppercorns.

MARGARITA

1 large cucumber, peeled and chopped

6 basil leaves

Juice of 6 fresh limes

Simple syrup

1 pint tequila

Pomegranate seeds for garnish

❯ Place the cucumber, basil, and lime juice into a blender. Process until smooth. Add the simple syrup. Mix until well combined. Pour into a shaker, and top with the tequila. Shake. Place the pomegranate seeds into a large glass jar or bottle. Pour the tequila-cucumber mixture into that container, and chill well.

❯ Shake well and pour into ice-filled glasses. Garnish with more pomegranate seeds, if desired.

Makes 8 servings.

COCKTAIL-MAKING TIPS

Throughout the chapters, you'll find an array of beverages—some alcoholic, some not—all of which derive inspiration from our gardens and cupboards.

Nancy Davidson, a professional food writer and mixologist, attended our potluck on one of her visits to Nashville. She shared with us her Garden Margarita and now shares these cocktail-making tips:

- Use the same principles as you do in cooking.
- Combine ingredients that complement one another.
- Include the basic cocktail flavors: sweet, sour, bitter, and strong (alcohol). Good cocktails have a balance of those four components.
- Mix them up as a big batch that can be transported in a nonreactive container, such as a large Mason jar or other sealable glass bottle or jug.

This soup is cooling to the eyes and the palate. Because taste can vary from melon to melon, sample this as you make it. The lime juice and sherry vinegar add dimension to the soup and counter the melon's natural sweetness. The honey brings balance.

COOLING CANTALOUPE SOUP

2 ripe cantaloupes, peeled, seeded, and cut into chunks (6 cups of fruit)

1-inch piece of fresh ginger, peeled and julienned

1 cup orange juice

4 tablespoons fresh lime juice

2 tablespoons sherry vinegar

4 teaspoons local honey

1 teaspoon salt

1/2 teaspoon black pepper

2 cups plain yogurt

Fresh mint leaves or basil for garnish

❯ Working in batches, place the cantaloupe chunks and ginger into a blender or food processor fitted with a chopping blade. Pulse and puree them, adding a little of the orange juice at a time. Pour into a large bowl.

❯ Add the lime juice, sherry vinegar, honey, salt, and pepper. Whisk until well blended. Whisk in the yogurt until thoroughly combined. Taste for seasonings and correct as needed. Cover and chill until serving time. Pour into bowls and top with mint leaves or basil for garnish.

Makes 2 quarts.

My first harvest of plums inspired this recipe. Sweet and sour Asian flavors infuse the chicken in this simple overnight brine.

PLUMGOOD ROAST CHICKEN

1 gallon water

1 cup firmly packed brown sugar

1 cup hoisin sauce

2 tablespoons chopped fresh ginger

1 teaspoon red pepper flakes

4 garlic cloves, chopped

1 cup sliced ripe plums

1 cup rice wine vinegar

1 whole chicken

12 fresh ripe plums, halved and pitted

1/2 to 1 teaspoon paprika to dust over the chicken

❯ In a large tub or small cooler mix the water, brown sugar, hoisin, ginger, red pepper flakes, garlic, sliced plums, and rice wine vinegar. Place the cleaned chicken into the tub and refrigerate overnight.

❯ Preheat the oven to 375 degrees.

❯ Remove the chicken from the brine, drain, and truss.* Lay chicken in the baking pan. Surround with the halved plums. Sprinkle paprika over the chicken. Bake uncovered for 60 to 70 minutes.

❯ Remove the chicken from the pan, reserving the fruit and juices, and place on a cutting board to rest for 15 minutes before carving. Snip and discard the twine. Cut off the wings and drumsticks and carve the breast and thighs into slices. Arrange slices, wings, and drumsticks on a platter. Spoon baked fruits and juices from the baking pan over the chicken.

Makes 6 servings.

*Trussing the chicken makes for a nice presentation and, more important, ensures a moister, more evenly cooked bird. See sidebar on page 8 for instructions.

TRUST TRUSSING

To truss, you'll need about 3 feet of kitchen twine. Place the chicken, breast side up, on your work board. Center the length of twine underneath the tail. Bring the twine around the chicken and crisscross the twine, looping it around the ends of the drumsticks. Pull tight to close the drumsticks together. Bring the twine around the sides of the chicken and over the wings. Flip the chicken over so the neck is facing you. Crisscross the twine around the neck, pulling tight. Tie the twine off around the neck. Trim excess twine. Flip the chicken to breast side up. The trussed bird is ready to roast.

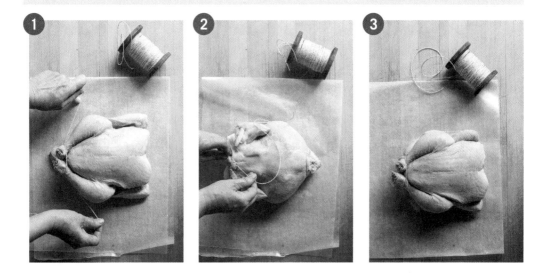

Fennel is a curious-looking plant, bulbous with wispy fronds. It is really making a comeback in gardens and at the market. Delicious braised or roasted, it's also excellent raw, shaved into salads and slaw. Here, the citrus enlivens fennel's subtle anise flavor. The "pyramid" layering makes a stunning presentation.

LAYERED ORANGE-FENNEL SALAD WITH ORANGE VINAIGRETTE

4 fennel bulbs, fronds removed, bulbs peeled, cored, and thinly shaved crossways

1 small sweet onion, thinly sliced

Orange Vinaigrette (recipe follows)

2 oranges, peeled and thinly sliced into rounds (13 slices)

1 bunch lemon basil, chopped*

A few curls of shaved Parmigiano-Reggiano cheese

❯ Mix the fennel and onion together in a large bowl, and use about half of the Orange Vinaigrette to lightly coat the vegetables. Place a layer of sliced oranges on a platter, 9 slices in 3 rows of 3. Layer with half the fennel-onion mixture. Top with a third of the lemon basil and half of the curls of Parmigiano-Reggiano.

❯ For the next layer, place 4 orange slices in 2 rows of 2, then the other half of the fennel-onion mixture, then a third of the lemon basil, and finally the rest of the cheese, until you've built a stacked pyramid! Drizzle with the remaining dressing. Garnish with the rest of the lemon basil, and serve.

Makes 8 servings.

*If you are not able to locate lemon basil, you may substitute regular basil and still have great taste.

ORANGE VINAIGRETTE

1 tablespoon orange zest

2 tablespoons orange juice

2 teaspoons dry mustard

1/4 cup white wine vinegar

1/2 teaspoon salt

1/2 teaspoon black pepper

1 cup extra-virgin olive oil

❯ In a small bowl mix the orange zest, orange juice, dry mustard, vinegar, salt, and pepper. While whisking, slowly drizzle in the olive oil until it emulsifies.

Makes 1 1/2 cups.

When Teresa took a trip to the Yucatán, she had a version of this vibrant salad in a restaurant in Mérida. She made it for us using cucumber and radishes from her little backyard garden. Sweet, tart, fresh, and crunchy—it is tasty on its own or served over grilled fish or steak.

TERESA'S CUCUMBER SALAD WITH A CARIBBEAN TWIST

25 radishes, trimmed, rinsed, and chopped

1 large cucumber, peeled, seeded, and diced

1 handful fresh cilantro, trimmed and chopped

1 small jicama or 1/2 large jicama, peeled and chopped

2 mangoes, peeled and chopped

Juice of 2 oranges

Juice of 2 limes

4 tablespoons olive oil

2 tablespoons balsamic vinegar

2 tablespoons local honey

1/2 teaspoon kosher salt

Freshly ground black pepper to taste

◉ Place the chopped radishes, cucumber, cilantro, jicama, and mangoes in a large bowl and toss well. In a small bowl whisk together the orange and lime juices, olive oil, balsamic vinegar, and honey. Add salt and a few grinds of black pepper and stir. Pour the vinaigrette over the salad mixture and toss until coated with the dressing. Cover and chill for at least 1 hour before serving.

Makes 20 (1/4 cup side or topping) servings.

Oven poaching in a lemony white wine bath imbues the fillet with flavor while ensuring moist, tender planks of fish. The salmon looks appealing, too, decorated with fresh dill and lemon and served with little side bowls of capers, diced onion, and dill sauce. You might enjoy serving this as an appetizer to your group.

OVEN-POACHED SIDE OF SALMON WITH YOGURT-DILL SAUCE

1 (2-pound) side of salmon

2 tablespoons extra-virgin olive oil

1 teaspoon salt

1/2 teaspoon black pepper

1/2 teaspoon paprika

1 cup white wine

1 cup water

2 lemons, 1 for juice, 1 sliced into thin rounds

1 medium shallot, thinly sliced

2 tablespoons chopped fresh dill, plus more for garnish

Finely chopped red onions for garnish

Capers for garnish

Yogurt-Dill Sauce
(recipe on page 12)

❯ Preheat the oven to 325 degrees.

❯ Coat the salmon with olive oil and sprinkle with salt, pepper, and paprika. Fill the bottom of a 9 x 13-inch casserole dish with the white wine, water, and the juice of 1 lemon. Add the sliced shallot, 2 tablespoons chopped dill, and lemon slices. Save a few lemon slices for garnish.

❯ Place the salmon into its poaching bath. Cover the dish with foil and place in the oven. Bake for 25 to 30 minutes. Remove and allow to cool before chilling in the refrigerator.

❯ When ready to serve, remove the skin (it should peel away easily) and discard. Place the side onto a long platter. Run a knife along the "spine" of the fillet, and make small diagonal incisions—serving slices—radiating off the length of the primary cut.

❯ Garnish the top with sliced lemon rounds and fresh dill. Serve with side bowls of finely chopped red onion, capers, and Yogurt-Dill Sauce.

Makes 6 to 8 servings as an entrée, or 12 to 15 (or more!) as an hors d'oeuvre.

This sauce pairs perfectly with the salmon, but you'll find that it also makes a terrific veggie dip or dressing for new potato salad.

YOGURT-DILL SAUCE

1 1/2 cups plain Greek yogurt

1 tablespoon coarse-grain mustard

1 tablespoon white wine vinegar

1 tablespoon extra-virgin olive oil

2 heaping tablespoons chopped fresh dill

1 tablespoon chopped fresh chives

1 1/2 teaspoons sea salt

1/2 teaspoon black pepper

❯ In a medium bowl combine the yogurt, mustard, vinegar, olive oil, dill, chives, salt, and pepper, and whisk until well blended. Cover and refrigerate, allowing an hour for the flavors to develop.

Makes 1 3/4 cups.

Mark started his risotto at home and finished it at the potluck. The cheese imparts smoky richness and keeps the texture extra creamy. This batch feeds a crowd—and leftovers can be formed into patties, dusted with flour, and pan-fried into delectable risotto cakes.

SMOKED GOUDA AND SPRING PEA RISOTTO

3 cups water

4 cups vegetable stock

2 tablespoons butter

1 medium onion, diced small

1 medium shallot, diced small

2 cloves garlic, minced

1/2 teaspoon salt

1/2 teaspoon white pepper

2 1/2 cups Arborio rice

1 cup white wine

3 cups early June peas (use fresh shelled or frozen)

2 cups shredded smoked Gouda cheese

◉ In a large saucepan over medium heat, mix the water and vegetable broth together. Bring to a simmer.

◉ In another large pot over medium heat, melt the butter and sauté the onion and shallot for 2 minutes. Add garlic and sauté for another minute. Season with salt and white pepper. Add the rice and stir until all the grains are coated. Cook for 2 more minutes, allowing the grains to get toasted. Stir in the white wine, a little at a time, until it is absorbed.

◉ Ladle in the warm water–vegetable stock solution, a few spoonsful at a time. Keep stirring throughout the cooking process. The rice will plump up and get a glossy look. It will also release its starches, making a creamy broth. Cook for 20 minutes and add the fresh shelled peas. (If you are using frozen peas, add them after 25 minutes.) Cook 10 more minutes, folding in the cheese during the last minutes of cooking. Taste for seasonings, adjust, and serve.

Makes 16 servings.

The inspiration for this savory pie came from a pie tasting in Dahlonega, Georgia, that one of our intrepid potluckers, Jennifer, attended. I recreated it based on her exquisite description of the dish. The cornbread crust and the caramelized ultra-sweet Vidalias are what make this pie remarkable or, in Jennifer's words, "crazy-good."

VIDALIA ONION PIE WITH CORNBREAD CRUST

CRUST

1/2 cup cornmeal (I used white cornmeal, but either will work)

1/2 cup all-purpose flour

1 teaspoon baking powder

1/2 teaspoon salt

1 large egg

2 tablespoons chilled butter

4 tablespoons ice-cold water

FILLING

1 tablespoon butter

3 medium Vidalia onions, sliced

2 large eggs

1 cup half-and-half

1/2 teaspoon salt

1/4 teaspoon black pepper

1 cup shredded white Cheddar cheese

1/2 cup kernel sweet corn (can be fresh or frozen)

4 sprigs fresh thyme

Freshly ground black pepper to taste

❯ Coat a 9-inch deep-dish pie pan with nonstick cooking spray.

❯ Sift the cornmeal, flour, baking powder, and salt together in a small bowl, and place in a food processor fitted with a pastry blade. Add the egg and butter, and pulse until mixed. Add the water 1 tablespoon at a time and pulse. This will form a sticky mass of dough. Press the dough into the prepared pie pan. If the dough is too sticky, add a little cornmeal. Set aside while you make the filling.

❯ Preheat the oven to 375 degrees.

❯ Heat a large skillet over medium heat and melt the butter. Add the onions and toss until lightly coated. Sauté the onions for about 15 minutes, stirring occasionally, until caramelized. Remove from the heat and allow to cool.

❯ In a small bowl beat the eggs, half-and-half, salt, and pepper together well, until there is no trace of the yolk. Layer the bottom of the pie crust with about half of the shredded cheese. Sprinkle with the corn kernels, then add the onions. Pour the egg custard mixture over this. Top with the remaining Cheddar, the leaves from the sprigs of thyme, and a few grindings of black pepper. Bake for 35 to 40 minutes. The top will feel set and be nicely browned.

Makes 8 to 10 servings.

Allen Benton, of Madisonville, Tennessee, has become legendary for his thick-slab cut, slow-smoked bacon, sought out by chefs nationwide. We're lucky that a few area markets carry it, although Benton's offers prompt mail order. That bacon and its drippings bring smoky Southern goodness to this German potato salad.

WARM GERMAN-STYLE POTATO SALAD WITH BENTON'S BACON

4 pounds new potatoes

12 ounces thick-slab cut bacon (such as Benton's)

1 cup chopped well-cleaned leeks, white and some green parts

1/2 cup cider vinegar

1 tablespoon yellow mustard seeds

1 tablespoon local honey

Coarse ground black pepper to taste

1 bunch fresh chives, chopped, for garnish

1 bunch fresh parsley, chopped, for garnish

❯ Bring a large pot of salty water almost to a boil over high heat. Place the unpeeled new potatoes in the pot. Make sure the water covers the spuds. Boil until the potatoes yield to a knife pierce—tender, but not overcooked, about 7 to 10 minutes, depending on the size of the potatoes. Drain the potatoes and allow them to slightly cool. Cut into 1/4-inch slices and return to the pot. Cover and set aside.

❯ In a 10- or 12-inch skillet over medium-high heat, cook the bacon until crisp. Drain on paper towels and chop into bite-size pieces.

❯ Add the leeks to the remaining bacon drippings in the skillet and sauté until soft. Stir in the cider vinegar, mustard seeds, honey, and a few grindings of black pepper, scraping up the browned bits into the hot vinaigrette. Cook for 2 to 3 minutes.

❯ Pour the sauce over the sliced potatoes. Add the bacon pieces. Stir and fold, coating the potatoes. Taste for seasoning. Garnish with chopped chives and parsley. Serve warm.

Makes 12 servings.

Otherwise known as gnocchi, these creamy little pillows are much loved for their simplicity and versatility. They mix up in a pinch and are a great complement for this lively pesto.

ITALIAN CHEESE DUMPLINGS WITH 3-HERB AND ARUGULA PESTO SAUCE

2 pounds ricotta

2 1/2 cups all-purpose flour, plus more for flouring the sheet

1 1/2 cups grated Romano or Parmesan cheese

1/4 teaspoon salt, plus more for the pasta water

1/4 teaspoon black pepper

3-Herb and Arugula Pesto Sauce (recipe on page 18)

◉ Bring a 6-quart pot full of water to a boil over high heat. Lightly flour a surface for rolling out the dough and a baking sheet.

◉ In a large bowl mix together the ricotta, flour, cheese, salt, and pepper until a soft dough forms. Break off a small handful of dough, and on the lightly floured surface roll into a log about 1/2 inch thick. Cut the log into 1/4-inch pieces. Toss half of the pieces with flour on the baking sheet. Try not to let them touch to keep them from sticking to each other. Repeat with the rest of the dough.

◉ Season the pot of water with salt. In batches, drop the dumplings into the boiling water. Reduce the heat to medium and cook until they float to the surface. This should take 2 to 3 minutes. Then let them cook for 1 minute more. Remove with a slotted spoon and place into a large serving bowl. Reserve 1/2 cup of the dumpling cooking water for the pesto sauce. Gently coat the dumplings with the 3-Herb and Arugula Pesto Sauce.

Makes 10 to 12 generous servings.

You'll find other good uses for this fresh green sauce. Try it folded into a cheese omelet or spooned over grilled chicken.

3-HERB AND ARUGULA PESTO SAUCE

1 bunch fresh basil, stalks trimmed

1 bunch fresh mint, stalks trimmed

1 bunch fresh flat-leaf parsley

1 (5-ounce) package baby arugula

4 garlic cloves, chopped

3/4 cup olive oil

1 cup grated Parmesan or Romano cheese

Salt to taste

Black pepper to taste

1/2 cup reserved dumpling water

❯ Combine the basil, mint, parsley, arugula, and garlic in a food processor fitted with a chopping blade. Pulse until finely chopped. Add the olive oil while the motor is running, and process until all the olive oil is combined and the pesto is smooth.

❯ Pour the mixture into a large bowl. Stir in the cheese, and season with salt and pepper. Add the dumpling cooking water to make the pesto into a sauce that easily coats the dumplings.

Makes 2 cups.

Oh là là! John's chocolate dessert is sultry, smooth, and rich. Molded in a French ring, it makes an elegant presentation, especially with its center mound of raspberry whipped cream.

CHOCOLATE TRUFFLE RING WITH RASPBERRY WHIPPED CREAM

CHOCOLATE TRUFFLE RING

1 1/4 cups semisweet or bittersweet chocolate chips

1 cup sugar

1/2 cup boiling water

4 large eggs

2 tablespoons orange liqueur (such as Grand Marnier)

1 teaspoon pure vanilla extract

1/4 teaspoon salt

1 cup (2 sticks) butter, softened, plus more for the mold

❯ Preheat the oven to 350 degrees. Butter a French ring mold.*

❯ Place the semisweet morsels, sugar, and boiling water into the bowl of a food processor fitted with a chopping blade, and process until completely smooth. Continue processing, adding the eggs one at a time, then add the orange liqueur, vanilla, and salt. Continue processing and add the softened butter 1 or 2 tablespoons at a time until all the butter is incorporated and the mixture is smooth.

❯ Pour the mixture into the buttered French ring mold. Place the French ring mold into a larger baking pan and fill with water halfway up the side of the French ring mold pan. Bake for 50 to 55 minutes. Remove the French ring mold from the larger baking pan (be careful—the water will be very hot!), and place on a wire rack to cool for 30 minutes.

❯ Insert a thin knife 1/4 inch below the surface, and run it along the entire circumference of the exterior ring and the interior ring. Place a large plate on top of the ring pan, and turn it over quickly. Let it sit undisturbed for 30 minutes. Lift the ring pan gently. Refrigerate truffle ring for at least 1 hour.

RASPBERRY WHIPPED CREAM

1 cup heavy cream, well chilled

2 tablespoons sugar

3 tablespoons raspberry jam

❯ Chill a medium bowl and the beaters of an electric mixer. Pour the heavy cream into the chilled bowl, and using the chilled beaters, whip the cream until barely soft peaks form. Add the sugar and raspberry jam, and whip until stiff peaks form. Mound the whipped cream in the middle of the Chocolate Truffle Ring and serve.

Makes 8 to 10 servings.

*You can substitute a springform with a bundt insert for the French ring mold.

Quick, indeed! This dough, flecked with feta and fragrant dill, comes together easily. Stone-ground whole wheat flour, mixed in equal parts with unbleached white, gives nice texture to the crumb.

FRESH DILL-FETA QUICK BREAD

1 1/2 cups whole wheat flour

1 1/2 cups unbleached all-purpose flour

2 tablespoons baking powder

1 teaspoon salt

4 large eggs, lightly beaten

3/4 cup milk

1/2 cup olive oil

12 ounces crumbled feta cheese

6 heaping tablespoons chopped fresh dill

◗ Preheat the oven to 350 degrees. Lightly oil a 9 x 5-inch loaf pan.*

◗ In a large bowl whisk together both flours, baking powder, and salt. Add the eggs, milk, olive oil, feta, and fresh dill. Mix until all ingredients are well combined. Spoon the batter into the loaf pan. Bake for 25 to 30 minutes until done.

Makes 1 loaf.

*You can also use 2 medium loaf pans or a 12-cup muffin tin. Decrease the cooking time to 20 to 25 minutes for the medium loaves, and 12 to 15 minutes for the muffins.

The crème-de-la-crème creation! If you can find passion fruit, consider yourself blessed. Its fragrant citrus tang is nothing short of tropical bliss. But any assembly of fresh fruit— strawberries, blackberries, raspberries, or kiwi—would be both stunning and delicious nestled in the peaks of cream.

GIGI'S PAVLOVA*

8 large egg whites

1/4 teaspoon cream of tartar

1 1/4 cups sugar

1 tablespoon cornstarch

1 tablespoon white vinegar

1 tablespoon plus 2 teaspoons vanilla extract, divided

1 1/2 cups heavy cream, chilled

4 tablespoons confectioners' sugar

4 to 6 passion fruits, or 1 pint strawberries and 5 kiwis

❯ Preheat the oven to 400 degrees.* Line a baking sheet with parchment paper and draw a 10-inch diameter circle onto it.

❯ Using an electric mixer with the whisk attachment, beat the egg whites until soft peaks form. In a small bowl whisk the cream of tartar, sugar, and cornstarch together. Beat into the egg whites, a little at a time, until stiff peaks form. Fold in the vinegar and 2 teaspoons vanilla.

❯ Mound the meringue into the middle of the circle drawn on the parchment and, with a spatula, spread it out to the edges of the circle. Smooth the top and make a depression in the middle. Reduce the oven to 250 degrees.

❯ Place the meringue in the middle of the oven and bake for 1 hour. Turn off the heat and let the meringue rest in the closed oven. When cool, remove from the oven, invert, and carefully peel off the parchment. Place the meringue on a serving plate.

❯ In an electric mixer beat the chilled cream with the remaining tablespoon vanilla and confectioners' sugar until thickened with soft peaks. Mound the whipped cream into the center of the meringue and swirl out to the edges.

❯ Cut the passion fruits in half and scoop out the pulp and seeds onto the whipped cream. Or slice the kiwis and strawberries, arranging in appealing rings on top. Chill before serving.

Makes 10 to 14 servings.

*Created in the early 1920s to honor the renowned Russian ballerina Anna Pavlova, when she was touring Down Under, the "Pav" (as New Zealanders and Australians often call the dessert) is for celebrations. Its crisp meringue shell encasing a soft marshmallow-like interior is achieved by placing it in a hot oven that has been lowered to 250 degrees. Baking the Pavlova for an hour at this lowered temperature and allowing it to cool in the oven afterward will ensure a successful and delectable shell.

....

The BIG Tomato

WE TENNESSEANS ARE MIGHTY PROUD OF OUR TOMATOES, AND THAT PRIDE GETS TRANSFORMED INTO giddy excitement around the Fourth of July, the time when tomatoes start coming in by the bushels. Early Girls and Better Boys, Bradleys, Brandywines, Sun Golds, Sweet 100s, Park's Whoppers, Mortgage Lifters, Green Zebras, Cherokee Purples, heirlooms, and hybrids—there's love enough for all.

Sometime in the mid-1990s, in what now seems like the way-back machine in the life of our Nashville Farmers' Market, the search for the best homegrown tomatoes had its limitations. The plethora of vibrant heirlooms had not arrived on our agri-scene. You could count on Smiley's Farm for Bradleys. The Howells had Beefsteaks. On occasion, smaller vendors would show up with their garden varieties and set up stands in the back market shed.

There, we discovered that the tastiest tomatoes also happened to be the ugliest.

This we gleaned from one vendor—a gentleman with a shock of white hair and twinkly blue eyes who hawked his malformed "maters" along with his chow-chow and pepper sauces.

"Over here we got the best for the best price," you'd hear him say as his voice carried across the market shed. "Not a pretty face, but got a pretty taste. Come get your catface tomatoes."

Who could resist that call? You had to check it out.

He had quite the homely collection of reds: gnarled, scarred, with strange protuberances, overall resembling more the other end of the cat. But the price was right, and our man was convincing. We took a chance on a box of catface tomatoes.

Our white-haired friend explained that the "catfacing" happened early on in the development of the fruit—something about cooler temperature and watering issues—and that the later fruits of the plant "grew proper."

"Even if they don't look it," he said, "they still have the flavor."

Indeed. Those wonky catfaces had intense acid-candy sweetness. They passed the true test, the tomato sandwich. Sliced, salted, and slapped between two pieces of white bread—with a healthy swipe of good mayo—this is the essence of summer. And we loved them almost as well roasted with garlic and thyme into a glistening red sauce, spooned over pasta.

These days, we don't hear about the catfaces. The resurgence of cultivating heirlooms has introduced such a dazzling array of tomato colors and tastes, keeping us entranced with all those possibilities. There are countless ways of preparing them. Some have the right pop and zing for salads. Others amplify when simmered into a sauce. That is why we look forward to Third Thursday in the heart of summer. A tomato-inspired supper? Absolutely!

A tomato sampler platter alone would be delicious. But consider Lemon Boys in a Spicy Golden Mary cocktail, Cherokee Purples in a strata, roasted Romas in a tart, Green Zebras in gazpacho, and a tomato rice bake with a rainbow ensemble.

Come potluck time, we'll enjoy them all.

JULY: **THE BIG TOMATO**

Cornbread Panzanella with Real Ranch Dressing

Spicy Golden Mary

Tomato and Goat Cheese Tart with Olive Oil Crust

Zesty Gazpacho with Shrimp

Fresh Three-Bean Salad with Chunky Herbed Vinaigrette

Honeycrust Fried Chicken Tenders and Make It Nashville Hot

Caroline's Warm Eggplant Salad

"Posh Squash" Soufflé Casserole

Cast-Iron Heirloom Tomato and Rice Bake

Blueberry-Peach Coffee Cake

Buttermilk Peach Ice Cream with Salted Caramel Sauce

Bourbon Pecan Bars

A Southern take on an Italian summer favorite. Cornbread croutons, market-fresh Bradley tomatoes, cucumbers, and ranch dressing combine to make an unbeatable salad.

CORNBREAD PANZANELLA WITH REAL RANCH DRESSING

CORNBREAD CROUTONS

1 1/2 cups cornmeal

1 cup all-purpose flour

1 tablespoon sugar

1 teaspoon salt

2 teaspoons baking powder

2 large eggs

1/2 cup (1 stick) butter, melted

1 cup milk

❯ Preheat the oven to 350 degrees. Butter a baking sheet.

❯ In a large bowl whisk together the cornmeal, flour, sugar, salt, and baking powder. Whisk in the eggs, melted butter, and milk until well incorporated. Do not overbeat. Pour onto the baking sheet. Bake until set—golden brown—about 20 minutes. Allow to cool. Cut into cubes and spread out onto a lightly oiled baking sheet. Toast for about 15 minutes. Allow to cool.

Makes 2 cups.

REAL RANCH DRESSING

1/2 cup buttermilk

1/2 cup mayonnaise

2 tablespoons fresh lemon juice

2 green onions, chopped finely, tops included

1 heaping tablespoon chopped fresh flat-leaf parsley

1/2 teaspoon granulated garlic

1/4 teaspoon salt

Pinch of black pepper

❯ In a medium bowl combine the buttermilk, mayonnaise, lemon juice, green onions, parsley, garlic, salt, and pepper. Whisk until smooth and creamy. Taste for seasonings and adjust. This will keep, refrigerated, for a week.

Makes 1 generous cup.

PANZANELLA

1 1/2 cups diced Bradley tomatoes

1/2 cup peeled, seeded, and cubed cucumbers

1/2 cup sliced red onion

1/2 cup chopped fresh basil

Salt and black pepper to taste

❯ In a large bowl combine the tomatoes, cucumbers, onion, basil, salt, and pepper. Add 2 cups of cornbread croutons. Pour the Real Ranch Dressing over the croutons and toss well. Serve immediately.

Makes 8 to 10 servings.

We liked this "less bloody" version. It's no less zingy and appealing, and it's a clever use for an abundance of yellow heirlooms.

SPICY GOLDEN MARY

4 to 5 pounds very ripe yellow tomatoes, cored and chopped (about 7 cups)

1 1/2 cups good-quality vodka (we used Tito's from Austin, Texas)

2 teaspoons prepared horseradish

Generous pinch of sea salt to taste

Freshly ground black pepper to taste

1 tablespoon serrano chili lime sauce (or 2 teaspoons hot sauce, such as Tabasco)

3 tablespoons fresh lemon juice

1 tablespoon Worcestershire sauce

Lime slices to serve

Celery sticks to serve

❯ Puree the chopped tomatoes in a food processor fitted with a chopping blade until smooth. Strain through a fine sieve into a large bowl. Add the vodka, horseradish, salt, pepper, chili sauce, lemon juice, and Worcestershire and mix well. Taste and adjust for salt and spice. Decant into clear glass bottles or pitchers. Cover and chill until ready to serve. Serve over ice with a squeeze of lime and a crunchy celery stick.

Makes approximately 2 quarts.

The trick to this crust: place the olive oil in the freezer overnight (or 4 hours) so that it solidifies. Then work it into the dough. It imparts a wonderful flavor to the crust, which is a natural with the tomatoes, creamy goat cheese, and oregano.

TOMATO AND GOAT CHEESE TART WITH OLIVE OIL CRUST

CRUST

1/3 cup olive oil

1 1/4 cups all-purpose flour, plus more for rolling the dough

1/2 teaspoon salt

1/2 teaspoon baking powder

1 teaspoon white wine vinegar

3 to 4 tablespoons icy water

○ Pour the olive oil into a glass jar and place it in the freezer for at least 4 hours. Within a few hours, it will become cloudy and thick, like molasses.

○ In a medium bowl sift the flour, salt, and baking powder together. Place the flour mixture into the bowl of a food processor fitted with a chopping blade or pastry blade. Add the olive oil mass and the vinegar. Pulse a few times. Continue pulsing the mixture as you add the icy water, 1 tablespoon at a time. When the dough ball forms, remove it and wrap it in plastic wrap. Refrigerate until it is well chilled, about 1 hour.

○ Preheat the oven to 350 degrees.

○ Dust your counter with flour, roll out the dough to the desired thinness, and place into a 9-inch pie pan. Prick the bottom and sides of the crust with a fork. Refrigerate until the oven is preheated.

○ Bake for 5 to 7 minutes. Cool before adding the filling.

FILLING

1 (10.5- to 11-ounce) log plain goat cheese, at room temperature

Sea salt to taste

Black pepper to taste

3 large heirloom tomatoes

3 tablespoons fresh oregano leaves

1 to 2 tablespoons extra-virgin olive oil

○ Slice the goat cheese log into rounds, and cover the bottom of the cooled crust. Spread to the sides. Sprinkle with sea salt and black pepper.

○ Core and slice the tomatoes into rounds. Place the slices, slightly overlapping, over the goat cheese layer. Sprinkle with sea salt, black pepper, and oregano. Drizzle with the olive oil and bake for 25 minutes, until the tomatoes begin to release their juices, bubble, and brown.

○ Remove from the oven and allow to cool for 15 minutes before slicing into wedges.

Makes 8 to 10 servings.

Rhonda enlivened her already zesty gazpacho with plump shrimp, pan-seared in spices and cooled with a spritz of lime. We had an array of small punch cups in which to serve this summer soup.

ZESTY GAZPACHO WITH SHRIMP

8 ripe tomatoes, cored and cut into chunks

4 cucumbers, peeled and cut into chunks

3 sweet red peppers, seeded and cut into chunks

1 jalapeño pepper (unseeded for extra piquancy)

2 yellow onions, cut into chunks

4 cloves garlic

1 quart tomato-vegetable juice

1 pint tomato-clam juice

1/2 cup plus 2 tablespoons olive oil, divided

1/2 cup balsamic vinegar

1/4 cup fresh basil, chiffonade

1/4 cup fresh dill, chopped

1 tablespoon hot sauce (such as Crystal or Louisiana Hot)

1 pound large shrimp (26 to 30 count), peeled and deveined

1/4 teaspoon granulated garlic

1/4 teaspoon paprika

1/4 teaspoon sea salt

1/4 teaspoon cayenne pepper

Juice of 2 limes

Salt to taste

Cracked black pepper to taste

❷ Carefully wash and dry the tomatoes, cucumbers, and peppers. In a food processor fitted with a chopping blade, in batches pulse the tomatoes, cucumbers, and peppers so that they are coarsely chopped. Place into a large pot. Place the onions and garlic in the food processer and pulse, then add to the pot. Add the tomato-vegetable juice, tomato-clam juice, 1/2 cup olive oil, balsamic vinegar, basil, dill, and hot sauce. Stir well. Cover and refrigerate until well chilled.

❷ Warm the remaining 2 tablespoons olive oil in a skillet over medium heat. Place the shrimp in a bowl and sprinkle with the garlic, paprika, sea salt, and cayenne, tossing to thoroughly coat them. Drop the shrimp onto the hot skillet, taking care not to crowd them. Cook these in batches if necessary. Cook the shrimp on each side for about 1 minute. When pink and firm, sprinkle lime juice over the shrimp. Cool and chop into bite-size pieces. Stir into the chilled gazpacho. Taste for salt and pepper and adjust.

Makes 1/2 gallon (16 4-ounce servings).

We're all familiar with the jars of this picnic mix found on supermarket shelves. But once upon a time, folks made it fresh, with garden-picked beans, pintos simmered in garlic, and vinaigrette chunky with sweet red bell peppers. Mercy.

FRESH THREE-BEAN SALAD WITH CHUNKY HERBED VINAIGRETTE

3 cloves garlic, divided

1/2 pound dried pinto beans (or other meaty bean—we love Rancho Gordo heirloom beans)

1 bay leaf

Sea salt and black pepper to taste

Pinch of red pepper flakes

1 pound green beans

1 pound yellow wax beans

1 small red onion, diced small

1 small red bell pepper, diced small

1 batch Chunky Herbed Vinaigrette (recipe follows)

❯ Mince 2 garlic cloves and place them in a deep saucepan with the pinto beans and bay leaf. Cover with water by at least 2 inches. Season with salt, black pepper, and red pepper flakes. Bring to a boil over high heat, then reduce to medium-low and simmer, covered, for at least 2 hours, until the beans are tender but not mushy. Remove the bay leaf and allow to cool.*

❯ Slice the remaining garlic clove. Fill a large skillet with 2 inches of water. Season with salt and sliced garlic, and bring to a boil. Cook the green beans in the skillet for 1 to 2 minutes (until crisp-tender) and plunge into an ice bath. Cook the yellow wax beans for 4 to 5 minutes, then chill them in the ice bath as well. Add additional ice to the water if needed.

❯ Drain and dry off the blanched, chilled beans. Cut on the diagonal into pieces. Combine with the cooled pintos, red onion, and red bell pepper. Toss well with the Chunky Herbed Vinaigrette. Makes a nice big bowl for potluck.

Makes 12 servings.

*This step can be done the day before.

CHUNKY HERBED VINAIGRETTE

1 clove garlic, minced

3 tablespoons finely chopped red bell pepper

3 tablespoons finely chopped red onion

3 tablespoons finely chopped fresh flat-leaf parsley

4 tablespoons red wine vinegar

Sea salt to taste

Cracked black pepper to taste

Pinch of red pepper flakes

1 cup extra-virgin olive oil

◗ In a medium bowl add the garlic, bell pepper, onion, parsley, vinegar, salt, pepper, and red pepper flakes. Vigorously whisk to combine. Slowly drizzle in the olive oil while whisking to emulsify the dressing.

Makes 1 cup.

The best fried chicken I ever ate came from a long-gone Nashville restaurant called Cayce's, Home of the Honeycrust Chicken. There's no honey in the crust; the name alludes to its golden crisp coating and gush of salty-sweetness. This recipe recreates that honeycrust goodness. While Cayce's always butchered and fried the whole chicken, the recipe works great for tenders, which are easy to serve at potluck.

HONEYCRUST FRIED CHICKEN TENDERS

3 pounds boneless chicken breast tenders

2 cups buttermilk

1 cup water

2 teaspoons plus 1 tablespoon kosher salt, divided

1 teaspoon plus 1 tablespoon cracked black pepper, divided

3 cups all-purpose flour

1 tablespoon paprika

1 teaspoon granulated garlic

1/2 teaspoon thyme

1/2 teaspoon cayenne pepper

Canola oil or canola-peanut oil combination

❯ Wash the chicken and pat dry. In a large bowl mix the buttermilk, water, 2 teaspoons salt, and 1 teaspoon black pepper. Place the chicken in the buttermilk bath. Cover and refrigerate overnight.

❯ Remove the chicken from the refrigerator. In a large bowl combine the flour, the remaining 1 tablespoon salt, the remaining 1 tablespoon pepper, paprika, garlic, thyme, and cayenne. Place a cast-iron skillet on medium-high heat. Add enough oil to reach a 1-inch depth. Drain each piece of chicken and dredge in the seasoned flour.

❯ When the oil sizzles, carefully place the chicken tenders, dusted of excess flour, into the skillet. Do not crowd the pan. Work in batches if necessary. Tenders will cook 3 to 4 minutes per side. Place the cooked pieces on a wire rack to drain. Let the chicken rest 10 minutes before serving.

Makes 10 to 12 servings.

MAKE IT NASHVILLE HOT

It started as revenge: a woman fried up the meanest, hottest, cayenne pepper–doused chicken she could make for her carousing man. Turned out, he loved that chicken and begged for more. So did everyone who tried it at his restaurant. Now, Hot Chicken is a Nashville signature dish. Brush this fiery sauce onto a batch of your fried chicken tenders and offer both styles at the table!

2 tablespoons lard or grapeseed oil

2 to 3 tablespoons cayenne pepper

1 tablespoon paprika

1/4 teaspoon sugar

1 1/2 teaspoons salt

1 teaspoon granulated garlic

1/2 teaspoon onion powder

1/4 teaspoon turmeric

❯ Melt the lard or warm the oil in a saucepan over medium heat. Stir in the cayenne, paprika, sugar, salt, garlic, onion powder, and turmeric and mix until it becomes a fiery red paste. If the paste becomes too thick, whisk in a few drops of water. Brush onto cooked, hot fried chicken, entirely coating each piece.

NOTE: Make a double batch of the Real Ranch Dressing (page 29) and set out a bowl as a cooling dip for the Nashville Hot Chicken.

Eggplant, cubed and roasted to caramel crispness, tossed warm with juicy tomatoes—the flavors meld beautifully in this summer salad that will delight any palate, from vegan to omnivore! Add cubes of fresh mozzarella for a "meatier" vegetarian version.

CAROLINE'S WARM EGGPLANT SALAD

2 large eggplants, unpeeled, cut into 1-inch cubes

6 tablespoons olive oil

Coarse kosher salt and black pepper to season eggplant

5 to 6 large ripe heirloom tomatoes, cubed

5 to 6 garlic cloves, minced

1/2 cup fresh basil leaves, chopped

2 tablespoons extra-virgin olive oil

2 tablespoons sherry vinegar

1/2 teaspoon salt

1/2 teaspoon black pepper

1 cup fresh mozzarella, diced (optional)

❯ Preheat the oven to 350 degrees.

❯ In a large bowl combine the cubed eggplant with the olive oil in a large bowl and toss well to coat. Spread the eggplant out on a baking sheet. Sprinkle with kosher salt and pepper. Bake for 12 minutes. Turn the eggplant over and bake until soft, with browned edges, about 12 minutes longer.

❯ While the eggplant is cooking, toss the cubed tomatoes, minced garlic, and chopped basil together in a large salad bowl. Add the extra-virgin olive oil and sherry vinegar along with 1/2 teaspoon salt and 1/2 teaspoon pepper. Toss gently to blend.

❯ Allow the eggplant to cool slightly, about 5 minutes. Add warm eggplant to the tomato mixture and toss. Let this sit at room temperature for about an hour before serving to allow the flavors to marry.

❯ Right before serving, add 1 cup diced fresh mozzarella, if desired. Toss and serve.

Makes 10 servings.

Simple to make and oh-so-rich, this bakes into a golden soufflé-like puff. Of all the yellow squash casserole recipes, this is the one that everyone requests, including those who claim they don't like squash.

"POSH SQUASH" SOUFFLÉ CASSEROLE

4 pounds yellow squash, sliced into medium-size pieces

4 large eggs

2 cups mayonnaise

2 cups grated Parmesan cheese

1 teaspoon sea salt

1/2 teaspoon freshly ground black pepper

1/2 teaspoon granulated garlic

1/2 teaspoon paprika

2 medium onions, diced

Preheat the oven to 350 degrees.

Bring a large pot of water to a boil over high heat. Add the squash and boil until tender, about 12 minutes. Drain and cool.

In a medium bowl whisk together the eggs, mayonnaise, Parmesan, salt, pepper, garlic, and paprika. Fold in the onion, then the cooled squash. Place the mixture in a 9 x 13-inch casserole dish or a 6-cup soufflé dish. Bake for 30 minutes until puffed and golden brown.

Makes 8 to 10 servings.

A beautiful and savory way to showcase a variety of tomatoes. Serve it right in the cast-iron skillet in which it bakes. Be sure to use a short-grain rice like Arborio, which absorbs all the tomato juices as it plumps up.

CAST-IRON HEIRLOOM TOMATO AND RICE BAKE

1 tablespoon tomato paste

2 cups water

1 tablespoon butter

1 tablespoon olive oil

1/2 medium onion, diced small

1 tablespoon minced garlic

1 1/4 cups Arborio rice

2 tablespoons paprika

1/4 cup red wine*

Salt to taste

Black pepper to taste

1 1/2 pounds assorted heirloom tomatoes (such as Brandywine, Lemon Boy, and Green Zebra), sliced into wedges

◉ Preheat the oven to 425 degrees.

◉ In a medium bowl dissolve the tomato paste in the water. Place an oven-safe 9-inch skillet that is at least 2 inches deep over medium heat. Add the butter and olive oil. Add the onions and sauté until translucent. Add the minced garlic. Stir in the rice and paprika, stirring until the grains are coated. Add the tomato-water and wine and stir well. Season with a little salt and black pepper. Bring to a simmer.

◉ Remove from the heat and cover the top well with the tomato wedges. Place the skillet in the oven and bake for 15 minutes, uncovered. The tomatoes will brown and caramelize, their juices encasing the rice. The rice is done when the grains are firm but nicely puffed.

Makes 8 servings.

*You can substitute water for the wine.

AN ASIDE ON PEACHES

This is the big tomato month, but another summer love shows up at about the same time: the peach.

Georgia peaches are legendary, but our experience of them had been lackluster. The ones that showed up at our Nashville markets did not have that fragrant scent, supple give under the press of your thumb, or gush of peach sweetness when you took a bite. We would bypass them in favor of the ones from Alabama and South Carolina.

And then The Peach Truck came to town. Make no mistake: not *a* peach truck, but *The* Peach Truck.

Each week, June through August, Nashvillian Stephen Rose would drive his '64 Jeep Gladiator pickup laden with crates of just-picked peaches from his uncle's farm in Crawford, Georgia, and park in a lot only blocks from my house.

I discovered him early one Saturday morning on my way to the garden. He was busy setting up a display table, draping it with a vintage cloth. On the hood of the old green truck with wooden sideboards were a few brown sacks. A chalkboard sign set at the sidewalk read "Fresh Georgia Peaches. $6 Bag."

I had to stop. The garden would wait. Could these be what I had been missing?

The first test of a peach is in its scent. I opened up a bag, and there it was. Sweet and faintly floral. I lifted one out. It had the right heft, its blushed fuzzy velvet skin yielding when pressed. Already I was sold.

Then Stephen carved out a wedge for me to taste. Ambrosial. I was over the moon. And I knew where I would be next Saturday morning.

Perhaps best enjoyed purely out of hand, peaches do remarkable versatile work in salads, salsas, chutneys, preserves, cakes, pies, cobblers, and, of course, ice cream. In the weeks that they are available, we take advantage of them in all forms.

Amy's secret is Fiori di Sicilia extract, which imparts a beguiling citric and floral essence to the batter.

BLUEBERRY-PEACH COFFEE CAKE

1 cup (2 sticks) butter, softened

3 cups vanilla sugar, divided*

4 large eggs

2 cups sour cream

1 teaspoon vanilla extract

1 teaspoon Fiori di Sicilia extract**

4 cups all-purpose flour

2 teaspoons baking powder

2 teaspoons baking soda

1 teaspoon salt

1 tablespoon ground cinnamon

5 to 6 ripe peaches, peeled, pitted, and sliced

2 pints fresh blueberries, washed and drained

1 cup pecan pieces

◗ Preheat the oven to 350 degrees. Grease two 9-inch square baking pans.

◗ In the bowl of an electric mixer cream together the butter and 2 cups vanilla sugar. Beat in the eggs, one at a time, followed by the sour cream, vanilla, and Fiori di Sicilia extract. In a large bowl sift the flour, baking powder, baking soda, and salt together. Slowly add the flour mixture to the egg mixture and mix until the batter is smooth. Do not overbeat.

◗ Whisk the remaining 1 cup of sugar and cinnamon together in a small bowl. Spread half of the batter into the 2 greased pans. Add a layer of half of the sliced peaches and blueberries. Sprinkle with half of the cinnamon sugar. Repeat using the rest of the batter and remaining fruits. Top with cinnamon sugar and pecan pieces. Bake for 45 to 50 minutes. Serve warm or at room temperature.

Makes 2 cakes.

NOTE: This recipe can be halved with fine results.

*Amy keeps a canister of vanilla sugar (vanilla bean–infused white sugar) on hand to use in her baking. But if you don't have this, you can use plain sugar instead.

**Amy orders this from King Arthur Flour, but feel free to make your own Fiori di Sicilia extract substitute: mix 2 tablespoons vanilla extract, 2 teaspoons orange extract, and 2 teaspoons lemon extract.

The buttermilk in Rick's peach ice cream adds a tangy overlay. If you're inclined, grate some fresh nutmeg into the batch. You'll be glad you did.

BUTTERMILK PEACH ICE CREAM WITH SALTED CARAMEL SAUCE

adapted from *The Homesick Texan*

6 cups peeled, pitted, and chopped peaches (about 12 ripe peaches)

2 cups sugar

3 cups heavy cream

3 cups whole buttermilk

1 tablespoon vanilla bean paste*

1 teaspoon grated fresh nutmeg, if desired

❯ Place the peaches in a large bowl. Pour the sugar over the pieces and stir. Cover, refrigerate, and allow the fruit to macerate for at least 2 hours. You can macerate it overnight if you have the time. The peaches will release more juices.

❯ Place 4 cups of peaches in a blender and puree. Pour into a separate large bowl. Add the heavy cream, buttermilk, and vanilla paste to the pureed peaches. Add the nutmeg.

❯ Pour the mixture into the bowl of a 6-quart ice-cream maker. Churn according to manufacturer's directions. When the mixture is almost completely churned, fold in the reserved 2 cups of sliced peaches. Finish churning. Remove the bowl, cover, and freeze.

Makes 3 quarts.

NOTE: To cut the recipe in half, use 3 cups peeled, pitted, and chopped peaches (6 ripe peaches) divided (2 cups and 1 cup), 1 cup sugar, 1 1/2 cups heavy cream, 1 1/2 cups buttermilk, 1 1/2 teaspoons vanilla, and 1/2 teaspoon nutmeg.

*You can substitute 1 tablespoon vanilla extract or the scrapings of a whole vanilla bean.

"An apple is an excellent thing, until you have tried a peach."

——George du Maurier

Spooned over buttermilk peach ice cream, this sauce gives credence to the phrase "gilding the lily." But what a gild. You'll find many other uses for this addictive sauce.

SALTED CARAMEL SAUCE

1 cup sugar

1 cup heavy cream

1 tablespoon vanilla extract

1 teaspoon Maldon sea salt or French gray sea salt

❯ Place a large skillet over medium heat. Spread the sugar evenly over the bottom of the skillet. Occasionally shake the skillet as the sugar heats. Soon the sugar will melt clear. Begin rotating the skillet as the sugar starts to turn amber, stirring with a wooden spoon as needed. When the sugar becomes a caramel-colored liquid, remove the pan from the heat and stir in the cream and vanilla. The liquid sugar will sputter and seize and some of the pieces will harden, but don't worry! Continue stirring and return the pan to low heat. The caramel will begin to loosen and become a creamy-dreamy sauce.

❯ Sprinkle sea salt over the sauce and stir. Serve warm or room temperature in a bowl alongside the peach ice cream. Leftover caramel can be kept in a lidded jar in the refrigerator for 2 weeks (as if it would last that long).

Makes 1 cup.

Pecans cooked in a bourbon-laced caramel filling, in a crisp shortbread crust—what's not to love? We use Steen's Cane Syrup, the only mass-producing mill in the United States.

BOURBON PECAN BARS

SHORTBREAD CRUST

1/2 cup (1 stick) butter, softened

1/4 cup raw sugar (such as turbinado or demerara)

1 1/2 cups all-purpose flour

1 large egg

1/4 teaspoon salt

⊙ Place butter, sugar, flour, egg, and salt into a food processor fitted with the chopping blade. Pulse until the mixture becomes incorporated into a large mass. Form into a ball, cover in plastic wrap, and refrigerate for 15 minutes while you make the filling.

FILLING

1 cup cane syrup*

1/2 cup raw sugar (such as turbinado or demerara)

2 large eggs

2 tablespoons bourbon

1 teaspoon vanilla extract

6 tablespoons butter, melted and slightly cooled

2 cups pecan halves or pieces

⊙ Using an electric hand mixer or hand-held immersion blender, mix the cane syrup with the sugar, eggs, bourbon, and vanilla. Beat in the melted butter a little at a time, mixing well until the filling is well emulsified.

⊙ Preheat the oven to 350 degrees.

ASSEMBLY

⊙ Roll out the shortbread crust. Don't worry if it breaks off into pieces—these will piece back together when pressed onto the baking pan. Place the dough in the bottom of a 9 x 13-inch baking pan and bring the edges up the sides about 3/4 inch.

⊙ Cover the bottom with the pecan halves or pieces. Pour the filling mixture over the pecans. Bake for 20 to 25 minutes. Allow to cool thoroughly on a rack before cutting into bars or squares.

Makes 20 to 24 squares.

*If you can't find cane syrup, you can substitute 1/2 cup dark and 1/2 cup light corn syrup.

YES YOU CAN CAN TOMATOES!

For decades, I avoided canning. The reasons shifted, serving as a litmus test of where I was in my culinary development: *Canning? How uncool.* Or, *Canning? You've got to be kidding. I've got no time for that.* Or, *Canning is too scary. The terms "process bath" and "botulism" freak me out.* And, *Canning? A messy ordeal. I'll roast and freeze, thank you.*

These days, with a little more time on my hands and a lot less freezer space, I understand the wisdom of canning. And now the relative ease.

Tomatoes do *not* require a pressure cooker to safely can, just a "hot water bath." So, on to Demystifying the Process.

All you need is the right equipment—Mason jars, lids and rings, a large lidded pot with a rack for the bottom, canning tongs, a wide funnel . . . and a couple of leisurely hours. Your ingredients are simply your assortment of lovely, ripe tomatoes and kosher salt. Fresh basil, too, if you are so inclined.

It's much easier if you work in small batches. You don't have to make a day of it.

1. Place a canning rack or tethered canning rings on the bottom (this makeshift rack cushions the jars) of your 12-quart pot and fill with water. Cover and bring to a boil.
2. Heat a 3-quart pot of water to blanch your tomatoes. Have a bowl of chilled water ready to halt the cooking, post-blanch.
3. Clean canning jars and lids with hot, soapy water. Rinse well and place the jars into your canning vessel to sterilize. Let them boil for at least 10 minutes. Turn off the heat, but let your jars remain there until it is time to fill them. It's best to "hot-pack" hot tomatoes (or jams, ketchup, preserves) into hot jars. Place the lids and rings in a small saucepan over medium-high heat. Bring the water to a boil and allow the lids and rings to boil for 5 minutes.
4. Select ripe tomatoes, wash them, and then dip into boiling water for 30 seconds—or until skins crack. Plunge into icy water and remove. Core the tomatoes and slip off the skins. Cut into quarters and place into a 3-quart saucepan.
5. After you have cored, skinned, and quartered all your tomatoes, bring them to a boil.
6. Remove hot jars from the canning vessel. Drain. Place 1/2 teaspoon kosher salt into each pint jar (1 teaspoon salt if using quarts). Place a sprig of fresh basil into some, if you like.

7. Using a wide-mouthed funnel, ladle the tomatoes into each jar. Leave about a $1/2$-inch gap at the top of the jar.
8. Carefully wipe off the outer rim of each jar, place a seal and ring on top, and tighten.
9. Lower the jars into the large pot of boiling water. The jars shouldn't touch one another or the sides of the pot. About 2 inches of water should cover the tops—add more hot water if necessary. Return to a boil. Process for 20 minutes—counting your time from when the water begins boiling (in our case, that took about 2 minutes).
10. Remove the jars with canning tongs. Set out on the counter to cool. After a few minutes, you will hear a distinctive *POP*—that's the seal being made.

That's it! Tomatoes for sauces, soups, and stews: the sweet taste of summer ready to enjoy in the dead of winter!

....

For the Love of Figs

WHEN GIGI PLANTED A FIG TREE ON THE BORDER OF HER URBAN GARDEN, SHE HAD NO IDEA THAT IT
would take to the place with such ardor. But the tree settled right into its new home, rapidly
spreading upward and outward. In just four years, a sprawl of great leafed branches was
producing hundreds of honeyed knobs of fruit.

"It seems very happy here," we both observed. "This could be the year of the fig."

Throughout July, I'd get messages from Gigi—field reports you might say—about the
status of the figs.

"If these all ripen, well, this is one rockin' fig tree," was one update.

"Thousands of figs! I picked two 5-pound baskets in less than an hour," was another.

Over the next few weeks, as the summer heat became more severe, Gigi cultivated a
relationship with the beloved tree. To me, it seemed like a reverence: "It's unbearably hot, and
I keep telling her how wonderful she is, making all this fruit."

Gigi set up a special watering system. "I told her I'd take care of her. I know she's thirsty."

Before long, *she* had produced enough figs to make one hundred pints of preserves.

I had to get over to the garden and do some picking myself.

Gigi had set up a system of ladders and planks within the inner sanctum of the tree,
cloaked under the leafy branches. It was with childlike glee that I clambered up and around
the limbs, concealed from the outer world, immersed in the heady enclave of fig leaves and
fruit.

There is a mystery to the allure of figs. Ancient, exotic—it touches on something
primal. That nectarous gush and soft-seeded texture triggers a memory of a memory, an

elusive feeling or image that I can almost capture, but it vanishes just as I get a glimpse of it. Nonetheless, it leaves me, and other fig-lovers I know, with the longing for more.

I picked a large bowlful of figs, most dark purple, some yellow-green with a flush of rouge, all exquisite, ripe, and beautiful. My hands were sticky from the milky white liquid stored in the stems.

It was time to try something new with our prized fruit for the potluck. In the past, I'd made preserves with lemon and spread it over the top of a small round of Camembert. Gigi had already been playing with different recipes: cutting back on the sugar, adding ginger to some

batches, orange juice in another, and white balsamic vinegar in yet another. All methods were cooked on the stovetop.

While each batch was good, none had the figgy caramel syrup she was seeking.

Then I got a text: "Roasting is the way."

Why, of course! But wait, another text followed. "No olive oil. Sugar and white balsamic vinegar only. 425 degrees."

We like the economy of a texted recipe!

After carefully rinsing my figs, I placed them on a baking sheet, along with a few wedges of lemon—my addition. Then I dusted them with sugar, spritzed white balsamic vinegar over the batch, and put them into that hot oven to roast. It didn't take long—ten minutes or so—and the figs got puffed, releasing their juices. I gently stirred them as they became coated in a rich caramel created from the melting of the sugar, vinegar, and natural fig juices. It was incredible.

After scraping them into jars, I processed some in a hot water bath, but kept one jar in the fridge—ready for the flatbread pizza we'd planned on making for Third Thursday.

"To eat figs off the tree in the very early morning, when they have been barely touched by the sun . . ."
—Elizabeth David

AUGUST: FOR THE LOVE OF FIGS

A food writer and a culinary consultant, both visiting from New York City and in town to judge a Jack Daniels cooking contest, made a detour to our potluck. They helped create this terrific late-summer cocktail as their Third Thursday contribution. Let's Get Figgy is a riff on a traditional gin cocktail that is made with marmalade, imparting sunny Mediterranean flavors.

LET'S GET FIGGY COCKTAIL

1 pint gin (good quality such as Bombay, Henrick's, or Beefeater)

Juice of 4 lemons (Meyer lemons preferred)

1/4 cup local honey

1/2 teaspoon balsamic vinegar

1/2 cup fig jam or preserves*, plus additional for garnish

Ice

In a large bowl combine the gin, lemon juice, honey, and balsamic vinegar. Whisk in the fig jam, mixing well to make sure the jam is incorporated. Decant into a bottle or glass jar. Chill until ready to serve. Pour into a shaker with ice and shake vigorously. Serve over ice with an extra dollop of fig jam.

Makes about 2 1/2 cups.

NOTE: In individual glasses, placing the fig jam on a spoon makes a festive presentation while adding an extra bit of sweet. It can be slowly stirred into the cocktail or just licked off the spoon.

* See our recipe on page 159.

Joy notes that her slow-roasted tomatoes improve after cooling and refrigerating overnight—this gives time for the flavors to "settle in." Bring them to room temperature before serving. Set out a plate of the tomatoes and their juices with a crusty baguette, sliced into rounds and toasted, and a bowl of grated Parmesan to dust over the halves. So good!

JOY'S SLOW-ROASTED ROMAS

2 pounds Roma tomatoes

4 cloves garlic, minced

Olive oil

1 1/2 teaspoons dried oregano

Kosher salt to taste

Freshly ground black pepper to taste

1 teaspoon sugar

1 loaf crusty French bread

1/4 cup olive oil

1/2 cup grated Parmesan cheese

1 bunch fresh basil (about 12 leaves)

Preheat the oven to 250 degrees.

Slice the tomatoes in half lengthwise and place into a 9 x 13-inch casserole dish in a single layer, skin side down. Distribute garlic evenly over the tomatoes. Drizzle with olive oil and generously sprinkle with oregano, salt, pepper, and sugar. Bake for 2 to 3 hours. After cooling, refrigerate overnight.

Preheat oven to 375 degrees.

Slice the bread into 1/4-inch rounds and arrange on a baking sheet. Brush the tops with olive oil and toast until lightly brown—about 12 minutes. You may need to rotate the pan halfway through toasting. Allow to cool on the baking sheet, as slices will continue to crispen.

Roll up the basil leaves tightly and chiffonade. To serve, top each piece of bread with a roasted tomato half, a sprinkle of Parmesan, and a pinch of basil.

Makes 20 to 24 servings.

NOTE: This recipe is also very good chopped and tossed over hot pasta.

Covered with roasted figs, shaved gorgonzola, leeks, and ripples of prosciutto, this flatbread pizza has become our favorite—one we gladly repeat every August. A few sprigs of rosemary and a drizzle of the figgy syrup give it a distinctive boost.

ROASTED FIG, PROSCIUTTO, AND GORGONZOLA PIZZA

1 (.25-ounce) envelope active dry yeast

1 cup warm water

1 3/4 cups unbleached all-purpose flour, plus more for rolling and shaping

1/2 cup rye flour

2 teaspoons sea salt

2 tablespoons olive oil, divided

Roasted Figs in Syrup (recipe follows)

3 to 4 ounces sliced prosciutto

1 cup sliced well-cleaned leeks

6 ounces shaved or crumbled gorgonzola cheese

2 tablespoons fresh rosemary

❯ Sprinkle the yeast into a small bowl and pour the warm water over it. Stir well and let stand for 5 minutes to activate the yeast. Place the all-purpose and rye flours, salt, and 1 tablespoon olive oil into a large bowl. Using a wooden spoon, stir in the yeast water. Mix by hand until it forms into a ball. Knead the dough by hand for 10 minutes, until it becomes smooth and elastic. (If you have an electric mixer, you can use it with the dough hook attachment to mix the yeast water into the flour mixture until the dough ball forms and continue the mechanical kneading for 10 minutes.)

❯ Place the dough into another large bowl coated with the remaining tablespoon of olive oil. Cover with a damp towel and allow to rise in a warm place until doubled in size—1 to 1 1/2 hours.

❯ Transfer the dough to a lightly floured work surface. Divide the dough into two balls; each ball makes a pizza. Wrap and refrigerate 1 ball. Let the other ball stand out for 30 minutes.

❯ Preheat the oven to 450 degrees. Roll the dough into whatever pizza shape—round, oblong, rectangle—suits you. Use additional flour as needed to prevent sticking. Place the dough onto a baking sheet. Cover with the figs and syrup, prosciutto, leeks, cheese, and rosemary.

❯ Bake until browned and bubbly, about 10 minutes. Remove from oven and allow to cool slightly before slicing into wedges or squares.

Makes 8 to 10 servings.

ROASTED FIGS IN SYRUP

15 ripe figs, rinsed and dried

1 lemon, sliced into thin wedges (about 10 to 12 pieces)

1/4 cup sugar

2 to 3 tablespoons white balsamic vinegar

❯ Preheat oven to 425 degrees.

❯ Lay the figs out on a baking sheet. Scatter the lemon wedges around the figs. Sprinkle the sugar over the figs and lemon wedges. Sprinkle white balsamic vinegar over the sugared figs. Place into the oven and roast for 10 to 12 minutes, checking and rotating the pan after 5 to 6 minutes. Cook until the figs become puffed and release their juices.

Makes 1 1/2 cups.

A luscious centerpiece to a potluck dinner.

CIDER-BRAISED PORK SHOULDER WITH PEARS

1 (6-pound) pork shoulder, trimmed

Salt to taste

Black pepper to taste

3 tablespoons fresh thyme, divided

2 to 3 tablespoons olive oil

2 ripe, firm pears, sliced

1 yellow or white onion, sliced

3 carrots, diced

1 to 2 leeks, cleaned well and chopped

4 cloves garlic, minced

1 1/2 cups apple cider

❯ Liberally rub the pork with salt, pepper, and 2 tablespoons thyme. Heat a large Dutch oven over medium heat, add the olive oil, and brown the shoulder on all sides. Turn the heat down to low and add the sliced pears, onions, carrots, leeks, garlic, and remaining tablespoon of thyme. Pour in the cider.

❯ Cover and simmer over low heat for 3 hours. Flip the roast. Cover and simmer at least another 2 hours. The meat will pull away easily when it is ready and the bone will come out with just a little tug.

Makes 12 to 15 servings.

Stone-ground cornmeal, such as that from Falls Mill in Belvidere, Tennessee, is key to these flavorful puffs. Flecks of black pepper give them the right bite.

BLACK PEPPER BUTTERMILK CORNCAKES (GLUTEN-FREE)

2 cups stone-ground cornmeal

1 1/2 teaspoons baking powder

1/2 teaspoon baking soda

1 teaspoon salt

1/2 teaspoon black pepper

1 1/2 cups buttermilk

2 large eggs, lightly beaten

4 tablespoons (1/2 stick) butter, melted

❯ In a large bowl whisk together the cornmeal, baking powder, baking soda, salt, and pepper. In a medium bowl whisk the buttermilk, eggs, and butter together. Pour the buttermilk mixture into the cornmeal mixture and stir until combined. The batter will be thick. (If too thick, thin with a little more buttermilk.)

❯ Place a skillet over medium-high heat. Drop tablespoons of the batter into the skillet, creating 2-inch round cakes. Allow the edges to brown before flipping.

Makes 15 corncakes.

Roasting brings out the caramel sweetness of summer veggies. Arrange the slices in overlapping circles in the tart pan to create a pretty concentric ringed design.

ROASTED SUMMER VEGETABLE TART

CRUST

1 cup all-purpose flour

1/4 teaspoon salt

6 tablespoons butter, chilled and cut into small pieces

4 tablespoons ice water

1 tablespoon coarse-grain mustard

❂ Place the flour and salt in a medium bowl. With a pastry blender, cut the butter into the flour mixture until it becomes like coarse meal. Add the water, 1 tablespoon at a time, and mix well with a wooden spoon.

❂ With your hands, gather the dough up into a ball, pressing, rolling, and shaping until it is smooth and round. Flatten slightly, seal in plastic wrap, and place in the refrigerator for at least 1 hour.

❂ Roll the dough out on a lightly floured surface into an 11- or 12-inch circle. Drape the dough over a 9- or 10-inch quiche or tart pan. Press the dough to the bottom and sides, taking care not to stretch it. Rub the coarse-grain mustard onto the pastry surface and place it in the refrigerator for about 30 minutes.

❂ Preheat the oven to 375 degrees. Prick the crust with a fork. Line the crust with aluminum foil, pour beans or pie weights into the bottom, and place the pan in the oven to bake for 12 minutes. When the crust is nicely browned, remove and allow to cool.

ROASTED VEGETABLES

1 zucchini, cut into 1/2-inch rounds

2 yellow squash, sliced lengthwise in 1/2-inch pieces

1 red bell pepper, sliced into strips

1 medium onion, sliced "pole to pole"

12 to 15 cherry tomatoes

2 to 3 garlic cloves, in their skins

Olive oil

Sea salt to taste

A few sprigs of fresh thyme

❂ Increase the oven temperature to 400 degrees. Spread out the zucchini, squash, bell pepper, onion, tomatoes, and garlic on a baking sheet and brush with the olive oil. Sprinkle with sea salt and fresh thyme. Roast until the veggies are golden brown, about 12 minutes. Allow to cool. Pop the garlic cloves out of their skins and slice.

SAVORY CUSTARD

1 1/4 cups half-and-half

3 large eggs

1/2 cup grated Parmesan cheese

1/4 teaspoon salt

1/4 teaspoon black pepper

ASSEMBLY

1 cup shredded Gruyere cheese

> While the vegetables are roasting, beat the half-and-half, eggs, Parmesan, salt, and pepper together in a medium bowl until the eggs are well incorporated into the liquid.

> Reduce the oven temperature to 350 degrees.

> Lay the cooled roasted vegetable pieces in the tart shell in concentric circles. Sprinkle with the Gruyere cheese. Pour the custard mixture over the vegetables. Bake in the center of the oven for 25 minutes. The custard will set and the top will be nicely browned. Serve warm or at room temperature.

Makes 8 to 10 servings.

You can cook this chicken on your outdoor grill, but sometimes that's not possible. Mark's overnight brine and sticky sauce create a yummy oven alternative.

MARK'S STICKY ONION OVEN-BARBECUED CHICKEN

1 gallon water

1 cup kosher salt

1/2 cup firmly packed brown sugar

1/2 cup sorghum (or molasses)

1 cup sherry

1 onion, quartered

1 orange, quartered

1 apple, quartered

A few sprigs of fresh rosemary

1 tablespoon cracked black pepper

2 whole chickens, butchered into parts (16 pieces)

Sticky Onion Barbecue Sauce (recipe follows)

TO PREPARE THE CHICKEN: Pour the water into a large plastic tub (large enough to hold the chicken pieces and the brining liquid). Add the salt, brown sugar, sorghum, sherry, onion, orange, apple, rosemary, and pepper. Stir well. Place the chicken pieces in the brine. Cover and refrigerate overnight.

TO COOK THE CHICKEN: Preheat the oven to 375 degrees. Remove the chicken from the brine and pat dry. Lay the pieces out on a baking sheet. Pour 3 cups of the Sticky Onion Barbecue Sauce into a medium bowl. Brush the chicken liberally with the sauce and place in the oven.

❯ Bake for 15 minutes and baste with more sauce. Continue baking, basting every 10 to 15 minutes for 50 to 60 minutes. Rotate the baking sheet to ensure even browning of the pieces. When the chicken is done, remove from oven. Arrange pieces on a platter and serve.

Makes 12 servings.

STICKY ONION BARBECUE SAUCE

1/2 cup butter

5 cups diced yellow onions

5 garlic cloves, minced

1 1/2 teaspoons salt

1/2 cup firmly packed brown sugar

1/4 cup red wine vinegar

2 tablespoons Worcestershire sauce

2 tablespoons hot sauce (such as Crystal or Louisiana)

2 teaspoons dry mustard

1 1/2 cups (12 ounces) ketchup

2 1/4 cups (18 ounces) chili sauce

❯ In a heavy-duty pot over medium heat, melt the butter. Add the onions and sauté until soft and translucent, about 7 minutes. Add the garlic and salt. Stir well. Continue sautéing. The onions will begin to caramelize.

❯ Add the brown sugar, vinegar, Worcestershire, hot sauce, and dry mustard. Stir well and simmer for 10 minutes. Add the ketchup and chili sauce. Stir well and continue simmering over medium heat for another 10 minutes. Remove from heat. Cool and refrigerate.

Makes 6 cups.

This protein-rich salad came about because of Gigi's trial crop of turtle beans. We had no idea that they would grow so well in Tennessee. Although, after spending hours shelling the impressive pile—not to mention her time planting, weeding, and harvesting—she wasn't sure if she would grow them again. It definitely increased her already huge respect for farmers.

SOUTHWEST BLACK BEAN AND QUINOA SALAD

2 tablespoons olive oil

1 large onion, diced

1 poblano pepper, diced

2 cloves garlic, minced

1 teaspoon cumin

1 teaspoon coriander seed, toasted and crushed*

2 teaspoons salt, divided

2 cups fresh black beans, rinsed and picked over**

1 cup quinoa, rinsed three times and drained

1 1/2 cups water

1/2 teaspoon red pepper flakes

2 tablespoons extra-virgin olive oil

1 lime

1 medium avocado, diced

1 medium tomato, diced

4 green onions, chopped

❯ Pour the olive oil into a 2-quart saucepan over medium heat. Add the onions and poblanos and cook until the onions are translucent. Add the garlic. Season with the cumin, coriander, and 1 teaspoon of the salt. Sauté for 5 minutes. Add the beans and stir until they are well coated. Add enough water to cover the beans by 2 inches and cover. Lower the heat and simmer for 30 minutes.

❯ Skim off any foam that accumulates on the top and stir. Fresh beans will cook rather quickly. If using dried beans, simmer for about 2 hours. Continue simmering until the beans are soft but still intact. This part of the dish can be prepared the day before and refrigerated.

❯ Place a skillet over medium heat and add the well-rinsed quinoa. Stir to toast the grain, about 5 minutes. Add the water and stir. Season with the remaining 1 teaspoon salt and red pepper flakes. Cover, reduce the heat to low, and cook for 30 minutes. Remove from the heat and allow the quinoa to rest before fluffing with a fork.

❯ Pour the extra-virgin olive oil into a large bowl. Zest and juice the lime and add both to the bowl. Add the diced avocado, tomatoes, and chopped green onions. Gently toss.

❯ Drain the black beans and fold them into the quinoa mixture. Fold the quinoa mixture into the avocado–tomato mixture. Taste for salt and spice, and adjust as needed.

Makes 12 to 15 servings.

*To toast coriander seed, sprinkle seed into a shallow skillet over medium-high heat. Shake the seeds as they heat up and crackle. This will take just a minute or two. Remove from heat and scrape the seeds out of the pan into a small bowl to cool. Use a mortar and pestle or spice grinder to crush the toasted seeds.

**If using dried beans, soak them for at least 3 hours. Drain and rinse.

Watermelon demonstrates its potluck versatility in this recipe, the foundation of a large refreshing salad in its own serving bowl. The sharp and pungent tastes imparted by the red onion and feta meld with the gush of cool melon sweetness. A splash of sherry, along with the sherry vinaigrette, really enlivens the flavors.

WATERMELON SALAD IN A WATERMELON BOWL

1 medium-size ripe watermelon

1 medium red onion, sliced paper-thin

A handful of fresh oregano leaves, chopped

1/2 teaspoon salt

1/2 teaspoon black pepper

1/4 cup dry sherry

Sherry-Oregano Vinaigrette (recipe follows)

1 cup crumbled feta cheese

Fresh Thai basil, chiffonade, plus extra for garnish

❯ Place your watermelon on the counter with the flat side down, so that it is stable. Draw a line about one-third of the way down from the top. Then draw your cutting line around the circumference of the watermelon. Using a sharp knife, make an angled incision along the line.

❯ Separate the watermelon and carve or scoop the melon out of its rind in big, manageable chunks from both pieces. If you want to make a watermelon bowl, keep the rind of the larger half for the watermelon bowl intact.

❯ Cut the melon chunks into rectangular shapes about 2 1/2 to 3 inches long and 3/4 inch wide. You'll need 6 cups of cut watermelon.* Place the melon, onion, and oregano in a large bowl. Sprinkle with salt and black pepper. Let the mixture sit for 15 minutes and drain off any excess liquid. Add the dry sherry and toss.

❯ Pour the Sherry-Oregano Vinaigrette over the mixture. Then add the crumbled feta and the Thai basil. Gently toss. Place onto a bed of salad greens or into the watermelon bowl (see sidebar for instructions). Garnish with additional basil and serve.

Makes 10 to 12 servings.

*The melon may yield more than 6 cups, depending on its size. Reserve the extra for another use, such as our Watermelon-Lemongrass Refresher on page 76.

SHERRY-OREGANO VINAIGRETTE

6 tablespoons sherry vinegar

2 teaspoons fresh oregano

1/2 teaspoon coarse-grain mustard

1/2 teaspoon salt

1/4 teaspoon red pepper flakes

1 cup plus 2 tablespoons extra-virgin olive oil

❂ Mix the vinegar, oregano, mustard, salt, and red pepper flakes in a small bowl. Whisk in the olive oil, 1 tablespoon at a time, until the oil and vinegar combine. Taste for seasonings and adjust if needed.

Makes 1 1/2 cups.

MAKE A WATERMELON BOWL

After you have cut the watermelon into two pieces and removed the flesh, you can easily make a watermelon bowl. Using a large spoon, scrape clean the interior sides of the larger watermelon half—the bowl. Pour off any accumulated liquid. You can reserve this and drink it!

Wipe the exterior of the watermelon dry. With a sharp paring knife, make V-shaped cuts, up and down, along the rim of the watermelon bowl. Before filling with the salad, invert the bowl for several minutes to drain off excess water. (Yes, watermelons are very watery!)

These days you are likely to find several varieties and colors of sweet potatoes at the market with names like Jewel, Garnet, Boniato, Star Leaf, or Beauregard. It's fun and flavorful to roast red, white, and orange wedges together. Each cooks in the same time, yet retains its distinct taste. To serve, arrange them in a dish and top them with this tangy glaze.

SWEET POTATO TRIO WITH DRIED APRICOTS, LEEKS, AND BALSAMIC GLAZE

2 Garnet sweet potatoes

2 Jewel sweet potatoes

2 Boniato sweet potatoes

6 tablespoons olive oil, divided

Kosher salt to taste

1/2 cup dried apricots, cut into slivers

1/4 cup balsamic vinegar

1 leek, cleaned well and cut into 1/2-inch pieces

1/2 cup fresh flat-leaf parsley, chopped, plus extra for garnish

Coarse ground black pepper to taste

○ Preheat the oven to 375 degrees.

○ Scrub, rinse, and dry the sweet potatoes. Cut into planks or wedges, like steak fries, and place on a large baking sheet. Toss with 2 tablespoons olive oil and sprinkle with kosher salt. Bake until tender with crispy browned edges, about 25 minutes.

○ Place the apricots in a small bowl. Heat the balsamic vinegar in a small saucepan over medium heat and pour over the apricots.

○ Warm a skillet over medium heat and add the remaining 4 tablespoons olive oil. Add the leeks and sauté until softened and somewhat translucent, about 4 minutes. Stir in the parsley and then the apricots in balsamic. Remove the pan from the heat.

○ Arrange the sweet potato wedges in a layered circular fashion in a round casserole dish, spooning the leek mixture over each layer and on top. Season to taste with salt and black pepper. Garnish with parsley, if desired. Serve warm or at room temperature.

Makes 10 servings.

Rosemary leaves placed in the center of the lemon-glazed shortbread give Marla's cookies a simple elegance. You'll love the herbal and citrus tastes interspersed throughout the buttery crisps.

GLAZED LEMON-ROSEMARY SHORTBREAD COOKIES

SHORTBREAD

1 cup (2 sticks) butter, softened

3/4 cup sugar

1 tablespoon grated lemon zest

1 tablespoon chopped fresh rosemary

1 large egg

1 teaspoon fresh lemon juice

1 teaspoon vanilla extract

1 teaspoon salt

3 cups all-purpose flour

GLAZE

1 cup confectioners' sugar

2 tablespoons olive oil

1 teaspoon fresh lemon juice

2 to 3 tablespoons water

Fresh rosemary sprigs for garnish

TO MAKE THE SHORTBREAD: In the bowl of an electric mixer, cream the butter and sugar together on medium speed for 3 minutes. Add the zest, rosemary, egg, lemon juice, vanilla, and salt, and beat for 1 minute. Scrape down the bowl. At low speed, add the flour and mix just until combined; do not overmix. Roll the dough out between 2 large sheets of parchment paper to 1/4 inch thick. Chill the dough for 30 minutes.

❯ Preheat the oven to 350 degrees. Line several baking sheets with parchment paper.

❯ Cut the dough using your favorite cookie cutters. Place the dough shapes onto baking sheets and bake for 16 to 18 minutes or until the edges are golden. Remove to a wire rack to cool.

TO MAKE THE GLAZE: Combine the confectioners' sugar, olive oil, and lemon juice in a medium bowl. Add enough water to achieve a spreadable consistency. Drizzle and spread the glaze over each cooled cookie and top with a fresh rosemary sprig.

Makes 35 to 40 cookies.

It took a couple of seasons, but Jen became as busy as her bees, harvesting frame after frame of fragrant honey. You could practically taste a garden of flowers in her jar, which carried over into this humble cake. Seek out locally made honey where you live. You'll be surprised and pleased with the results when you cook with it.

BROWN BUTTER HONEY CAKE

CAKE

1 cup (2 sticks) butter

1 tablespoon fresh thyme leaves

2 1/2 cups all-purpose flour

2 teaspoons baking powder

1/2 teaspoon baking soda

1/2 teaspoon salt

Juice of 1 lemon
(about 2 tablespoons)

1 tablespoon vanilla extract

1 cup milk

1 cup local honey

3 large eggs

Honey Cream Cheese Icing
(recipe below)

1/2 cup pistachios, coarsely chopped, for garnish

❯ Preheat the oven to 350 degrees. Line a 9-inch cake or springform pan with parchment paper and coat with nonstick cooking spray.

❯ Slowly cook the butter in a skillet over medium heat, stirring occasionally, until it becomes toasty brown. Toss the thyme leaves into the warm brown butter and remove from heat.

❯ Sift the flour, baking powder, baking soda, and salt together in a medium bowl.

❯ Pour the lemon juice and vanilla into the cup of milk and stir. Let it stand and slightly thicken/curdle.

❯ When the butter has cooled, pour it into a large bowl of an electric mixer and beat in the honey with the whisk attachment, or use a hand mixer. Beat in the milk mixture, then the flour mixture. Beat in the eggs, one at a time, until each is well combined and the batter is smooth. Pour the batter into the cake pan.

❯ Bake for 25 to 30 minutes. When cake is set, remove from oven and cool on a wire rack. When cooled, unmold. Split the layer in half.

HONEY CREAM CHEESE ICING

1/2 cup (1 stick) butter, softened

1 (8-ounce) package cream cheese, softened

3 to 4 tablespoons local honey

❯ In a medium bowl use a hand mixer to beat the butter and cream cheese together until smooth, light, and fluffy. Beat in the honey, 1 tablespoon at a time. The mixture will be creamy smooth.

❯ Place a layer of cake on a serving platter and spread on half of the icing. Top with the second layer of cake and spread on the remaining icing.

❯ Garnish with chopped pistachios.

Makes 10 to 12 servings.

What could be better with Brown Butter Honey Cake?

POTLUCK PISTACHIO ICE CREAM

2 cups unsalted shelled pistachios, plus 1 cup toasted and chopped medium fine

1 1/2 cups sugar, divided

1 quart (4 cups) whole milk

6 large eggs

1 teaspoon vanilla extract

1/2 teaspoon almond extract

1 pint (2 cups) heavy cream

TO INFUSE THE PISTACHIOS: Using a food processor fitted with a chopping blade, grind the 2 cups pistachios and 1 cup sugar until fine. Be careful not to over-process, as that could result in "pistachio butter."

❯ Pour the milk into a large saucepan over medium heat and stir in the ground pistachio–sugar mixture. Bring to just under a boil. Remove the pan from the heat.

TO MAKE THE CUSTARD: In a large bowl beat the eggs and remaining 1/2 cup of sugar together. Add the vanilla and almond extracts and continue beating. The mixture will be frothy. Slowly add the hot milk mixture.

❯ Pour the egg mixture back into the large saucepan over medium heat. Bring the mixture to a simmer, stirring constantly with a wooden spoon as the custard begins to thicken. When the custard coats the back of the spoon (about 10 to 12 minutes cooking), remove the pan from the heat.

❯ Strain the custard into a large bowl and let cool. When cooled to room temperature, cover and place the bowl in the refrigerator for at least 2 hours or overnight. The mixture must be well chilled.

READY TO CHURN: Whisk in the heavy cream and chopped toasted pistachios and pour the mixture into your ice-cream maker. Churn according to the manufacturer's directions. Then remove and freeze until serving time.

Makes 2 quarts.

Burger Power

AMERICANS + BURGERS = LOVE

Americans have a long-standing love affair with the hamburger. It's iconic. These days, that love has never been bigger, and the desire to know where the meat in that burger came from has never been stronger. Veering away from industrial produced beef and all its incumbent risks, we focus on local ranchers raising happy herds: Cows free to roam and eat grasses. Cows free from antibiotics and hormones.

The shift back to old-school cattle raising obliges us to reeducate our palates and cooking techniques.

Gigi and I met Doug and Sue Bagwell from Walnut Hills Farm at our Nashville Farmers' Market. They were enthusiastic about their operation, fifty rolling acres in Middle Tennessee, where their Limousin cattle, heritage pigs, and chickens all enjoy a true free-range life. The farm had been fallow for years when the Bagwells purchased it in 2003. It was an overgrown mess, Doug attested, but the upside was that no herbicides or pesticides had been used on the land during that time, a tradition that the Bagwells were pleased to continue.

They also told us how best to prepare the meat.

Foremost we learned that grass-fed, dry-aged beef is both leaner and denser, making it lower in calories and saturated fats, but higher in those healthy omega-3s. It also contains less water than grain-fed. As such, it requires minimal seasoning and minimal cooking. The Bagwells suggest brushing the meats with olive or grapeseed oil to prevent sticking. You can also turn down the heat and cut back on your cooking time by 30 percent. Because you can trust the source of the beef, it is safe—and preferable—to cook steaks and burgers to medium-rare. The meat remains juicier and more flavorful. We purchased five (1-pound) packages of Walnut Hills ground beef and planned our mini-burger feast.

While Gigi fired up the grill, I hand-formed small patties, 2-ounce "slider-size" burgers. I brushed them with olive oil, splashed them with Worcestershire sauce, and sprinkled on some salt and black pepper. In seasoning and cooking, the less-is-more philosophy applies. When the coals became ashen, I started the process. Once the patties hit the grill, don't move or mash them down. Let them sizzle and char before flipping. It really didn't take long to turn out dozens of plump grilled burgers.

Having a platter full of these lightly charred patties, along with all manner of sauces and relishes, made for a fun, picnic-like potluck.

A big part of the burger allure is how it gets embellished: the fixin's. This is where creativity comes in, and this American icon gets sauced, slathered, and stacked with any number of ingredients. Our potluck spread had zucchini pickles, fried green tomatoes, blue cheese-chive mayo, caramelized onions, farmstead pimento cheese, and that king of condiments: ketchup. No kitchen pantry or fridge is complete without a bottle or two—especially if you have a ketchup fiend living in your house. Beyond the usual suspects—burgers and fries—a certain member of our household is known to slap some red onto his scrambled eggs, cottage cheese, white beans, stir-fried rice . . . Does anyone recall when the USDA labeled ketchup as a vegetable?

I had always been curious about making ketchup, and had been told that it was easy-peasy to make. With "paste" tomatoes (meaty plum-shaped tomatoes with few seeds) abundant at the market, it seemed like a good time to make a batch. I was as excited about the prospect of real-deal ketchup at the potluck as I was about our local burgers.

My recipe research turned up many variations, but I chose to use cider vinegar, brown sugar, and whole spices in the batch. A piece of cinnamon stick, a few beads of allspice, and bits of clove would impart more vibrant piquancy than dried-and-powdered to my pot of tomatoes, onions, garlic, and peppers.

Oh my.

With all those fine ingredients, I'd felt certain that it would be very good. But the ketchup experiment far exceeded my expectations. This is what it should really taste like! Our potluckers agreed. Packed with tomato sweetness—yet not too sweet—it was layered with pungent spice and complex flavors. The king of ketchups—almost worthy of that USDA vegetable label.

Power to the burger!

"It is the Americans who have managed to crown minced beef as hamburger, and to send it round the world so that even the fussy French have taken to *le boeuf hache, le hambourgaire*."

—JULIA CHILD

SEPTEMBER: BURGER POWER

With ripe watermelon and an unruly lemongrass plant in her garden, Teresa conjured up this Indian summer cocktail.

WATERMELON-LEMONGRASS REFRESHER

1 cup water

1 cup sugar

2 stalks lemongrass, cut into pieces

2 to 3 hot and mild chilies (such as serrano or anaheim), cut in half

1 medium seedless watermelon (basketball size)

Juice of 2 limes

2 cups melon rum

Fresh mint for garnish

◉ Place the water, sugar, lemongrass, and chilies into a saucepan over medium heat. Stir until the sugar is melted. Set aside to cool. When cooled completely, strain into a container.

◉ Cut the watermelon in half and remove the pulp with an ice-cream scoop. Working in batches if necessary, process watermelon pulp in a food processor fitted with a chopping blade until it becomes liquid. Strain into a large bowl. Add the lime juice, rum, and strained syrup. Stir, taste, and adjust. Decant into bottles or a large pitcher. Chill before serving over ice with a sprig or two of mint.

Makes approximately 2 quarts.

Lean and flavorful grass-fed beef grills quickly to rosy succulence. You don't want to overhandle it or overcook it.

THE LOCAL BURGER

5 pounds local, grass-fed ground beef

1/4 cup Worcestershire sauce

1/4 cup olive oil

Coarse sea salt to taste

Coarse ground black pepper to taste

The Fixin's (list to follow)

❯ Preheat the oven to low (180 to 200 degrees).

❯ Form small meat patties by rolling the meat into golf ball–size shapes; roll and pat, keeping the burger thick. Place onto a baking sheet.

❯ In a small bowl whisk together the Worcestershire and olive oil. Brush both sides of the meat patties with the oil mixture and season liberally with salt and black pepper.

❯ If you are using a gas grill, turn your heat to medium-high. Allow 5 to 10 minutes for the grate to get hot. If using charcoal, wait until the coals are ashen before grilling, about 30 minutes. If you are cooking indoors, heat your grill pan on medium-high.

❯ Cook the burgers approximately 3 minutes per side. Don't mash or press the patties! As the burgers are cooked, move them into a shallow roasting pan. Cover and keep warm in the oven until serving time.

❯ Split dinner rolls and place into a linen-lined basket. Mound butter lettuce leaves onto one section of a large platter. Lay out slices of tomatoes and slices of onion. Assemble other condiments into serving bowls.

Makes 40 (2-ounce) mini burgers.

THE FIXIN'S

40 round dinner rolls

1 head butter lettuce, washed, spun dry, and broken into leaves

6 to 8 small ripe tomatoes, washed, dried, and cut into 1/4-inch slices

2 small red onions, thinly sliced

Maggie's Refrigerator Zucchini Pickles (see page 81)

Kenny's Farmhouse Pimento Cheese (see page 80)

Ketchup for Real (see page 79)

Fried Green Tomatoes with Bacon-Horseradish Cream Sauce (see page 82)

Spicy Old-World Mustard (see page 104) or Stout Mustard (page 109)

Making your own ketchup is not difficult and is really fun. Its vibrant taste will win over those used to the store-bought, high-fructose corn syrup–laden types.

KETCHUP FOR REAL

2 pounds paste tomatoes (such as plum or Roma), coarsely chopped

1 pimento or red bell pepper, chopped

1 jalapeño pepper, sliced

4 cloves garlic, sliced

1 medium onion, chopped

1/2 cup firmly packed brown sugar

1/2 cup cider vinegar

1 cup water

1 stick cinnamon

2 teaspoons whole allspice

6 whole cloves

2 teaspoons salt

A few grinds of black pepper

Special equipment: food mill

◐ Place the tomatoes, peppers, garlic, onion, brown sugar, and cider vinegar into a 5- or 6-quart large pot over medium heat. Add the water. Place the cinnamon stick, whole allspice, and cloves in a piece of cheesecloth. Tie the cheesecloth with culinary string and add it to the pot. Season with salt and pepper. Stir and cover. Simmer for at least 1 hour.

◑ Uncover, stir, and simmer uncovered for 30 minutes, stirring occasionally. Remove the cheesecloth and continue cooking for about 1 hour. The mixture will become very thick. Allow to cool.

◒ Run the mixture through a food mill. This will separate the skin and seeds from the batch. (Sometimes I run the "dregs"—the leftover skins—through a second time to extract more juices.) Pour the ketchup into warm sterile* jars.

Makes almost 2 pints.

NOTE: If you increase this recipe to make a large quantity for canning, process in a hot water bath as you would for canning tomatoes.

*For directions on sterilizing jars, see our Canning Tips sidebar on page 49.

Fresh pimento peppers have a charming heart-shaped body and thick, meaty flesh that when oven-caramelized make the best pimento cheese—especially when combined with shredded white Cheddar cheese from Kenny's Farmhouse Cheeses in Kentucky. A few spoonfuls of Duke's mayonnaise complete this true Southern delicacy. Pimento cheese is held in lofty esteem and is showing up in mac 'n' cheese, grits casseroles, and stuffed eggs. Might we also suggest a dollop on a burger?

KENNY'S FARMHOUSE PIMENTO CHEESE

1 large pimento or sweet red bell pepper, halved

Olive oil

Sea salt to taste

1/2 teaspoon cider vinegar (optional)

1 pound sharp white Cheddar cheese

4 tablespoons mayonnaise (such as Duke's or Hellman's)

1/4 cup minced red onion

1/2 teaspoon granulated garlic

1/2 teaspoon black pepper

❥ Preheat the oven to 450 degrees.

❥ Place the pepper halves on a baking sheet and brush with olive oil and sprinkle with salt. Roast until the skin is blistered, about 15 minutes. When cool enough to handle, remove the peels, chop, and place in a small bowl. Add the vinegar. Set aside.

❥ Shred the cheese and place in a large bowl. Add the mayonnaise, red onion, garlic, black pepper, and peppers. Fold the mixture until the pimentos are laced throughout the cheese and the mayonnaise has moistened and helped bind the cheese. Taste for salt and adjust as needed. Serve with crackers, on finger sandwiches, or dolloped onto a burger. DEE-LISH.

Makes 3 cups.

This recipe is a great way to deal with a "zeal of zucchini." Maggie tested this idea the first summer her prolific squashes took over the garden, and it worked like a charm.

MAGGIE'S REFRIGERATOR ZUCCHINI PICKLES

6 pounds zucchini, sliced 1/4 inch thick

2 pounds onions, sliced into 1/4-inch thick rings or half rings

4 cups sugar

2 cups cider vinegar

1 cup water

1/4 cup kosher salt

1 1/2 teaspoons celery seed

1 1/2 teaspoons mustard seed

1 teaspoon turmeric

◉ Layer the zucchini and onions into a gallon glass jar. In a large pot combine the sugar, vinegar, water, salt, celery and mustard seeds, and turmeric and bring to a boil over high heat. Boil for 5 minutes. Allow the mixture to cool, then pour over the zucchini and onions. Screw on the cap and refrigerate for a week to allow the flavors to develop. Pickles will keep for months, if they last that long.

Makes 1 gallon.

There's something special about fried green tomatoes that I did not come to appreciate until recent years. When fried, what appears to be firm and without flavor softens and releases a tangy citrus essence. A surprise with bite! And then there's that salty crackle of cornmeal batter.

FRIED GREEN TOMATOES WITH BACON-HORSERADISH CREAM SAUCE

Vegetable or canola oil for frying

1 cup cornmeal

1/4 cup all-purpose flour

1 teaspoon salt

1/2 teaspoon black pepper

1/4 teaspoon cayenne pepper

1 cup buttermilk

4 firm green tomatoes, sliced 1/4 inch thick

Bacon-Horseradish Cream Sauce (recipe follows)

❯ In a skillet over medium-high heat, pour enough oil to reach 1/2 inch high. In a shallow pan or bowl mix the cornmeal well with the flour, salt, black pepper, and cayenne. Pour the buttermilk into another shallow bowl. Dip the tomato slices into the buttermilk. Then dredge in the cornmeal mixture.

❯ When the oil sizzles, add the tomato slices and fry 2 to 4 minutes per side, until golden brown. Drain on paper towels. Serve with Bacon-Horseradish Cream Sauce.

Makes 16 to 20 slices.

Bacon and tomatoes, the ideal pairing! Fold some crisp smoky bits throughout the horseradish cream sauce to make a fitting dip for fried green tomatoes.

BACON-HORSERADISH CREAM SAUCE

1 cup sour cream

1/2 cup mayonnaise (such as Hellman's or Duke's)

2 heaping tablespoons prepared horseradish

1 teaspoon fresh lemon juice

1/2 teaspoon hot sauce

1/2 teaspoon salt

1/4 teaspoon cayenne pepper

4 strips bacon, cooked crisp, drained, and chopped

❯ In a small bowl whisk together the sour cream, mayonnaise, horseradish, lemon juice, hot sauce, salt, cayenne, and bacon until well blended. Taste for horseradish and add more if necessary.

Makes almost 2 cups.

We potluckers like impetuous deviled eggs—devils with personality, pizzazz. Each version from this lively trio has its distinct, assertive devilish style.

MAKING DEVILMENT: DEVILED EGG TRIO

CAJUN DEVILS

12 large eggs, hard-boiled and peeled (see Hard-Boiled Tips on page 85)

1/2 cup mayonnaise (such as Duke's)

4 tablespoons Dijon mustard

1 teaspoon hot sauce (such as Crystal or Louisiana)

1/2 teaspoon Worcestershire sauce

1/2 teaspoon salt

1/2 teaspoon coarse ground black pepper

1/4 teaspoon granulated garlic

1/4 teaspoon cayenne pepper

Paprika for garnish

◉ Slice the eggs in half lengthwise. Place the yolks in the bowl of a food processor fitted with a chopping blade. Place the halves on a platter. Add the mayonnaise, Dijon mustard, hot sauce, Worcestershire, salt, pepper, garlic, and cayenne to the food processor. Pulse, then process until smooth. Taste for spice and adjust as needed.

◉ Spoon the yolk mixture into a pastry bag fitted with a star tip. Pipe the filling into the hollows of the eggs. Sprinkle the tops with paprika.

Makes 2 dozen.

RELISHED AND CAPERED

12 large eggs, hard-boiled and peeled (see Hard-Boiled Tips on page 85)

7 tablespoons mayonnaise

5 tablespoons sweet pickle relish

1 tablespoon capers

2 teaspoons Dijon mustard

1/4 teaspoon salt

Pinch of black pepper

Minced fresh parsley or dill for garnish

◉ Slice the eggs in half lengthwise. Place the yolks in the bowl of a food processor fitted with a chopping blade. Place the halves on a platter. Add the mayonnaise, pickle relish, capers, mustard, salt, and pepper to the food processor. Pulse, then process until somewhat smooth. Taste for seasonings and adjust as needed.

◉ Spoon the yolk mixture into a pastry bag fitted with a large open tip. Pipe the filling into the hollows of the halves. Garnish with minced parsley or dill.

Makes 2 dozen.

PIMENTO BACON

12 large eggs, hard-boiled and peeled (see Hard-Boiled Tips below)

4 slices bacon, cooked crisp, divided

4 green onions, divided

1 cup pimento cheese (see page 80 for Kenny's Farmhouse Pimento Cheese)

1 tablespoon coarse-grain mustard

◗ Slice the eggs in half lengthwise. Place the yolks in the bowl of a food processor fitted with a chopping blade. Place the halves on a platter. Pulse the yolks briefly to break them up. Crumble 3 slices bacon and finely chop 3 green onions. Add the pimento cheese, mustard, bacon crumbles, and chopped green onion to the yolks. Process until well combined but still chunky.

◗ Spoon the mixture into the halves. Crumble remaining bacon strip, chop remaining green onion, and garnish the tops.

Makes 2 dozen.

HARD-BOILED TIPS

We've all experienced it: stubborn hard-boiled eggs that refuse to peel, resulting in a mess of rag-tag eggs difficult to cut and stuff.

Here are some tips to ensure that eggs slip right out of their shells. And no icky gray-green ring—a sign of an overcooked egg—around the yolk either.

Use older eggs. It seems counterintuitive, but fresh farm eggs can be the culprits. Older eggs have time to form more of an air pocket between the white and the shell. I learned this from a friend who raises chickens. As she gathers and crates eggs, she dates them before refrigeration. When she wants to make deviled eggs, she uses the ones that are 2 to 3 weeks old.

Place eggs into a large pot (so they won't crowd and potentially crack!) filled with cool water that covers the eggs by 3 inches. Do not put a lid on the pot yet.

Bring the water to a boil over medium heat. Once the water comes to a rolling boil, place a lid on the pot and remove from the heat. Let the eggs sit undisturbed for 15 minutes.

Drain the water and cover the eggs with cool water. Let cool about 10 minutes. Crack and peel and carry on.

A luscious savory pie first made in honor of East Nashville's Tomato Arts Fest. The crust gets its unique flavor from pesto brushed on and baked into the surface. You'll love the pairing of lemon tomatoes and lemon basil, but the pie is just as delicious with Bradley tomatoes and Genovese basil.

DEEP-DISH LEMON TOMATO AND LEMON BASIL PIE

PESTO-PINE NUT PASTRY CRUST

1 cup all-purpose flour

6 tablespoons butter, chilled and cut into small pieces

1/4 teaspoon salt

4 tablespoons ice water

3 tablespoons pesto

1/2 cup pine nuts

◉ Preheat the oven to 350 degrees.

◉ Place the flour, butter, and salt in the bowl of a food processor fitted with the pastry blade. Pulse until the mixture is like coarse meal. Add the ice water, 1 tablespoon at a time, and process until the mixture gathers into a mass. Shape into a ball, wrap in plastic, and place in the refrigerator for at least 1 hour.

◉ Roll the dough out on a lightly floured surface into a 12-inch circle. Drape the dough over a 9-inch deep-dish pie pan or springform pan. Press the dough to the bottom and sides, taking care not to stretch it. Brush the pesto onto the pastry surface, prick the pie bottom with a fork, and scatter with pine nuts, which double as pie weights.

◉ Bake for 10 to 12 minutes. Remove and cool before adding the filling.

FILLING

2 large eggs

1 1/2 cups mayonnaise

1 1/2 cups grated Parmesan cheese

1/2 teaspoon granulated garlic

1/2 teaspoon salt

1 teaspoon black pepper

4 to 6 ripe lemon-colored or yellow tomatoes, such as Lemon Boys, sliced 1/2 inch thick

1 1/2 cups chopped fresh lemon basil leaves

1 cup shredded Monterey Jack cheese

1/2 cup shredded sharp white Cheddar cheese

◉ Preheat the oven to 350 degrees.

◉ In a medium bowl whisk the eggs, mayonnaise, Parmesan, garlic, salt, and pepper. Cover the bottom of the prebaked piecrust with a layer of sliced tomatoes. Top with half of the chopped basil. Spoon about half of the egg mixture over the basil, and top with half of the shredded cheeses. Repeat the layering. Decorate the top with tomato slices and basil leaves.

◉ Bake for 45 to 50 minutes, until golden. Serve warm or at room temperature.

Makes 12 to 15 servings.

This layered casserole is a great way to use those end-of-the-season zucchinis and tomatoes. The grits cook up rich and soufflé-like. Around here, we all love the grits from Falls Mill; they are stone ground in the time-honored tradition for excellent texture and taste. The grits have more "grit."

ITALIAN FLAG GRITS

ZUCCHINI LAYER

2 medium zucchinis, sliced 1/4 inch lengthwise

Olive oil

Salt to taste

10 to 12 fresh basil leaves

❯ Preheat the oven to 425 degrees.

❯ Brush the zucchini slices with olive oil. Sprinkle with salt. Roast until the edges are browned, about 15 minutes. Remove from the oven and allow to cool.

GRITS SOUFFLÉ LAYER

4 cups water

1 cup stone-ground grits

1 teaspoon salt

1/2 teaspoon black pepper

1 teaspoon granulated garlic

2 eggs, lightly beaten

1/2 cup milk

1 cup grated Pecorino-Romano cheese

❯ Pour the water, grits, salt, pepper, and granulated garlic into a large saucepan over medium heat. Bring to a boil, stirring well, and then simmer until thickened, about 20 minutes. Remove the pan from the heat. In a small bowl beat the eggs and milk together, and vigorously whisk the mixture into the cooked grits. Fold in the grated cheese.

ROASTED TOMATO LAYER

4 whole, ripe tomatoes

Olive oil

1 small onion

3 cloves garlic

A few sprigs of fresh thyme

Salt

Black pepper

◉ Preheat the oven to 425 degrees.

◉ Core the tomatoes, slice in half, and place on a baking sheet, skin side up. Brush with olive oil. Slice the onion pole to pole into 1/4-inch strips. Scatter the sliced onions onto the baking sheet, along with the whole garlic cloves and a few sprigs of thyme. Dust with salt and pepper.

◉ Roast for 15 to 20 minutes. The tomato skins will be blackened, puffed, and easy to slip off. When cooled, remove the tomato skins. Garlic cloves can be squeezed out of their casings. Coarsely chop the tomatoes, onions, and garlic together, and place them, along with any accumulated roasting juices, in a medium bowl.

ASSEMBLY

◉ Preheat the oven to 350 degrees.

◉ Cover the bottom of a 9 x 13-inch casserole dish with the zucchini slices, overlapping slightly where needed. Place the basil leaves over the zucchini slices. Pour the grits over the zucchini. Place more basil leaves over the top. Bake for 40 minutes. The grits will become firm, golden brown, and bubbly. Remove from the oven and spoon the roasted tomato mixture over the top.

Makes 10 to 12 servings.

Wendy enhances the potatoes' flavor by boiling them in water seasoned with garlic, bay leaf, and celery leaves. Show off the appealing layers in a glass bowl.

OLD-FASHIONED LAYERED PARSLEYED POTATO SALAD

8 medium-to-large red potatoes

1 garlic clove

1 bay leaf

A few celery tops

1 (8-ounce) container sour cream

1 1/2 cups mayonnaise*

1 heaping tablespoon prepared horseradish

1 tablespoon celery seed

2 medium Vidalia onions, chopped

1 cup fresh flat-leaf parsley, chopped

Salt to taste

Black pepper to taste

⊘ Place the potatoes, garlic, bay leaf, and celery tops in a large pot. Add enough water to cover the potatoes and bring to a boil over high heat. Cool, peel, and slice the potatoes.

⊘ In a medium bowl mix the sour cream, mayonnaise, horseradish, and celery seed. In another medium bowl mix together the onions and parsley. Layer half of the sliced potatoes in a clear glass bowl or casserole dish. Sprinkle with salt and pepper. Spoon half of the sour cream mixture on top of the potatoes and half of the onion mixture on top of the sour cream mixture. Repeat.

Makes 8 servings.

*Wendy uses Hellman's canola mayo.

Maybe this should be called "Pork Belly with Purple Hull Peas," because more time is involved in cooking the unctuous meat than the fresh peas, which simmer to tenderness in 30 minutes. The time spent browning and rendering the pork belly is well spent—it makes a wonderful foundation for the peas and its stewing juices, or as we say around here, "pot likker." And then Brian pushes it over the top—he stirs in a little heavy cream at the end. Wow.

BRIAN'S PURPLE HULL PEAS WITH PORK BELLY

1 pound piece pork belly

Salt to taste

Black pepper to taste

1 small onion, diced

2 cloves garlic, minced

2 carrots, finely chopped

2 celery ribs, finely chopped

2 cups water

4 cups freshly shelled purple hull peas, rinsed well

2 tablespoons sorghum

1 teaspoon red pepper flakes

1 bay leaf

1/2 cup heavy cream

❯ Score the top and bottom of the pork belly. Salt and pepper it generously and place it in a heavy-duty pot over medium-low heat to slowly render its fat and brown. Rotate the piece so that it eventually browns on all sides. This could take 30 minutes.

❯ After the pork belly browns, remove it from the pot. Increase the heat to medium and add the diced onions, garlic, carrots, and celery to the pan with the rendered fat, and sauté until they are soft.

❯ When the vegetables are softened, return the pork belly to the pot. Add 2 cups of water. Stir everything around, scraping up any browned bits. Cover and simmer for 30 minutes.

❯ Stir in the purple hull peas, sorghum, and red pepper flakes. Add more liquid, if necessary, to cover the peas. Toss in a bay leaf. Simmer uncovered until the peas are tender, about 30 minutes. Skim off any foam that may form when the peas first begin to cook.

❯ Before serving, discard bay leaf. Remove the pork belly to a cutting board. Stir in the heavy cream. Shred the meaty bits of the pork belly (discard hunks of fat) and return them to the pot. Taste for seasoning and add a little black pepper or a dash of hot sauce if necessary. Let everything rest for at least 30 minutes before serving.

Makes 12 to 15 servings.

The magic of this cobbler is in the crust: it begins as batter at the bottom of the pan, with fruit filling poured over the top. While baking, the two magically swap places: the batter rises to become a golden brown crust, leaving bubbly sweet filling underneath.

You can make magic with any variety of cooked fruits such as peaches, blueberries, strawberries, or plums. Just swap out the cherries and blackberries in equal quantities.

CHERRY-BERRY MAGIC COBBLER

1/2 cup (1 stick) butter, melted

4 cups pitted fresh cherries and blackberries

1 1/2 cups sugar, divided

1/4 cup water

1 cup all-purpose flour

1 1/2 teaspoons baking powder

3/4 cup milk

❯ Preheat oven to 350 degrees. Pour the melted butter into a 9 x 13-inch casserole pan.

❯ In a medium saucepan over medium heat, add the cherries, blackberries, 1/2 cup sugar, and water. Cook until the berries release their juices and the sugar cooks into the liquid. This could take 10 minutes. Remove the pan from the heat.

❯ In a medium bowl mix the remaining 1 cup sugar, flour, baking powder, and milk together. Pour the mixture over the melted butter in the casserole pan. Do not stir. Spoon the fruit and juices all over the top. Bake for 30 to 35 minutes. The magic cobbler crust will rise to the top and brown. Serve on its own or with Rick's Very Vanilla Bean Ice Cream (page 94).

Makes 12 servings.

Warm cobblers beg for a scoop of vanilla ice cream. Rick's recipe, which uses vanilla bean paste and extract, delivers the intense vanilla taste we crave.

VERY VANILLA BEAN ICE CREAM

6 cups half-and-half

3 cups whole milk

2 cups sugar

2 tablespoons vanilla bean paste*

1 tablespoon vanilla extract

1/2 teaspoon salt

◉ In a large heavy-duty pot over medium heat, add the half-and-half, milk, sugar, vanilla bean paste, vanilla extract, and salt. Stir well to dissolve the sugar and disperse the vanilla paste throughout the mixture. When small bubbles begin to form along the edge of the pan, remove from the heat. Allow to cool to room temperature, then pour the mixture into a lidded container. Refrigerate overnight.

◉ Churn the mixture in your ice-cream maker according to manufacturer's directions. When the mixture achieves soft-serve texture, remove and place it in the freezer to harden for at least an hour.

Makes 3 quarts.

NOTE: For a smaller quantity, churned in a 2-quart ice-cream maker, cut the ingredients in half and follow the same method: 3 cups half-and-half, 1 1/2 cups whole milk, 1 cup sugar, 1 tablespoon vanilla bean paste, 1 1/2 teaspoons vanilla extract, and 1/4 teaspoon salt.

*If you can't locate the paste, scrape a couple of vanilla beans instead.

Growing Roots

IF YOU'VE SCROLLED THROUGH OUR MENUS, YOU MAY HAVE NOTICED A SPECIAL ICE-CREAM DESSERT appearing most months. This is because no Third Thursday gathering feels complete without one of Rick Rockhill's creamy-dreamy confections. He's the Ice Cream Man. It's a worthy title for a man who was unaware of his churning talents until he started attending the potlucks.

Rick owned a six-quart White Mountain Creamery ice-cream maker, hardly used, and decided to give it a try. He began with a basic: vanilla. His first pass was respectable, and subsequent churns just kept getting better. He told us, "I've worked on that recipe three or four times. I believe I have it mastered."

Buoyed by success, he expanded his repertoire to include fruit-based ice creams, using the season's pick as his palette. Month by month, we were treated with lush blends of fresh peaches, local strawberries, and blueberries plucked from Gigi's garden.

Then he got edgier—Mexican chocolate sparked with cinnamon and cayenne, and puckery key lime pie ice cream, sidled by a clever bowl of graham cracker crumbs. His own harshest critic, Rick is the first to voice his pleasure or disapproval. A daring honey-rosemary ice cream got the Rockhill thumbs-down. "It tastes like conifers," he said, grimacing. Maybe it didn't match his vision for the dish, but the rest of us loved his "Conifer Cream."

Rick is always open to new ideas. When I suggested that "Rockhill's Rocky Road" would be a natural, he took it to heart. He showed up at the next potluck bearing an over-the-top batch of chocolate custard swirled with slivered almonds, coconut, mini marshmallows, and chunks of bittersweet chocolate. Have mercy.

Could I pick a favorite? Doubtful. But, if pressed, I'd have to choose the Ginger Cookie and Lemon Ice-Cream Sandwich. And not because of the clean, refreshing tang of the lemon or the soft molasses-deepened cookies that surrounded it. Don't get me wrong—both were exceptional executions, and the resulting ensemble was stellar.

It endeared itself to me because of the collaborative effort that went into its creation.

You see, unbeknownst to us, Rick and another avid dessert maker, Amy, had put their heads together at one potluck and formed a plan. The following month, Amy arrived with a container of her freshly made ginger spice cookies, and Rick brought in his lemon ice cream, laced with bright yellow curls of zest.

While we were finishing up the main part of meal, Amy and Rick set up their ice-cream sandwich assembly line. Amy laid out her cookies in rows as Rick slathered on his lemon ice cream. Amy followed behind, capping each with another gingered disc. Soon, they passed trays of these luscious sandwiches, to the wide-eyed delight of all.

From the realized talent to the creative collaboration to the shared result, that singular ice-cream sandwich embodies the spirit of Third Thursday.

"Without ice cream, there would be darkness and chaos."
—Don Kardong

OCTOBER: GROWING ROOTS

Diane Stopford's Autumnal Cocktail

Leisa's Witchy Brew

An Artisanal Cheese Platter

Jessi's German Pretzels with Spicy Old-World Mustard

Crowder Pea Salad with Benton's Ham and Lemon-Herb Vinaigrette

Easy Grilled Chicken-Apple Sausages with Braised
Cabbage, Sage-Onion Jam, and Stout Mustard

Pecan-Crusted Glazed Baked Ham with Apricot Mustard

Acorn Squash Rings Stuffed with Sorghum Apples and Pecans

Sweet Potato Biscuits

Deep-Dish Sweet Potato and Pecan Pie

The Collaborative Ice-Cream Sandwich: Amy's Ginger
Cookie and Rick's Lemon Zest Ice Cream

"Autumnal
Cocktail"

contains:
Pears, Cinnamon
Anise orange
Rum, Pom
seeds & S

"To Ta
Chill

Pears, cinnamon sticks, and star anise infuse wonderful aromatics and fall flavors into this pretty beverage.

DIANE STOPFORD'S AUTUMNAL COCKTAIL

PEAR SIMPLE SYRUP

1 ripe pear

2 cinnamon sticks

3 star anise

Juice and peel from 1 orange

1 cup water

1 cup sugar

COCKTAIL

Pear Simple Syrup

1 pint rum

1/4 cup Triple Sec

1 cup orange juice

Fresh pomegranate seeds from 1/2 pomegranate

Orange slices for garnish

1 liter seltzer water (optional)

TO MAKE THE SIMPLE SYRUP: Slice the pear lengthwise in half. Remove the stem and core. Dice the pears and place in a saucepan over low heat. Add the cinnamon sticks, star anise, orange juice and peel, water, and sugar. Stir well. Simmer to melt the sugar into the liquid. Remove the pan from the heat and let the syrup cool. Remove the cinnamon sticks, star anise, and orange peel from the simple syrup and discard. Do not remove the pears.

TO MIX THE COCKTAIL: Pour the pear simple syrup into a 2-quart container with a tight-fitting lid. Add the rum, Triple Sec, orange juice, and pomegranate seeds. Cover and shake well.

❯ Pour over ice and garnish with a slice of orange. Top with a splash of seltzer to lighten.

Makes 8 servings.

Leisa gives this spiced cider a kick with the addition of lemon ginger echinacea juice made by Knudsen. Her versatile brew could change names given the holiday at hand. Call it Pilgrim's Punch in November and Christmas Cheer in December.

LEISA'S WITCHY BREW

2 quarts apple cider

1 quart orange juice

1 (32-ounce) bottle lemon ginger echinacea juice

10 whole cloves

3 cinnamon sticks

◉ Pour the cider, orange juice, and lemon ginger echinacea juice into a 6-quart pot over low heat. Add the cloves and cinnamon sticks and allow to slowly warm. Stir occasionally.

Makes 1 gallon.

AN ARTISANAL CHEESE PLATTER

Long before she opened her business, The Bloomy Rind, Kathleen was a cheese maven. She introduced us to artisanal cheeses that she had discovered around the region and gave us tips on how to put together a balanced yet intriguing platter.

When you are assembling a cheese platter, look to include a hard or semi-firm cheese; a fresh, creamy cheese; a "bluesy" cheese; and a bloomy rind cheese. Your variety can include goat's and sheep's milk cheeses, along with cow's milk cheeses.

Fruits, dried and fresh, nuts, and a couple of sweet or savory embellishments, such as honey, chutney, pesto, or hot sauce, are all wonderful accompaniments and help make your cheese sampling a real pleasure. And always include a selection of breads and crackers.

SELECTION OF CHEESES

Hard and Semi-firm

> Sweetwater Valley Farm: Buttermilk Cheddar farmstead
> Looking Glass Creamery: Chocolate Lab washed rind
> Sequatchie Cove Farm: Coppinger washed rind

Fresh and Creamy

> Noble Springs: Chèvre
> Bonnie Blue: Chèvre
> Manyfold Farm: Brebis

Bloomy Rind

> Chapel Hill Creamery: Carolina Moon
> Sweet Grass Dairy: Green Hill
> Looking Glass Creamery: Ellington (ash)
> Sequatchie Cove Farm: Cumberland

Bluesy

> Kenny's Farmhouse: Barren County Bleu
> Sweet Grass Dairy: Asher Blue

SELECTION OF EMBELLISHMENTS

> Local Honey
> Balsamic Syrup
> Pesto
> Fruity Olive Oil
> Sriracha Hot Sauce
> Preserves or chutney (see pages 157 and 169 for recipes)

FRUITS AND NUTS

> Dried Fruits: apricots, dates, figs
> Toasted Nuts: pecans, Marcona almonds, walnut halves
> Fresh Fruits: sliced apples, pears, grapes, assorted berries

Jessi successfully recreated the pretzels that she and her husband loved in Germany. Dipping the pretzels into the diluted lye solution is what gives them their distinctive even browning and flavor. Amazing!

JESSI'S GERMAN PRETZELS WITH SPICY OLD-WORLD MUSTARD

1 1/2 teaspoons active dry yeast

2 cups warm water, divided

5 cups bread flour

2 1/2 teaspoons salt

2 1/2 tablespoons butter, softened

1/2 cup food-grade lye*

10 cups water

Coarse sea salt to taste

❷ Dissolve the yeast in 1/4 cup warm water.

❷ Place the bread flour into the bowl of an electric mixer fitted with the dough hook. Add the salt, softened butter, activated yeast, and remaining 1 3/4 cups water. Mix until combined. Knead the ingredients until the dough is elastic, about 10 minutes.

❷ Cover with a towel and let the dough rest for 5 minutes. Cut into 12 equal pieces and form into balls. Let rest for 5 minutes. Roll each ball into a thin rope (about 16 inches long). Make into an upside-down U, and twist the ends around each other to create the distinctive pretzel shape. Place pretzels on a parchment paper–lined baking sheet and refrigerate uncovered for a minimum of 2 hours or overnight.

❷ Preheat the oven to 400 degrees. Line a baking sheet with parchment paper.

❷ In a stainless-steel bowl, dissolve the lye in the water. Dip each side of the pretzels into the lye mixture for 15 seconds and remove to the baking sheet. Sprinkle each pretzel with coarse salt. Bake for about 17 minutes. Immediately remove the pretzels from the parchment onto a wire rack to cool.

Makes 12 pretzels.

*Jessi's Notes:

• You can find food-grade lye at a number of online sources. I ordered mine from http://www.essentialdepot.com/servlet/categories.

• Only use stainless-steel pots, bowls, and utensils when working with lye. No plastic. No wood. It is wise to wear gloves when dipping the pretzels into the diluted lye solution.

• Don't be afraid of the lye mixture—just be prudent. It's pretty diluted and really the key to making the outside of the pretzel firm and browned evenly.

• I also like to do just the pretzel rolls. Snip or score the top of the rolled ball after dipping in the lye solution.

MIGHTY MUSTARD-MAKING TIP

This month's menu is spiced up with a trio of homemade mustards. While each possesses a distinct flavor profile, all three begin with three basic ingredients:

- Yellow mustard seeds
- Brown (or black) mustard seeds
- Powdered (dry) mustard

The creativity comes in using your array of pantry staples: vinegars, brown sugar, honey, dried apricots, allspice, kosher salt . . . You can easily turn your kitchen counter into a savory mustard-making laboratory.

Perhaps you'd like to add tarragon to one of your batches. Or lemon juice instead of vinegar. Or habanero peppers (whoa!). Or peach preserves.

Check your fridge for a stray bottle of beer or the last few glugs of Sauvignon Blanc. White wine mellows in the Dijon-style mustard. A bit of Guinness enlivens the Stout mustard.

Here's the coolest part: there is no cooking required!

SPICY OLD-WORLD MUSTARD

1/2 cup white wine

3 tablespoons white wine vinegar

4 tablespoons yellow mustard seeds

2 tablespoons black mustard seeds

4 tablespoons powdered mustard

2 teaspoons salt

◉ Place the wine, vinegar, yellow and black mustard seeds, powdered mustard, and salt in a nonreactive (such as glass or ceramic) bowl. Stir well and cover with plastic wrap. Keep at room temperature and allow the liquid to soften the mustard seeds for 48 hours.

◉ Uncover and churn with an immersion blender until it makes a smoother (but not entirely smooth) mustard. Taste for salt and spice. Place in a jar with a tight-fitting lid, cover, and refrigerate. This will keep for up to three months.

Makes 1 scant cup.

At our farmers' market, we were lucky to have Tammy, who shelled all manner of fresh peas and beans on-site. You can also make this salad with purple hull peas, black-eyed peas, or October beans. Using fresh is key. Benton's ham is very much like prosciutto and brings a subtle smoky bite to the salad.

CROWDER PEA SALAD WITH BENTON'S HAM AND LEMON-HERB VINAIGRETTE

1 tablespoon olive oil

2 cloves garlic, minced

1 pound fresh shelled crowder peas

1 teaspoon salt

1 bay leaf

4 to 6 cups water

3 carrots, finely chopped

3 ribs and leaves celery, finely chopped

3 large scallions, including green tops, chopped

Lemon-Herb Vinaigrette (recipe follows)

2 ounces sliced Benton's ham or prosciutto, julienned

4 to 6 pieces red leaf lettuce, sliced into thin strips

Black pepper to taste

◗ Add the olive oil to a large saucepan over medium heat. Stir in the minced garlic and sauté for 2 minutes. Add the crowder peas, salt, and bay leaf. Add enough water to cover the peas by 2 inches. Simmer for 40 minutes, until peas are tender but still intact. Remove the bay leaf. Drain the peas and chill.

◗ In a large serving bowl combine the carrots, celery, and scallions. Add the Lemon-Herb Vinaigrette and stir until all the ingredients are well coated. Add the crowder peas and ham. Gently fold these into the mixture until everything is well coated with the vinaigrette. Fold in the shreds of lettuce. Taste for seasonings and add black pepper.

Makes 10 servings.

LEMON-HERB VINAIGRETTE

6 tablespoons olive oil

1 heaping tablespoon lemon zest

1/4 teaspoon salt (or more to taste)

A few grindings of fresh cracked black pepper

Pinch of red pepper flakes

2 tablespoons fresh lemon juice

1 tablespoon white balsamic vinegar

1 heaping tablespoon chopped fresh flat-leaf parsley

4 to 6 sprigs of garlic chives or chives, snipped into small pieces

◐ Pour the olive oil into a small bowl. Add the zest and allow it to infuse the oil for a few minutes. Then add the salt, black pepper, red pepper flakes, lemon juice, vinegar, parsley, and chives. Stir together well.

Here's a dish that is indeed greater than the sum of its stellar parts. Gigi and I found these chicken-apple sausages to be lean yet full flavored, especially when chargrilled. But they really elevate when accompanied by these tasty "supporting players" that you can easily make. Serve the sausages on a bed of braised cabbage spiked with sage-onion jam and a side of your own homemade stout mustard. Add a pot of whipped potatoes, and you've got a version of bangers and mash. So good!

EASY GRILLED CHICKEN-APPLE SAUSAGES WITH BRAISED CABBAGE, SAGE-ONION JAM, AND STOUT MUSTARD

The humble cabbage becomes sweet and tender in this simple braise.

BRAISED CABBAGE

2 tablespoons butter

1 large head green cabbage, washed, cored, and cut into wedges

1/2 teaspoon salt

1/4 teaspoon red pepper flakes

1/4 cup water

◉ Melt the butter in a 5- to 6-quart pot over medium heat. Add the cabbage wedges. Sprinkle with salt and red pepper flakes. Toss gently. Add the water. Cover, reduce the heat to low, and cook for 15 minutes. Stir, cover, and cook until tender, another 10 minutes. The liquid will become absorbed and the cabbage almost meltingly tender. Taste for seasonings and adjust as needed.

Delicious on the grilled sausage, but we also recommend spreading this savory jam on a roast turkey or pork sandwich.

SAGE-ONION JAM

4 tablespoons olive oil

5 large yellow onions, thinly sliced pole to pole

1 teaspoon kosher salt

12 to 15 fresh sage leaves, finely chopped

◉ Heat a large heavy-bottomed pot over medium heat and add the olive oil. Add the onions and salt, stirring to coat the pieces with oil. Reduce the heat to low and cook, uncovered, for 1 hour, stirring occasionally. The onions will soften, release their juices, and slowly cook down and caramelize. When the mixture is glazy-sweet and brown, stir in the fresh sage leaves and cook for another 10 minutes. Remove from the heat.

NOTE: This jam will keep in the refrigerator in a sterile jar for a month or more.

STOUT MUSTARD

1/2 cup Guinness stout

1/3 cup red wine vinegar

5 tablespoons black mustard seeds

2 tablespoons yellow mustard seeds

1 tablespoon raw sugar (such as turbinado or demerara)

1/4 teaspoon ground allspice

2 teaspoons kosher salt

○ Pour the stout and vinegar into a nonreactive bowl. Add the black and yellow mustard seeds, sugar, allspice, and salt. Stir to combine. Cover with plastic wrap and let the bowl sit out at room temperature for 48 hours. Stir. Use an immersion blender to blend until fairly smooth. Spoon into a clean, lidded jar and refrigerate.

NOTE: The mustard will keep in the refrigerator for at least three months.

THE SAUSAGES

15 Chicken-Apple Sausages

ON THE GRILL: Split the sausages lengthwise and place on a hot barbecue grill. Cook until chargrilled on one side, 5 to 7 minutes, and flip. Grill on the other side until done. Remove.

IN THE OVEN: Preheat the oven to 400 degrees. Split the sausages lengthwise and lay out on a baking sheet. Oven roast for 10 to 12 minutes. Flip the sausages over and continue cooking for another 10 to 12 minutes. Sausages will sizzle and brown.

ASSEMBLY

○ Put hot braised cabbage into a large shallow serving bowl. Spoon half of the sage-onion jam over the cabbage. Arrange grilled sausages over the vegetables. Serve with a side bowl of stout mustard.

Makes 15 servings.

More mustard making in this sweet nod to the South. The glaze combines apricot mustard, cane syrup, and allspice, and seals in the ham's juices as it bakes. An outer dusting of pecan pieces toasts to a nice crunch. Serve with the remaining apricot mustard and Sweet Potato Biscuits (page 115).

PECAN-CRUSTED GLAZED BAKED HAM WITH APRICOT MUSTARD

6 to 8 pounds sugar-cured ham (shank or butt portion)

1/2 cup Apricot Mustard (recipe follows)

1/2 cup cane syrup

2 teaspoons ground allspice

1 cup water, plus additional as needed

1/2 cup pecans, finely chopped

Preheat the oven to 350 degrees.

Trim the ham, removing tough outer hide pieces and any excess fat. Leave a thin layer of fat to help seal in the juices of the meat. Score the ham in crisscross fashion, cutting into, but not all the way through, that thin layer of fat.

In a small bowl whisk together the Apricot Mustard, syrup, and allspice. Liberally coat the entire ham with this glaze. Place the ham in a roasting pan. Pour the water into the bottom of the pan. Coat the upper glazed surface with finely chopped pecans. Bake, uncovered, allowing 15 minutes per pound. An 8-pound ham will take 2 hours. Check periodically, adding a little more liquid so that the sugars don't burn. If the glaze is browning too much, you may loosely cover the ham with an aluminum foil tent.

Allow the meat to rest at least 15 minutes before carving. The ham can be baked in advance and kept warm. It is also delicious served room temperature.

Makes 15 entrée servings or 3 dozen ham biscuits.

APRICOT MUSTARD

1/2 cup dried apricots

2 tablespoons local honey

2 tablespoons raw sugar (such as turbinado or demerara)

6 tablespoons white balsamic vinegar, divided

1/4 cup water

5 tablespoons yellow mustard seeds

3 tablespoons powdered yellow mustard

1/2 cup white wine

2 teaspoons salt

● In a medium nonreactive bowl, add the dried apricots, honey, sugar, 4 tablespoons vinegar, and the water. Stir to combine, cover, and soak for 2 days at room temperature.

● In a small nonreactive bowl, add the mustard seeds, powdered mustard, wine, remaining 2 tablespoons vinegar, and salt. Stir to combine, cover, and soak for 2 days at room temperature.

● After 2 days, spoon the mustard mixture into the apricot mixture and use an immersion blender to churn the apricots into the mustard. Taste for salt and desired sweetness. Spoon into a lidded jar and refrigerate. This will keep for up to three months.

Makes about 1 cup.

This dish makes for an attractive presentation. Sorghum coats the apples with a mineral-sweet glaze.

ACORN SQUASH RINGS STUFFED WITH SORGHUM APPLES AND PECANS

2 large acorn squashes

Olive oil

2 large baking apples (such as Granny Smith, Golden Delicious, or Ginger Gold)

2/3 cup chopped shallots

2/3 cup pecan pieces

1/4 cup sorghum

3/4 teaspoon salt

1/2 teaspoon black pepper

◗ Preheat the oven to 350 degrees. Line a baking sheet with parchment paper.

◗ Slice the squashes into rings about an inch thick. Depending on the size of the squash, you should be able to get 5 to 6 rings from each one. Scoop out the seeds and lay the rings on the baking sheet. Brush the rings with olive oil.

◗ Wash, core, and dice the apples into 1/2-inch chunks. Place into a medium bowl. Add the shallots, pecans, sorghum, salt, and pepper. Toss so that all the pieces are coated with the sorghum. Mound the sorghum apple mixture into the center of each ring. Bake for 25 minutes.

Makes 10 to 12 servings.

NOTE: For serving a large group, you can slice the rings in half after they are cooked.

Mashed sweet potatoes bring such good flavor, color, and body to biscuits. Wonderful when stuffed with slices of pecan-crusted ham and a touch of apricot mustard.

SWEET POTATO BISCUITS

2 medium sweet potatoes (to make 2 cups cooked sweet potatoes)

4 cups self-rising flour

1/3 plus 1/4 cup raw sugar (such as demerara or turbinado), divided

1 teaspoon ground ginger

1 teaspoon ground nutmeg

1/2 teaspoon ground cloves

1/2 cup plus 2 tablespoons buttermilk, divided*

10 tablespoons cold butter, cut into pieces

1/4 cup pecan pieces (optional)

○ Preheat the oven to 425 degrees.

○ Wash and dry the sweet potatoes. Place them on a baking sheet in the oven and bake until soft, 35 to 40 minutes. Remove, allow them to cool, and then scoop out the insides.

○ Line a baking sheet with parchment paper. In a large bowl add the self-rising flour, 1/3 cup sugar, ginger, nutmeg, and cloves. Add the sweet potatoes, 1/2 cup buttermilk, and butter pieces. Working with your hands, mix all the ingredients, rubbing the butter pieces into the flour. Work quickly; soon it will all come together in a mass. If it is too sticky, add a bit more flour. Beware of overworking the dough—it will toughen.

○ Dust a cutting board or counter with flour. Roll out the dough to 1/2 inch thick and cut into rounds with a biscuit cutter. Place on the baking sheet close together (sides touching is fine).

○ Place pecan pieces into a food processor fitted with a chopping blade. Pulse the nuts until they become finely ground. Pour into a small bowl. Add the 1/4 cup sugar and whisk until well combined.**

○ Brush the biscuit tops with the remaining 2 tablespoons buttermilk and sprinkle them with the ground pecan and sugar mixture. Bake for 10 to 12 minutes.

Makes 3 dozen 2-inch-round biscuits.

*If you don't have buttermilk, you can make your own. Add 1 tablespoon fresh lemon juice to the same quantity (1/2 cup plus 2 tablespoons) of whole milk.

**You may omit this step if desired.

Sometimes decisions are difficult. Should I have pecan pie or sweet potato pie? How about the best of both in one slice? Be sure to use a deep-dish pie pan to accommodate the delectable layers.

DEEP-DISH SWEET POTATO AND PECAN PIE

PIE CRUST

1 cup all-purpose flour

1/4 teaspoon salt

6 tablespoons butter, chilled and cut into pieces

3 to 4 tablespoons ice water

❯ Place flour, salt, and cold butter pieces in the bowl of a food processor fitted with a chopping or pastry blade. Pulse until the butter is cut into the flour and resembles little peas. Add the ice water, 1 tablespoon at a time, with the motor running. The dough will gather into a ball.

❯ Remove and form the ball into a slightly flattened disc shape. Wrap in plastic wrap and refrigerate for at least 15 minutes.

SWEET POTATO LAYER

2 medium sweet potatoes (to make 2 cups cooked sweet potatoes)

1/2 cup firmly packed brown sugar

1/2 cup buttermilk

1 tablespoon vanilla extract

1 teaspoon ground ginger

1/2 teaspoon ground cinnamon

1/2 teaspoon ground nutmeg

1/4 teaspoon salt

Pinch of ground cloves

2 large eggs

❯ Preheat the oven to 425 degrees. Wash and dry the sweet potatoes and place them on a baking sheet, and into the oven. Bake until soft, 35 to 40 minutes. Remove and allow to cool. Scoop out the insides to measure 2 cups.

❯ Place the sweet potatoes into the bowl of a food processor fitted with the chopping blade and process until smooth. Add the brown sugar, buttermilk, vanilla, ginger, cinnamon, nutmeg, salt, and cloves and process. Add the eggs one at a time, processing after each addition, and process until very smooth.

PECAN LAYER

2 large eggs

1 cup dark corn syrup

2 teaspoons vanilla extract

1/4 teaspoon salt

4 tablespoons butter, melted and slightly cooled

1 1/2 cups pecan halves or pieces

With a hand mixer or in an electric mixer with a whisk attachment, beat the eggs, syrup, vanilla, and salt together until no streaks of yolk can be seen. Beat in the melted butter.

ASSEMBLY

Preheat the oven to 350 degrees. Remove the dough from the refrigerator. Sprinkle a cutting board or the counter with a little flour and roll out the dough to fit into a 9-inch deep-dish pie pan. Fit the dough into the pan and crimp the edges. Fill the pie with the sweet potato mixture. Sprinkle the pecan halves in circular fashion on top. Spoon the pecan pie filling over the pecans.

Bake for 35 to 40 minutes. Test in the center for doneness (tester stuck into the center should be clean when removed). Allow to cool before slicing.

Makes 10 servings.

You'll love the tart creamy lemon nestled between these ginger sandwiches, made more potent with zest in the ice cream and crystallized ginger bits in the cookie.

THE COLLABORATIVE ICE-CREAM SANDWICH: AMY'S GINGER COOKIE AND RICK'S LEMON ZEST ICE CREAM

GINGER COOKIES

4 cups all-purpose flour

1 tablespoon baking soda

2 tablespoons ground ginger

2 teaspoons ground cinnamon

1 teaspoon ground cloves

1/2 teaspoon white pepper

2 cups (4 sticks) butter, softened

2 1/2 cups raw sugar (such as demerara or turbinado), divided

1/2 cup molasses

2 large eggs

1 1/2 cups crystallized ginger, chopped (optional)

○ In a large bowl whisk the flour, baking soda, ginger, cinnamon, cloves, and pepper together. In an electric mixer with a paddle attachment, cream the butter, 2 cups sugar, and molasses together until fluffy. Beat in the eggs. Beat in the flour mixture, a little at a time. Then beat in the crystallized ginger. Cover the bowl and chill the dough for 30 minutes.

○ Preheat the oven to 350 degrees. Line baking sheets with parchment paper.

○ Place the remaining 1/2 cup sugar into a small bowl. Scoop up a golf ball–size round of dough and shape into a ball. Roll each ball in the sugar and place on the baking sheets, slightly flattening. Leave 2 inches between each cookie. Bake on the middle rack of the oven for 12 minutes.

Makes 60 cookies or 30 ice-cream sandwiches.

LEMON ZEST ICE CREAM

6 to 8 lemons

1 1/2 cups sugar

2 cups whole milk

1 quart heavy cream

○ Zest 6 of the lemons, and juice all the lemons to make 1 cup of juice. Place the zest in the bowl of a food processor fitted with a chopping blade. Add the sugar and pulse the mixture until both the zest and sugar become fine. Add the lemon juice and pulse to dissolve the sugar.

○ Pour the milk and cream into a large bowl. Whisk in the lemon mixture until all the ingredients are well combined. Cover and refrigerate for 2 hours, allowing the flavors to marry.

○ Churn in ice-cream maker according to manufacturer's directions. Freeze until you are ready to scoop and fill the ice-cream sandwiches.

Makes 2 quarts.

ASSEMBLY

❯ Set out half of the cookies in rows. Place a small scoop of ice cream onto each cookie.

❯ Place the sandwich top on the ice cream and gently press. Serve immediately.

ICE CREAM TIPS

Once you get that "churning desire," you'll learn, as Rick has, that there are many ways up the ice-cream mountain. Will you use egg yolks, whole eggs, or no eggs? In what combinations will you blend the heavy cream, half-and-half, whole milk, buttermilk, or sweetened condensed milk? Or perhaps you'll use no dairy at all, and fruit juices or coconut milk will come into play. The possibilities are endless.

As Teresa jokes, "You can freeze just about anything!"

In researching and testing recipes, Rick found that when he was increasing his quantities suitable for his 6-quart ice-cream maker, he could reduce the number of yolks without sacrificing the creaminess of the churn. He would back off the quantity of heavy cream, often substituting half-and-half and whole milk. Too much heavy cream results in a "whipped cream" quality of ice cream that can be a little overbearing in butterfat.

Once you master some basics, you'll be ready to get creative with your batches. Some rules of thumb:

- If you are making a custard base with egg, always strain it before chilling.
- Chill well! Well-chilled custards and mixes will churn more readily in well-chilled containers.
- Extras such as chopped nuts, caramel sauce, shredded coconut, macerated fruits, syrups, and chocolate shavings or chunks are best folded in during the last few minutes of churning.

Autumn Bounty

FOR MOST AMERICANS, THE FOURTH THURSDAY OF NOVEMBER SIGNALS THE KICK-OFF FOR THE HOLIDAY season. At Third Thursday, we feel like we have a jump on that. Exactly one week before America's annual celebration of plenty, we get together for our final potluck of the year.

No, we don't meet in December. Because everyone has so many holiday-related demands during the month, we decided that it was good sense to take a break.

It makes this potluck especially festive. Knowing that we won't see one other until after the New Year compels us to share best wishes along with our best efforts at the table.

It reminds me of a challenge, a playful "food battle" that writers Kim Severson and Julia Moskin staged a few years ago: When it comes to the Thanksgiving feast, what's it all about, the turkey or the sides? For Moskin, it is the myriad side dishes that make the dinner memorable and worthwhile. But Severson insists, no: the bird is the word.

I'm not one to take sides; I want 'em all. One is incomplete without the other. But, if I had to pass judgment, I'd go with Moskin. I'd prefer a table full of exciting accompaniments over a roast turkey.

Good thing, at potluck, that challenge is never an issue. Recognizing the noble bird's imminent arrival on most Thanksgiving tables, we tend to sidestep turkey for beefier prospects. One year, Beef Tips Burgundy, simmered with onions, carrots, mushrooms, and red wine, became our meal's centerpiece. Another year, it was a round of beef, slow roasted to succulence under a blanket of garlic and fresh herbs.

But the Turkey versus Sides challenge is, in a way, about Tradition versus the New. We all cherish rituals and customs. We find comfort in cycles and seasons, the return to the table for a holiday meal, and the foods associated with it. I know there are certain things that I look forward to each year—and may only eat on this one occasion: Cranberry relish. Pumpkin pie. And, of course, roast turkey, gravy, and cornbread dressing.

But I like change too. Tastes, diets, and needs shift over time. If you're like me, you have family members who are either vegetarian or vegan, or who have certain health concerns that mean low sodium or no gluten in the things that they eat. When it comes to honoring traditions, that means walking a razor's edge between expectation and desire for the new. With side dishes, those supporting players to the Big Feast, there's the opportunity to introduce variety. And please everyone.

At potluck, intriguing side dishes and desserts abound. It's become the venue to try out new recipes with some variations on the Thanksgiving theme. I've always found inspired contributions that I'd like to include in my family's holiday meal. Consider our Yukon Gold and

Sweet Potato Gratin, or Brussels sprouts roasted with red pear and hazelnuts, or our Not Your '70s Green Bean Casserole. I might even forgo pumpkin pie for cane syrup cake topped with Rick's Pumpkin Pie Ice Cream.

It's fun to bring something new to the table and enliven the tried and true while still upholding treasured traditions.

And, challenges aside, what it's all about is the expression in tangible form of that interconnected quality: gratitude. Here in the South we like to call it "A Gracious Plenty."

NOVEMBER: AUTUMN BOUNTY

Poire et Jacques Cocktail

Bacon-Wrapped Pear-Stuffed Dates

Four-Lettuce Salad with Pears, Water Chestnuts, and Toasted
Pumpkin Seeds with Brown Sugar Vinaigrette

Rich and Garlicky Roast Round of Beef with Horseradish Mousse

Not Your '70s Green Bean Casserole

Red Beet Quinoa

Butternut Squash and Leek Lasagna

Yukon Gold and Sweet Potato Gratin

Brussels Sprouts with Red Pear, Shallots, Hazelnuts, and Sage

Mme. Vienneau's Gateau de Sirop (Cane Syrup Cake)

Pumpkin Pie Ice Cream

Rustic Apple Galette

Teresa's ode to the holidays is delicious poured over ice, but on chilly evenings, you can heat it on the stovetop for warming comfort. The whole pears infusing the cocktail, she notes, can be eaten at a later time, for a "tipsy" dessert.

POIRE ET JACQUES COCKTAIL

6 cups pear cider

2 cups honey whiskey (such as Jack Daniel's Tennessee Honey)

1 cup pear liqueur

2 tablespoons ginger preserves

1 to 2 ripe pears, peeled

◗ Pour the pear cider, whiskey, and pear liqueur into a large bowl. Add the ginger preserves and stir well. Place the whole peeled pear into a large pitcher. Pour the cocktail mixture over the pear and chill until ready to serve.

Makes 10 cups.

We all love bacon-wrapped treats, but Kristina's trick, a dash of ground cloves on the pears, is what makes these smoky-sweet bites exceptional.

BACON-WRAPPED PEAR-STUFFED DATES

1 ripe pear

1/4 teaspoon ground cloves

24 pitted dates

12 slices bacon

Maple syrup (optional)

❯ Preheat the oven to 400 degrees. Nestle a baking rack into a baking sheet.

❯ Slice the pear into small rectangular pieces—a shape that will fit inside the dates. Place the pear slices in a bowl and sprinkle with the ground cloves. Gently toss. Stuff the pear pieces into the dates.

❯ Slice the bacon in half, making 24 slices. Wrap one piece of bacon around each date and secure with a toothpick. Put the wrapped, stuffed dates on the rack. This will allow the bacon to get crisp while the drippings fall away. Bake for 15 to 20 minutes, until bacon is brown and crispy.

❯ If you desire, once the bacon is crisp, remove the pan from the oven and lightly brush each piece with maple syrup. Return to the oven for another 5 minutes to caramelize.

❯ Serve warm.

Makes 24 appetizers.

The sweet-sour taste of the dressing is terrific drizzled onto this fall salad.

FOUR-LETTUCE SALAD WITH PEARS, WATER CHESTNUTS, AND TOASTED PUMPKIN SEEDS WITH BROWN SUGAR VINAIGRETTE

2 firm, ripe pears

1 lemon

1 head Bibb lettuce, washed and spun dry

1 head red leaf lettuce, washed and spun dry

1 bundle frisée, washed and spun dry

1/4 pound (4 ounces) arugula, washed and spun dry

1 can whole water chestnuts, drained, rinsed, and thinly sliced

1/2 cup pumpkin seeds, toasted*

Brown Sugar Vinaigrette (recipe follows)

◉ Cut the pears in half. Core and slice them into thin wedges and place into a medium bowl. Cut the lemon in half and squeeze the juice over the pear slices. Cover until ready to use.

◉ Break the Bibb and red leaf lettuce leaves into small pieces and place in a large salad bowl or on a platter. Add the frisée and arugula and toss. Arrange the pear slices and water chestnut slices over the greens. Sprinkle with pumpkin seeds, and serve with Brown Sugar Vinaigrette on the side.

Makes 10 servings.

*See how to toast pumpkin seeds on page 144.

BROWN SUGAR VINAIGRETTE

6 tablespoons white balsamic vinegar

1 teaspoon celery seed

1 teaspoon paprika

1/4 cup firmly packed brown sugar

1/4 medium onion

2 teaspoons Dijon mustard

1 teaspoon salt

1/2 teaspoon black pepper

1 cup vegetable oil

◉ Place the vinegar, celery seed, paprika, brown sugar, onion, mustard, salt, and pepper into the bowl of a food processor fitted with a chopping blade. Pulse until the onion is pureed into the mixture. While the processor is running, slowly pour in the oil. It will incorporate nicely into the vinaigrette. Dijon mustard keeps the dressing emulsified.

Celebratory! For best results, coat the beef generously with the herb and garlic rub and refrigerate overnight. It will permeate the meat and deepen the flavors while the beef roasts.

RICH AND GARLICKY ROAST ROUND OF BEEF WITH HORSERADISH MOUSSE

6 to 8 large garlic cloves

4 tablespoons fresh thyme leaves

2 tablespoons olive oil

1 teaspoon coarse sea salt or kosher salt, plus more to taste

1 teaspoon black pepper, plus more to taste

1 tablespoon red wine vinegar

1 (8-pound) boneless top or inside round of beef or sirloin tip

1 cup water

Horseradish Mousse (recipe follows)

❂ Combine garlic, thyme, olive oil, salt, pepper, and vinegar in a food processor fitted with a chopping blade. Pulse to make a pesto-like paste. Rub this mixture onto all sides of the roast. Wrap the meat in plastic wrap and refrigerater for 8 hours or overnight, to allow the paste to permeate the meat. Remove the meat from the refrigerator 1 hour before roasting.

❂ Preheat the oven to 350 degrees. Fit a rack into a roasting pan. Unwrap the beef and place it on the rack. Sprinkle with additional coarse salt and pepper.

❂ Roast, uncovered, allowing 15 minutes per pound for medium-rare meat. (An 8-pound roast should take 2 hours.) About halfway through the cooking time, rotate the roast in the oven. Add the water to the bottom to keep the juices from getting too browned.

❂ Insert a meat thermometer into the thickest part of the beef. When it registers 125 degrees, remove the pan from the oven. Lightly tent the meat with aluminum foil and let it rest at least 20 minutes before removing from the pan to the carving board.

❂ Deglaze the bottom of the roasting pan with additional water, if needed, to get all the savory drippings. Serve the roast with the Horseradish Mousse, a gravy boat of the pan juices, and small dinner rolls.

Serves 30 guests for a potluck buffet.

Plain whipped cream folded into highly seasoned mayonnaise makes this sauce airy, yet with an assertive horseradish bite.

HORSERADISH MOUSSE

1/2 cup mayonnaise (such as Hellman's)

1/3 cup prepared horseradish

1 1/2 teaspoons Worcestershire sauce

2 teaspoons fresh lemon juice

2 teaspoons hot sauce

1/2 teaspoon sea salt

1/2 cup heavy cream

In a medium bowl whisk together the mayonnaise, horseradish, Worcestershire, lemon juice, hot sauce, and salt. In another medium bowl whip the cream until firm peaks form. Fold the cream into the mayonnaise mixture. Refrigerate until serving.

Makes 1 cup.

NOTE: This can be made a day in advance.

Made with a light hand, this deconstructed version of a classic is a visual treat and lets each flavor shine through. You really taste the green beans, the mushrooms, and the crispy onions.

NOT YOUR '70s GREEN BEAN CASSEROLE

BEANS

1 clove garlic, sliced

1/4 teaspoon sea salt

2 pounds fresh young green beans

❯ Fill a large pot with water and bring to a simmer over medium-high heat. Season with garlic and salt. Place the beans into the pot and cook for 2 to 3 minutes. While the beans are cooking, prepare an icy water bath. Test a bean—it should be crisp-tender. When they are done, plunge the beans into the ice bath to stop the cooking process and set the bright green color.

MUSHROOM SAUCE

2 tablespoons butter (or olive oil, if preparing vegan)

1 (8-ounce) package mushrooms, cleaned and sliced (I use shiitakes, which are so meaty)

1 bundle scallions, white and green parts chopped

Salt to taste

Black pepper to taste

A few fresh thyme leaves

2 tablespoons all-purpose flour

2 cups mushroom broth

❯ Heat the butter in a skillet over medium heat. Add the mushrooms and scallions. Season with salt, pepper, and thyme, if desired.

❯ Cook until the vegetables are softened, about 5 minutes. Stir in the flour and allow it to coat the mushrooms and scallions. Keep stirring, scraping up the browned bits. When you can no longer see any traces of white flour, pour in the broth. Keep stirring until the mixture becomes creamy. Taste for seasonings and adjust if needed.

CRISPY ONIONS

1 small onion, thinly sliced

Olive oil

Sea salt to taste

❯ Preheat the oven to 400 degrees. Lightly coat the onion slices in olive oil. Lay them out on a baking sheet and sprinkle with sea salt. Roast for 10 to 12 minutes, until golden brown and crispy. Remove and allow to cool.

ASSEMBLY

❯ Preheat the oven to 325 degrees.

❯ Coat the bottom of a 9 x 13-inch casserole dish with the warm mushroom sauce. Cover with a layer of blanched green beans. Spoon more sauce over the beans and repeat layers. Finish the top with the oven-crisp onions. Bake until thoroughly heated, about 15 minutes, and serve.

Makes 8 to 10 servings.

NOTE: You may prepare the green beans and make the mushroom sauce ahead of time, refrigerate them in separate containers, and then assemble the casserole when you are ready to bake. Bake in a preheated 325-degree oven for about 30 minutes.

TIPS FOR HANDLING BEETS

Those sweet ruby beets possess real staining power. If you don't use kitchen gloves, here are some tips for peeling them, post-roasting, without turning your fingertips pinkish purple:

- When cool enough to handle, open the foil. Rub the beet back and forth in your hand, allowing the foil to do the work of removing the outer skin.
- Grab the beet with a paper towel and use it as a barrier between your hands and the beet as you slide off the skin. It will absorb the staining juice before it colors your fingers.

Allison says that anything with a color this brilliant has to be good for you! And it has a flavor to match. Fruit and spice notes add complexity to the earthy sweetness of the beets.

RED BEET QUINOA

4 medium beets

4 tablespoons boiled cider*

Juice of 1 medium orange

2 tablespoons orange zest

1/4 teaspoon salt

1/8 teaspoon ground cinnamon

1/8 teaspoon ground nutmeg

1/8 teaspoon ground cardamom

2 tablespoons extra-virgin olive oil

1 1/2 cups quinoa

3 cups water

1 (5-ounce) bag baby arugula

❯ Preheat the oven to 400 degrees.

❯ Wash each beet thoroughly and individually wrap in aluminum foil. Place on a baking sheet and bake for 1 hour.

❯ In a small bowl whisk together the cider, orange juice, zest, salt, cinnamon, nutmeg, and cardamom. Whisk in the olive oil.

❯ Remove the beets from the oven, remove the aluminum foil, and allow to cool just enough to handle. The skin will slide right off while the beets are warm.** Dice the beets and add them to the dressing. Cover the bowl and marinate overnight.

❯ The next day measure the quinoa into a medium bowl and cover with warm water. Let it sit for 20 minutes. Drain the quinoa through a fine-mesh sieve and wash until the water runs clear and doesn't look "soapy" anymore. This will get rid of any bitterness.

❯ Add 3 cups of water and the quinoa to a medium pot over medium-high heat and bring to a boil. Reduce heat to low and cook for 20 minutes. Drain any excess water. Add the beet mixture to the warm quinoa for the best results. The quinoa will soak up all of the dressing and distribute the color throughout. Serve over a bed of fresh arugula.

Makes 8 to 10 servings.

*Allison gets her boiled cider from Wood's Cider Mill in Springfield, Vermont. They take fresh apple cider and boil it down until it is extremely concentrated and oh so tasty! There are no additives to the apple cider, and the taste is truly unique. Check our source guide in the back of the book.

**See sidebar on handling beets (previous page) for tips on neat peeling.

This might be my favorite way to prepare butternut squash. The layering of the three components—roasted butternut squash puree, leek-ricotta béchamel, and stewed yellow tomatoes—make this recipe unique and utterly delicious.

BUTTERNUT SQUASH AND LEEK LASAGNA

ROASTED BUTTERNUT SQUASH PUREE

2 medium butternut squashes

Olive oil

Salt to taste

Black pepper to taste

Half-and-half, as needed

◐ Preheat the oven to 400 degrees.

◐ Cut the squash in half and scoop out the seeds. Brush both sides with olive oil and sprinkle with salt and pepper. Place skin side up onto a baking sheet and roast uncovered for 30 to 40 minutes. The outside skin will brown and blister slightly, and the whole squash will soften and collapse. When this occurs, remove the baking sheet from the oven and allow the squash to cool.

◐ When cooled, the skin will peel away from the meat of the squash. Where it doesn't peel away, scoop out the meat with a spoon. Place all the roasted squash into the bowl of a food processor fitted with the chopping blade and puree. Season to taste with salt and pepper. The mixture will be fairly thick and creamy. If it's too thick to spread, thin with a little half-and-half.

LEEK-RICOTTA BÉCHAMEL

3 tablespoons butter

4 leeks, cleaned well and chopped (white and green parts)

3 tablespoons all-purpose flour

1 1/2 cups half-and-half

1 cup ricotta

Salt to taste

White pepper to taste

◐ In a 3-quart saucepan over medium heat, melt the butter and add the leeks. Sauté for 5 to 7 minutes, stirring often, until the leeks soften and separate. Sprinkle in the flour and stir rapidly so that the leeks are well coated. When the flour has absorbed all the butter and cooked onto the leeks, pour in the half-and-half. Keep stirring. Soon the sauce will bubble and thicken. Add the ricotta and stir well. Season with salt and white pepper. The sauce will be rich tasting and somewhat sweet from the leeks.

STEWED TOMATOES

1 tablespoon olive oil

1 pint yellow or red tomatoes

1/2 teaspoon salt

1/2 teaspoon black pepper

⊙ Warm the olive oil in a small saucepan over medium heat. Add the tomatoes. Season with salt and black pepper. When thoroughly heated, remove the pan from the stovetop and use an immersion blender to puree the tomatoes.

ASSEMBLY

Olive oil

Leek-Ricotta Béchamel

1 (9-ounce) box no-boil lasagna

Roasted Butternut Squash Puree

1 handful fresh sage leaves, chopped

1 cup stewed tomatoes

4 ounces Pecorino-Romano cheese

1/4 cup walnut halves/pieces (optional)

⊙ Preheat the oven to 350 degrees.

⊙ Lightly coat a 9 x 13-inch baking pan or casserole dish with olive oil. Cover the bottom of the casserole with a layer of béchamel. Place the lasagna noodles on top. Spread a layer of butternut squash puree over that. Sprinkle chopped sage over the puree and spoon with another layer of béchamel.

⊙ Add a second lasagna noodle layer, then the stewed tomatoes. Grate half of the Pecorino-Romano over the tomatoes, dot with additional béchamel, and add a third lasagna noodle layer. Spread the puree over the lasagna, sprinkle with more chopped sage, and cover with the final layer of lasagna noodles. Cover the top with the remaining béchamel. Grate Pecorino-Romano over the top and sprinkle the walnut pieces over the lasagna, if desired.

⊙ At this point, you can refrigerate the assembled dish and bake it the next day, if you like. Otherwise, seal with foil and bake for 30 minutes. (This helps the casserole to steam up as it bakes, cooking the pasta.) Uncover and bake for another 10 minutes.

Makes 12 servings.

NOTE: You can make this with red tomatoes too. We had grown and canned yellow tomatoes, which aesthetically made a nifty layer in this lasagna. But we've made it with the reds with delicious results. That one layer of acid-sweet is one of the keys to this terrific recipe.

An update on potatoes au gratin. You'll enjoy the sweet potatoes interspersed with the Yukon Golds in this appealing casserole, enriched with Gruyere cheese.

YUKON GOLD AND SWEET POTATO GRATIN

5 tablespoons butter, softened, divided

2 shallots, diced

2 cups half-and-half

2 heaping tablespoons coarsely chopped fresh flat-leaf parsley

1 tablespoon finely chopped fresh chives

1 teaspoon sea salt

1/2 teaspoon white pepper

1 1/2 pounds Yukon Gold potatoes, cleaned

1 1/2 pounds sweet potatoes, cleaned

1 whole nutmeg

1 1/2 cups shredded Gruyere cheese, divided

1/4 cup grated Parmigiano-Reggiano cheese

> Preheat the oven to 375 degrees. Coat a 9 x 13-inch casserole dish with 1 tablespoon of butter.

> In a saucepan over medium heat, melt 3 tablespoons of butter and add the shallots. Sauté until translucent, 2 to 3 minutes. Add the half-and-half, parsley, chives, salt, and white pepper. Stir well until warmed. Remove the pan from the heat. Allow to cool.

> Peel the Yukon Gold and sweet potatoes and slice very thin (1/8 inch). Layer 1/3 of the potatoes and sweet potatoes in the bottom of the casserole dish in overlapping circles. It's fine to layer them randomly. Grate some fresh nutmeg over the slices.

> Stir the cooled half-and-half mixture and spoon a thin layer over the potatoes. Sprinkle with 1/2 cup Gruyere. Repeat with another layer of sliced potatoes, arranged in similar fashion. Follow with grated nutmeg. Cover again with more liquid, followed by 1/2 cup of Gruyere. Press down with the back of a wooden spoon to make sure the liquid is seeping through all the overlapping slices.

> Finish with a final layer of sliced potatoes, half-and-half mixture, the remaining 1/2 cup Gruyere, and the Parmigiano-Reggiano. Dot the top with the remaining tablespoon of butter.

> Cover the dish with aluminum foil and bake for 30 minutes. Remove the foil and finish baking for another 15 to 20 minutes, until the casserole is browned and the potatoes feel tender when pierced.

Makes 10 to 12 servings.

These maligned little cabbages have been redeemed! Gigi's inspired seasonal combination makes this an elegant side dish.

BRUSSELS SPROUTS WITH RED PEAR, SHALLOTS, HAZELNUTS, AND SAGE (VEGAN)

2 pounds fresh Brussels sprouts, washed, dried, and ends trimmed

Olive oil

Sea salt to taste

Black pepper to taste

4 shallots, diced small

1 cup chopped hazelnuts

1 bundle fresh sage leaves

2 large firm red pears, cored (not peeled) and diced medium

❯ Preheat the oven to 325 degrees.

❯ Place the Brussels sprouts on a baking pan and lightly coat with olive oil. Season with salt and pepper and roast for about 25 minutes. The outer leaves will get crispy and brown and the interior will be firm but tender.

❯ Pour 2 to 3 tablespoons of olive oil into a deep saucepan over medium heat. Add the shallots and cook until translucent, about 2 minutes. Stir in the hazelnuts and sage leaves, and continue to cook another 2 minutes. Add the diced pear and gently stir. The pear will break down slightly and get coated with the shallot–hazelnut mixture. Add the roasted Brussels sprouts to the saucepan, and stir to combine. Taste for seasoning and adjust as needed.

Makes 12 to 15 servings.

Have you ever cooked with cane syrup? We were recently introduced to this deep amber delicacy made by Steen's in Abbeville, Louisiana. Lighter than molasses, it has a unique, dark, almost bittersweet caramel taste that works well in sweet and savory recipes. This simple one-layer cake highlights it beautifully. Enjoy a slice unadorned, alongside a café au lait, or topped with a scoop of Rick's pumpkin ice cream.

MME. VIENNEAU'S GATEAU DE SIROP (CANE SYRUP CAKE)

2 cups cane syrup, divided

1/2 cup milk (whole or 2%)

1/4 cup strong black coffee

2 large eggs, lightly beaten

2 teaspoons vanilla extract

1/2 cup (1 stick) melted butter

2 cups all-purpose flour

1 1/2 teaspoons baking soda

1/2 teaspoon salt

1 teaspoon ground ginger

1/2 teaspoon ground cinnamon

1/4 teaspoon ground cloves

1 cup pecan halves, if desired

❷ Preheat the oven to 350 degrees. Butter a 9-inch springform pan and line the bottom with parchment.

❷ In a large bowl combine 1 1/2 cups cane syrup, milk, coffee, eggs, and vanilla. Whisk until ingredients are well combined. Beat in the melted butter. In a medium bowl sift the flour, baking soda, and salt together. Stir in the ginger, cinnamon, and cloves. Slowly add the flour mixture to the egg mixture and beat by hand until the batter is smooth. Pour into the prepared pan. Bake for 40 to 45 minutes.

❷ Remove and let the cake cool on a wire rack for 15 minutes. Unmold and brush the top with the remaining 1/2 cup cane syrup while the cake is still warm to give it a nice glazy sheen. Decorate with pecan halves, if desired.

Makes 10 to 12 servings.

You can make this ice cream with store-bought pumpkin puree, but if you have an extra hour or so, don't deprive yourself of roasting a fresh pumpkin. The sugars concentrate and the flavor intensifies. Plus, you'll have all those delectable seeds to season and toast afterward for snacking!

PUMPKIN PIE ICE CREAM

2 pie pumpkins (may substitute 3 cups canned pumpkin puree)

Olive oil

3 cups whole milk

2 cups sweetened condensed milk

1/2 cup firmly packed brown sugar

2 teaspoons ground cinnamon

1 teaspoon ground ginger

1/2 teaspoon fresh grated nutmeg

1/2 teaspoon ground cloves

1/4 teaspoon fine sea salt

- Preheat the oven to 425 degrees.
- Wash the exterior of the pumpkins and cut in half. Scoop out the seeds, reserving them, if you like, to make toasted pumpkin seeds (see sidebar on page 144). Place the halves upright on a baking sheet and brush with oil. Bake for 35 to 40 minutes. Test for doneness by inserting the tip of a sharp knife into the meat of the pumpkin. Test in a few spots and rotate the baking sheet if needed to ensure even cooking. Remove from the oven and allow to cool.
- While the pumpkin is cooling, pour the whole milk, sweetened condensed milk, brown sugar, cinnamon, ginger, nutmeg, cloves, and salt into a large bowl. Whisk until all ingredients are well combined.
- Scoop out the pumpkin flesh and puree in a food processor fitted with a chopping blade. Measure 3 cups and whisk the puree into the spiced milk mixture.*
- Cover and refrigerate until the mixture is thoroughly chilled, 2 to 3 hours or overnight.
- Churn in your ice-cream maker according to the manufacturer's directions and place the container in the freezer to allow the ice cream to further harden.

Makes 2 quarts.

*You may freeze leftover puree for up to two months.

TOAST YOUR OWN PUMPKIN SEEDS
(FROM KATH OF *THE ORDINARY COOK*)

Kath leaves bits of pumpkin flesh hanging on to the seeds, as it really adds to the flavor.

Scrape out the seeds from a fresh pumpkin, and remove most of the flesh from them. Spread the seeds onto a lightly oiled baking sheet so they are in a single layer. Sprinkle with a little more oil and sea salt and freshly ground black pepper.

Place into a preheated 300-degree oven and bake for 30 to 40 minutes. Check on them every 15 minutes, as the ones at the edge of the tray may start to burn and will need stirring into the middle. When the seeds have a good caramel color all over, they are ready. Allow to cool.

There's no cinnamon or spice in this rustic tart, which truly celebrates the apple. A delectable syrup made from cooking the apple cores and trimmings magnifies the pure apple taste.

RUSTIC APPLE GALETTE (ADAPTED FROM *MY BERLIN KITCHEN* BY LUISA WEISS)

CRUST

1 cup all-purpose flour, plus more for dusting

1/2 teaspoon sugar

1/8 teaspoon salt

6 tablespoons butter, chilled and cut into 1-inch pieces

3 1/2 tablespoons ice water

> Place the flour, sugar, and salt into the bowl of a food processor fitted with the pastry blade. Add the butter. Pulse until the butter is broken down into lima bean–shaped pieces. Add the water, a spoonful at a time, and pulse between additions. When the dough becomes a ball, dump it out onto a lightly floured work surface and gather it together. Flatten it into a 4-inch-wide disc, wrap in plastic, and refrigerate for a minimum of 30 minutes (up to 3 days).

> When ready to bake, preheat the oven to 400 degrees. Line a baking sheet with parchment paper.

> Remove the pastry dough from the refrigerator. Unwrap and roll out onto a flour-dusted work counter. Roll the dough, rotating to form an even 14- to 16-inch circle. Dust with more flour to prevent sticking, if necessary. Place the rolled dough round on the baking sheet.

APPLE FILLING

2 pounds crisp, firm apples (I use Ginger Gold and Honeycrisp), peeled, cored, and thinly sliced (reserve the peels and cores for syrup)

2 tablespoons butter, melted

3 to 5 tablespoons sugar

> Place the apple slices in overlapping circles on the dough, leaving a 2-inch border. Crowd as many apple slices as possible. They will cook down in the oven. Fold the edges of the dough over the apples, creating a rustic look, leaving the center of the tart exposed. Brush the dough and apples with melted butter and sprinkle with sugar.

> Bake in the center of the oven for 45 minutes, rotating the tart after 20 to 22 minutes. The crust will become golden brown, as will the edges of the apples. While the tart bakes, make the apple syrup.

APPLE SYRUP

Reserved apple cores and peels

1/2 cup sugar

● Put the cores and peels into a saucepan. Add the sugar. Pour in enough water to cover, and bring to a boil over high heat. Reduce heat to medium and simmer for 30 minutes. Strain the liquid and discard the apple trimmings. Return the liquid to the saucepan. Reduce the heat to low and cook for another 10 to 15 minutes, until it becomes thickened and syrupy.

● Remove the baked tart and let it cool for 15 minutes before brushing the apples and crust with apple syrup. Serve warm or room temperature.

Makes 8 servings.

Gifts and Tips

IN DECEMBER, LIFE CAN MOVE AT A HECTIC PACE. ANOTHER YEAR WINDS DOWN, ALMOST AT AN avalanching crescendo, as the winter season ramps up. Amid the bustle and hum particular to this time, we tend to look forward: What will the New Year bring? What would we like to do? Or change?

So often, food plays into our resolutions: "eat less red meat," "eat more whole grains," "eat less white sugar," "eat more leafy greens." To that list, how about adding "eat less frequently on the run" and "eat more often with friends"? Studies reinforce what we already intuitively know—that sharing food and dining together strengthens our connections. It makes us healthier, happier human beings.

Why not start your own Third Thursday potluck?

Here are some tips to help get you going.

HAVE A COHOST

Start your potluck community by asking someone to partner with you on the project. Two heads, and two sets of hands, are always better than one. Party planning and execution are far more enjoyable when you have someone to share in the work and the fun. It sparks the creative flow and broadens the pool of people to invite.

You and your cohost each have strengths, which you'll target in your division of labor. Gigi, the designer in our duo, creates the e-mail invitation each month. I figure out the food quantities and shopping list.

Because we alternate the potluck location between our homes, it balances the chore of readying the household for guests. It also keeps the rhythm of the potlucks interesting. Over the months, you can mix it up and hold the gathering at other venues. Some of our potluckers have served as guest cohosts, opening up their homes for the meal. We call those "Pop-Up Potlucks."

THE POTLUCKERS

When Gigi and I formed our initial guest list, we thought about our friends and acquaintances who enjoy gardening or cooking in some way. In creating community, cast a net! Consider your potluckers with the core idea of bringing like-minded people together to share good food.

Someone once told me, "Oh, it's an affinity group." Well, perhaps so. I don't think about our Third Thursday in such a formal way.

Decide on how many guests you feel comfortable having in your home. Then, push it a little. Not everyone will be able to come, nor will they be able to come each time.

What we've learned is that our potluck community mirrors the community at large. It is fluid. People will rotate in and out; some will be avid potluckers, never missing a Third Thursday, and some will come a few times a year. Over time, we've seen friends leave for graduate school, get married, have babies, get divorced, take a job in another city. Life! Knowing that change is ever the constant, you might like to keep refreshing your list, to keep the potluck vital.

Once you've decided on whom to invite, you'll create the e-mail list and e-vite. We cite date, time, and location, and ask people to bring a dish and beverage of choice. We keep it simple—no assigned dishes, no RSVP. In the beginning, we sent the invitations two weeks in advance. These days, everyone seems to know when Third Thursday is, so the e-vite goes out ten days ahead of time.

THEME?

From its onset, our potluck has been seasonally driven, which makes the harvest-of-the-moment our overriding theme. But, on occasion, Gigi and I have been more specific. When Third Thursday fell on Saint Patrick's Day, "Everything Green" became the order of the day. Another month, we had Breakfast for Dinner, a meal change-up that everyone likes. Say it's October, and you'd like to have Bavarian-style Oktoberfest? Go for it!

PLATES, FORKS, NAPKINS, GLASSWARE

You may not have twenty-five or more everyday dinner plates (or dessert plates!) in your cupboard, but you can find them at thrift stores, discount warehouses, or the Goodwill for little expense. You can amass the flatware in similar fashion.

Embrace the look of mix and match! There's real charm in a hodgepodge collection of china, silver, and linens.

Scout out places like Dollar Tree for low-cost wine glasses. Mason jars, in half-pint and pint sizes, are available everywhere. When you're not using them to "put up" your harvest, you can set them out alongside a pitcher of tea. For cloth napkins, bandanas make a colorful choice.

A viable alternative: ask each guest to bring her own plate and fork. We've heard of potlucks that take this approach, and we see the merit.

COOKING STRATEGY

In the week leading up to potluck, Gigi and I get together to brainstorm our part of the meal. While the element of surprise is a hallmark of our gatherings, we try to balance that uncertainty by making at least one anchor dish. Our choices can spring from a craving for an ethnic cuisine (Mexican! Let's have a taco bar!) or be sparked by a trend (Sliders! We'll grill mini burgers and make baby buns!) or a food memory (like the crisp, spicy falafels Gigi ate in London years ago).

More often than not, inspiration comes from whatever is flourishing in our gardens or in our backyards. Depending on our choices, we split up who will make what. Other times, one will help prep for the other.

A good rule of thumb is to prepare a dish that will feed ten to twelve.

CLEANUP

Yes, the ugly truth! But our guests always help with scraping and rinsing plates, stacking, and loading the dishwasher. Toss your soiled linens into the washing machine, give the table a dust-off, the floor a sweep, and your home will be restored in short order.

THE JOURNAL

Keep one. We have a little book of blank pages, now filled with the names and contributions of guests from each potluck. While it has been a bit haphazard (it can be hard to get everyone to sign in), it's a great way to compile the menus over time, along with recipe ideas. Looking back, you'll be amazed at the rich variety of dishes that have been shared at the table.

ANYTHING ELSE?

Relax. Enjoy your guests, food, and sharing.

Remember, it's no big deal. It's potluck.

GIFTS

Our potluck group does not exchange gifts—food is always the gift—one that we are always grateful to be able to share. However, there have been numerous occasions when someone has given out gifts, if for no other reason than the desire to give.

In the bounty of summer, Gigi would set out a basket of "overrun" vegetables—tomatoes, peppers, squashes—for folks to pick what they'd like and take home. The year the fig tree went crazy with fruit, she gave away dozens of jars of fig preserves.

Jessi, our herbal soap maker, showed up one potluck evening bearing a silver tray covered with little cubes of citrus-scented soap tied in ribbons. "Party favors," she beamed. Allison shared jars of her orange marmalade—which later became a prized ingredient in a cashew chicken dish. Urban beekeeper Jen's gift of honey inspired a luscious cake.

The gifts came unexpectedly, which made them all the more treasured. We've included recipes for a few of them. We believe that the gift of food is one of the most precious of all.

GIGI'S NAPKINS

After the first potluck, Gigi and I discussed the subject of name tags. Some of the guests suggested that it would be a good idea, certainly a tried-and-true method for people who don't know one another to be identified. We both resisted the notion. It felt too "organized" or corporate. It didn't feel right for our group. Introduce yourself to someone new. Strike up a conversation over the food. That seemed truer to the way of creating community.

But Gigi, ever the crafty one, conceived an ambitious project. Over a two-month period, she designed and sewed personalized napkins for each potlucker. Using natural linen as the backdrop, she transformed each fabric square into a work of art. Odd scraps of textured cloth, silk ribbons, and pieces of vintage print cotton were all shaped, cut, and stitched to create a napkin to suit each person. Rick's had ice-cream cones; our Italian chef, Paulette, had a '60s-style postcard vignette of Rome; a lush green tree design suited our staunch environmentalist advocate, Jenn.

GOOD DEEDS

As your potluck community grows and takes root, you may like to introduce the idea of doing a good deed. It could be participating in a food drive, where everyone brings nonperishables, canned and dry goods, to donate to the local food bank. Or it could be a volunteer effort, such as weeding at a community garden or meal prepping at a soup kitchen.

One month we sponsored a "Pass the Plate." This was a low-key fund-raiser for the Community Food Advocates, a local nonprofit that works to promote healthy food access in underserved neighborhoods. It is a simple way to do a good deed.

We announced our intent and gave guests the opportunity to put whatever amount they desired into the collection plate—which, in our case, was a breadbasket. We were able to present CFA with a few hundred dollars to assist with their programs. It may seem small, compared to fund-raising efforts by large nonprofits, but the small donations bring great value too: in the end, it all adds up, right?

DECEMBER: GIFTS AND TIPS

Wendy's Friendship Sweet Rolls

Allison's Organic Cara Cara Orange Marmalade

Jessi's Lavender-Oat Bath Soak

Fig Preserves, Lafayette-LA-Way

Teresa's Aromatic Sugars

Mark's Fifteen-Spice Steak Rub

FOR YOU:
Wendy's
Friendship
Sw

Lucky-lucky people have been the recipients of Wendy's sweet rolls, which she often bakes in big quantities for the holidays. Made with a potato-sourdough starter, these cinnamon-swirled treats have a wonderful texture. Wendy enhances her glaze with orange juice, vanilla, and almond extract.

WENDY'S FRIENDSHIP SWEET ROLLS

POTATO SOURDOUGH STARTER

3/4 cup sugar

3 tablespoons instant potato flakes

1 (.25-ounce) envelope active dry yeast

1 cup warm water

❯ Combine the sugar, potato flakes, yeast, and water in a large glass bowl. Cover with plastic wrap and pierce it 4 to 5 times with a sharp knife. Refrigerate for 3 to 5 days. The starter is ready on Day 3, and good to use through Day 5.

❯ Remove the starter from the refrigerator. Let stand at room temperature for 1 hour. Stir well and remove 1 cup for the recipe. The remaining starter needs to be "fed" with the starter food (see below for instructions) and reserved for the next baking.

STARTER FOOD

3/4 cup sugar

1 cup warm water

3 tablespoons instant potato flakes

❯ Stir the sugar, water, and potato flakes into the remaining starter. Let it stand uncovered for 8 to 12 hours at room temperature. Cover with plastic wrap and pierce 4 to 5 times with a sharp knife. Refrigerate 3 to 5 days.

❯ You can repeat this process 3 times. Use all of the starter or discard after 4 feedings, as the yeast will no longer be good. There is always a 3- to 5-day window between feedings where the starter will be good to use.

THE ROLLS

6 cups all-purpose flour

1/3 cup sugar

1 (.25-ounce) envelope quick-rising yeast

1 tablespoon salt

1 1/2 cups warm water

1 cup Potato Sourdough Starter (recipe above)

1/2 cup canola oil

❯ Mix the flour, sugar, yeast, and salt together in a stand mixer. In a saucepan over medium heat, mix the water, starter, and oil together until very warm. Add the warm starter mixture to the flour mixture and blend together with a dough hook. Turn the dough out and knead until smooth, 4 to 5 minutes. Cover the dough with a towel and let rest 10 minutes.

CINNAMON MIXTURE

2 to 3 tablespoons ground cinnamon

2/3 cup firmly packed dark brown sugar

1 cup chopped walnuts or pecans

1/2 cup (1 stick) butter

◉ Stir the cinnamon, brown sugar, and nuts together in a small bowl. Melt the butter and set aside in a separate small bowl for brushing on the dough.

ASSEMBLY

◉ Turn the oven to 200 degrees and keep on for 10 minutes to warm its interior. Turn off heat. Grease three 8-inch aluminum cake pans.

◉ Cut the rested dough in half. Roll half out into a rectangle shape on a lightly floured surface. Brush the dough with the melted butter and sprinkle with half of the cinnamon–nut mixture. Repeat with the remaining dough. Roll up each rectangle jelly roll–style. Cut each roll into 12 slices. Fit 8 rolls into each cake pan and drizzle with the remaining butter.

◉ Place the pans in the warmed oven. Boil a few cups of water and pour into a pan. Put on the bottom rack of the oven to aid rising. When the rolls have doubled in size, remove the pans of rolls and the pan of water. This can take 1 1/2 to 2 hours.

◉ Preheat the oven to 350 degrees. Bake the sweet rolls for 20 to 25 minutes.

ICING

2 tablespoons butter, melted

2 cups confectioners' sugar

1 teaspoon vanilla extract

1/4 teaspoon almond extract

1/4 cup orange juice

◉ Mix the butter with the sugar and vanilla and almond extracts. Add enough orange juice to make the icing somewhat runny. Drizzle over the cooled sweet rolls. Cover the rolls with festive plastic wrap. Tie up with a ribbon, and your delicious friendship gifts are ready.

Makes 24 sweet rolls.

Have you ever tried Cara Cara oranges? Very sweet and lower in acid, their flavor has been described as complex, underscoring the tastes of cherries, blackberries, and rose petals in the citrus. Allison stresses the importance of using organic, since the entire fruit will be eaten.

ALLISON'S ORGANIC CARA CARA ORANGE MARMALADE

8 organic Cara Cara oranges

2 organic lemons

5 cups filtered water

1 stick cinnamon

2 whole cloves

1 whole allspice

5 cups sugar

❯ Begin with sterilized jars, lids, and rings. See the directions for this in Step 3 of the Canning Tips on page 49.

❯ Slice the oranges and lemons $1/8$ inch thick using a mandolin. This will leave large slices, so cut them into quarters. Remove any seeds. Place into a 10-quart pot with high sides, fitted with a candy thermometer. Add the water. Place the cinnamon, cloves, and allspice into a muslin bag and add to the pot.

❯ Bring the pot to a boil over high heat for 10 minutes. Reduce the heat to medium and simmer until soft, about 40 minutes. Add the sugar and stir constantly for about 20 minutes. Don't walk away; it could burn! Cook until the mixture reaches 222 degrees on the candy thermometer.

❯ Remove the jars from the canning vessel and drain on a towel. Fill the hot jars with marmalade and screw the lids on tight. Lower the jars into the hot water bath and process for 10 minutes. Remove the jars from the water and place on a dish towel to cool.

Makes 10 to 12 8-ounce jars or 5 to 6 pints.

Our soap maker shares this simple bath soak to relax and revitalize.

JESSI'S LAVENDER-OAT BATH SOAK

1 cup Epsom salt

1 cup baking soda

1/2 cup crushed oats (crush in a food processor to release the natural oils)

2 tablespoons dried lavender buds

1 to 4 drops lavender essential oil

2 tablespoons grapeseed or olive oil for a more moisture-rich soak

◉ Mix the salt, baking soda, oats, lavender buds, and oils together in a large bowl. Package in a clean, pretty glass jar with a lid to keep out moisture.

Makes enough for 1 luxurious bath.

My friend Maggie taught me the way her mama made fig preserves. Where they lived in Lafayette, Louisiana, a great old fig tree graced their yard. Each year they looked forward to harvesting the fruit, either cooked into lush jam or plucked ripe and relished in the moment.

FIG PRESERVES, LAFAYETTE-LA-WAY

4 pounds figs, cleaned, stems left on

4 cups sugar*

1 1/2 to 2 cups water

1 1/2 lemons, sliced

◉ Place the figs into a deep skillet. Add the sugar and just enough water, about 2 cups, to dissolve the sugar. Place the lemon slices throughout. Bring to a simmer over medium-low heat, stirring and folding the figs carefully, sometimes shaking the skillet side to side. Skim off the foam as it accumulates.

◉ Simmer like this for at least 1 hour. The figs will change from purple to brown, the lemon will cook away, and the rind will candy. The syrup will become thick, brown, and glazy.

◉ Place into sterile, warm half-pint jars and seal. Either cool, then refrigerate, or process in a 10-minute hot water bath.**

Makes 8 half-pint jars.

*Rule of thumb: for every pound of figs, use 1 cup of sugar.

**Please see the canning notes on page 49 for information about sterilizing jars.

Many cooks place a whole split vanilla bean into a canister of sugar, which permeates the crystals, making a potent vanilla sugar. It is ideal for baking. Teresa uses that trick with other herbs and spices to flavor different sugars. The result: beautiful little jars of spiced sugars, ready to dust over cookies or spoon into a cup of hot tea.

TERESA'S AROMATIC SUGARS

COCONUT PALM SUGAR WITH STAR ANISE AND GREEN CARDAMOM PODS

1 cup coconut palm sugar*

3 to 4 star anise

1 tablespoon cardamom pods, slightly crushed

◗ Place the sugar, star anise, and cardamom pods into a jar with a tight-fitting lid. Shake well. Wait a week before using and shake the jar each day for the spices to become imbued into the sugar. Wonderful spooned into a cup of hot tea.

Makes 1 cup.

*You may substitute raw sugar (such as turbinado or demerara) if you can't locate this.

LEMON AND LAVENDER SUGAR

Peel from 1 lemon

2 (2-inch) air-dried lavender stems with leaves

1 cup granulated sugar

◗ Place the lemon peel and lavender stems into a jar with a tight-fitting lid. Pour the sugar over the pieces. Give the jar a shake every day, allowing a week for the aromatics to be absorbed into the sugar. Sprinkle onto shortbread cookies or stir into a steaming cup of Earl Grey tea.

Makes 1 cup.

- MARK'S -
15-Spice
Steak Rub

STAR ANISE
CARDAMON
SUGAR

LEMON
LAVENDAR
SUGAR

The list seems long but contains everyday ingredients that you have in your pantry. Massaged onto flank steaks and briskets, this heady blend grills to a nice crusty char, sealing the meat in complex heat and spice.

MARK'S FIFTEEN-SPICE STEAK RUB

1/4 cup paprika

1/4 cup chili powder

2 tablespoons kosher salt

1 tablespoon dried oregano

1 tablespoon dried sage

1 tablespoon dry mustard

1 tablespoon granulated garlic

1 tablespoon ground cumin

1 tablespoon sugar

2 teaspoons black pepper

1 1/2 teaspoons dried thyme

1 1/2 teaspoons red pepper flakes

1 1/2 teaspoons dried rosemary

1 teaspoon ground cinnamon

1 teaspoon cayenne pepper

In a large bowl combine the paprika, chili powder, salt, oregano, sage, dry mustard, garlic, cumin, sugar, pepper, thyme, red pepper flakes, rosemary, cinnamon, and cayenne. Using a whisk, stir until all the ingredients are well combined. Place into lidded jars until ready to use. Store in a cool, dry, dark place for up to a year.

Makes 1 1/3 cups.

"Food is symbolic of love when words are inadequate."
—Alan D. Wolfelt

Staying Warm

JANUARY IS A CAPRICIOUS MONTH. IT IS NOT UNCOMMON FOR NASHVILLE TO EXPERIENCE WILD WEATHER
swings—sunny, almost balmy days that trick you into thinking it couldn't possibly be winter,
followed by a brash descent of Arctic air, the chilling reminder that, indeed, we are in winter's
heart.

We Nashvillians are not cold natured. I'd like to say it's not in our DNA, but as a New York
transplant, I have to toss that theory out. Blessed with—or spoiled by—an abundance of warm
weather, we fare less well in frigid times. We tend to bundle up, hunker down, go all inward.
Our Southern sense of bonhomie gets tested. We become a bit dark and sullen.

And if there's snow? The threat of flurries sends us into a strange frenzy. Schools shutter
before the first flake is sighted. Grocery stores turn into wastelands. Jugs of milk vanish. Loaves
of bread practically leap off the shelves.

But I get ahead of myself.

Potluck, I've found, helps send that drab winter funk packing. It's no cure-all, but consider
getting together on what might otherwise be another random bleak evening and sharing an
array of foods bold in spice and long in comfort. Like Linda's kale chips or Jimbo's Creole for
a Crowd. And thank goodness for the wealth of citrus fruits—lemons, limes, ruby grapefruits,
clementines—bringing the color and sunlight from another place.

January is also a good time to remind yourself of the true joys of canning tomatoes. This
is why you spent those steamy afternoons in July and August coring, peeling, and processing.
The rumble of the hot water bath on your stovetop, the pristine lineup of Mason jars across your
counter. Because months later, when you crack open the first jar, there it is: all the sweetness

of summer-on-the-vine. Whether cooked into sauces or layered into stratas, that first taste immediately transports you out of the winter drear and into the tangle of an August garden.

One January, the snow did arrive late on a Third Thursday afternoon. I'd been tinkering with a stew—a long-simmered pot of pork, corn, beans, and poblano peppers, made with Southwest flair—when I heard the first rash of icy rain pellet the windows. Soon after, the snow made its grand entrance, quickly enveloping the neighborhood in whorls of white. By the time I had packed up my cornbread and stewpot to drive over to Gigi's, the streets were blanketed, concealing a treacherous glaze of ice underneath. Whoa! My car did a little fishtail dance up the hill to her house. Shouldn't we call this thing off?

"This time it might really be just you and me," Gigi said, eyeing our Santa Fe spread.

She had made a batch of sweet potato quesadillas and a chocolate cayenne cake. But, before long, we heard the stamping of snowy feet on the porch and a rap at the door. Apparently we had underestimated our intrepid potluckers. In came Caroline with a savory bread pudding and neighbors Webb and Jan with roasted winter vegetables. Our once-meager table filled.

"I didn't make anything. But I slipped into The Cocoa Tree before they closed up shop and bought some truffles," said Kidd. Hey, it's a local business, with handcrafted chocolate. That counts!

All in all, seventeen souls braved the weather. The snowfall had muffled the city, brought things to a standstill. I sympathized for those who'd been thwarted by it. But at that moment, we all felt a kind of exhilaration, a snug camaraderie that we'd made it. The snow was beautiful and a challenge. We were safe and warm and together.

JANUARY: STAYING WARM

Crimson Cocktail

Spicy Kale Chips

Warm Green Hill Cheese with Apricot-Cranberry Chutney

Winter Pastels: Ruby Grapefruit and Avocado Salad with Citrus-Champagne Vinaigrette

Tomato and Mozzarella Strata

Winter Squash, Chard, and Onion Bread Pudding

Sweet Potato Quesadillas with Lime Zest Crèma

Jimbo's Creole for a Crowd

Santa Fe Pork Stew

Winter Whites: Baby Yukon Potatoes, Hakurei Turnips, Cauliflower, and Onion

Maggie's Best Skillet Buttermilk Cornbread

Key Lime Ice Cream with Graham Cracker Crumb Topping

Flourless Chocolate Cayenne Cake with Cinnamon Whipped Cream

Vibrant color, astonishing taste: what an uplift! One of the more enjoyable ways we've found to drink fruits and vegetables. While its deep garnet color is perfect for the December holidays or February Valentines, we say serve it in the drab of January, if for no other reason than to splash some color onto the winter greys.

CRIMSON COCKTAIL

1 1/2 cups water

1 cup firmly packed dark brown sugar

6 whole star anise

3 large red beets

1 1/2 quarts pure apple juice

1 1/2 cups rye whiskey (such as Bulleit)

Apple or pear slices for serving

◗ Pour the water into a small saucepan over medium heat. Stir in the brown sugar and star anise and bring the mixture to a boil. Reduce the heat to low and simmer for 20 to 25 minutes, until somewhat syrupy. Cool and strain to remove the star anise. Pour into a lidded jar and refrigerate until ready to use.*

◗ Peel and chop the beets. Place the beets in a food processor fitted with a chopping blade and puree. Do this in batches if necessary. Strain the beet juice through a sieve, pressing the pulp with the back of a wooden spoon to release the juices.**

◗ Whisk together the beet juice, 1 cup star anise syrup, apple juice, and whiskey in a large bowl and pour into bottles or a large pitcher. Chill. Pour over ice and garnish with a slice of tart apple or pear. Salut!

Makes over 2 quarts.

*This syrup will keep for a month.

**After you've extracted the juice, you can freeze the remaining pulp for another use, such as in chocolate cake.

These are the best kale chips ever. Positively addicting! Everyone gobbles these up whenever Linda brings them to potluck. She's concocted a heady spice coating for the leaves and "cooks" them in her dehydrator. If you don't have a dehydrator, your oven at its lowest setting will do the trick.

SPICY KALE CHIPS

Juice of 1 lemon

1/2 cup coconut oil

1/2 cup tahini paste

1/2 cup cider vinegar

1/3 cup tamari sauce

1/3 cup Sriracha sauce

1/3 cup minced garlic

1/2 cup nutritional yeast

2 bunches of kale*

◉ Place the lemon juice, coconut oil, tahini paste, cider vinegar, tamari, Sriracha, garlic, and yeast into a food processor fitted with a chopping blade or a blender and blend until nice and creamy.

◉ Soak the kale in a bowl of ice water to revive and perk it up. Swish the leaves in the ice water, then rinse and drain them so they are clean. Strip the leaves off of the main stem, keeping the pieces fairly large, as they will shrink. Spin the leaves in a salad spinner until dry. Pour the dressing over the kale, turning and massaging until the leaves are thoroughly coated.

◉ Place the coated kale in single layers on the trays of a dehydrator and dry for 8 hours at 120 degrees, rotating the trays halfway through.

◉ If you don't have a dehydrator, place the coated kale on baking sheets lined with parchment paper and place in your oven, set to the lowest setting, for 4 to 5 hours. Check on them hourly. You want them dried, not cooked.

Makes 15 to 20 servings.

*Curly kale is best.

The cheese we like to use for this recipe is a Camembert-like cheese from Sweet Grass Dairy in Thomasville, Georgia. It has a mild rind and a creamy butter-yellow center. Spread the top with a simple yet piquant chutney made with dried apricots, cranberries, and ginger.

WARM GREEN HILL CHEESE WITH APRICOT-CRANBERRY CHUTNEY

1 tablespoon vegetable oil

2 cloves garlic, minced

1 (1-inch) piece of fresh ginger, peeled and minced to make 2 teaspoons

1 cup coarsely chopped dried apricots

1/2 cup dried cranberries

1 cup water

1/3 cup white wine vinegar

1/4 cup firmly packed brown sugar

1/4 teaspoon salt

Pinch or 2 of red pepper flakes

1 (8-ounce) round Camembert or Brie*

Crackers or baguette slices for serving

◗ In a medium saucepan over medium heat, add the oil, garlic, and ginger and stir for about 2 minutes. Add the apricots, cranberries, water, vinegar, brown sugar, salt, and red pepper flakes and stir well. Turn the heat to low and allow the mixture to cook for another 15 to 20 minutes as the dried fruits absorb the liquid and thicken. Stir occasionally. Remove from heat and allow to cool to room temperature.

◗ Preheat the oven to 350 degrees. Place the cheese on a baking sheet lined with parchment paper. Bake in the oven for 5 to 7 minutes, just enough to warm the cheese but still remain intact. Slide the cheese onto a serving plate. Spread the cooled chutney over the top and serve with crackers or baguette slices.

Makes about 1 1/2 cups of chutney.

*We use Green Hill cheese from Sweet Grass Dairy.

Walnut oil not only imbues its toasted nutty taste but also gives an extraordinary silken quality to the vinaigrette.

WINTER PASTELS: RUBY GRAPEFRUIT AND AVOCADO SALAD WITH CITRUS-CHAMPAGNE VINAIGRETTE

2 large heads butter lettuce, washed, dried, and broken up into large leaves

2 limes

3 avocados

3 large ruby grapefruit, peeled and sliced into thin wedges (reserve rinds for vinaigrette)

1 cup chopped walnuts, toasted

Citrus-Champagne Vinaigrette (recipe follows)

❯ Place the butter lettuce leaves onto a large plate. Zest the limes and reserve the zest for the vinaigrette. Squeeze the lime juice into a medium bowl. Slice the avocados into fan-like sections and dip into the lime juice. Scatter the slices of grapefruit and avocado over the lettuce and top with the toasted walnuts. Drizzle generously with the Citrus-Champagne Vinaigrette and serve.

Makes 10 to 12 servings.

CITRUS-CHAMPAGNE VINAIGRETTE

3 tablespoons champagne vinegar

3 tablespoons grapefruit juice (squeezed from your sliced rinds)

1 heaping tablespoon chopped chives

1 1/2 teaspoons reserved lime zest

1/2 teaspoon black pepper

1/3 teaspoon dry mustard

Pinch of salt

3/4 cup (12 tablespoons) walnut oil

❯ Pour the vinegar and grapefruit juice into the bowl of a food processor fitted with a chopping blade. Add the chives, lime zest, pepper, dry mustard, and salt. Process, adding the walnut oil 1 tablespoon at a time. The vinaigrette will become nicely emulsified. Refrigerate any unused portion, which will keep for a week.

Makes 1 1/4 cups.

Here's that perfect opportunity to use your canned tomatoes (see page 49)—summer in a jar!

TOMATO AND MOZZARELLA STRATA

3 tablespoons olive oil

1 large onion, thinly sliced

3 cloves garlic, minced

1 (24-ounce) jar peeled tomatoes and juice, chopped*

Salt to taste

Cracked black pepper to taste

Dash of red pepper flakes (optional)

4 1/2 cups cubed stale bread

6 large eggs

1 1/2 cups half-and-half

6 to 8 ounces fresh mozzarella, sliced

6 tablespoons pesto

❯ Preheat the oven to 350 degrees. Coat a 2-quart soufflé dish with olive oil.

❯ Heat a deep skillet or Dutch oven on medium. Add the olive oil, onions, and garlic and cook until translucent, about 2 to 3 minutes. Add the chopped tomatoes and their juices. Season with salt, black pepper, and a dash of red pepper flakes, if you like. Increase the heat to medium-high and simmer for 10 minutes. Remove the pan from the heat and stir in the stale bread cubes. Stir until all the bread is coated with the tomato mixture.

❯ In a medium bowl beat the eggs and half-and-half together until blended. Whisk in a little salt and pepper. Spoon a layer of half of the tomato–bread mixture into the prepared dish. Top with a layer of half of the sliced mozzarella. Spoon half of the pesto over the mozzarella. Repeat the layering.

❯ Carefully pour the egg mixture over the tomato–cheese layers. You can poke through the strata with a fork, or even a chopstick, to make sure the mixture gets through the layers.

❯ Bake until puffed and golden brown, 30 to 35 minutes.

Makes 8 to 10 servings.

*You may substitute a 28-ounce can of diced tomatoes in juice from the grocery store.

Heather and Caroline's savory bread pudding imparts many of the aromas associated with Thanksgiving dressing: sage, browned butter, bread cubes, and onion. They've made it a one-dish vegetarian meal by folding in earthy-sweet winter squash and Swiss chard.

WINTER SQUASH, CHARD, AND ONION BREAD PUDDING

6 cups diced winter squash (2 to 3 butternuts or 1 large hubbard)

4 tablespoons olive oil, divided

2 tablespoons butter

2 onions, diced

1 bunch Swiss chard, cleaned and leaves sliced into ribbons

6 large eggs

2 cups half-and-half

1 cup milk

3 tablespoons chopped fresh sage leaves

Salt to taste

Black pepper to taste

6 cups cubed bread (from sturdy loaves, like baguettes, farm breads, or sourdough)

1 cup grated Pecorino-Romano cheese

❯ Preheat the oven to 450 degrees. Grease a 9 x 13-inch casserole dish.

❯ Place winter squash on a baking sheet. Pour 3 tablespoons of olive oil over the pieces and toss to coat them well. Place into the oven to roast for 12 to 15 minutes. When the pieces are lightly brown, remove from the oven and allow to cool. Lower the oven temperature to 350 degrees.

❯ In a large skillet over medium heat, melt the butter with the remaining 1 tablespoon olive oil. Add the onions and cook for 2 to 3 minutes, until translucent. Add the Swiss chard and continue to cook until the leaves are collapsed, about 5 minutes. Pour the sautéed mixture into a large bowl and toss with the roasted squash pieces.

❯ In a medium bowl whisk the eggs with the half-and-half, milk, sage leaves, salt, and pepper. Pour the egg mixture over the squash–chard mixture. Add the cubed bread and toss until everything is well coated. Spoon into the prepared dish and top with the cheese. Bake for 30 minutes until puffed but firm and nicely browned.

Makes 12 servings.

The flavors of spices magnify, or "bloom," in warm olive oil, which plays a big part in making this quesadilla filling so delectable.

SWEET POTATO QUESADILLAS WITH LIME ZEST CRÈMA

4 medium sweet potatoes (enough to make 4 cups mashed)

4 tablespoons olive oil

1 tablespoon ground coriander*

2 teaspoons cumin

2 teaspoons salt

1 cup diced onion

4 cloves garlic, minced

1 cup diced red bell pepper

1 cup diced poblano pepper

2 cups frozen corn kernels

1/4 to 1/2 teaspoon cayenne pepper**

2/3 cup vegetable stock

16 (8-inch) tortillas

Lime Zest Crema (recipe follows)

❯ Preheat the oven to 425 degrees.

❯ Scrub the sweet potatoes and place them on a baking sheet. Bake until they yield to gentle pressure, about 35 minutes.

❯ While the sweet potatoes are baking, place the olive oil in a large skillet over medium heat. Add the coriander and cumin and allow to bloom in the oil. This takes about 30 seconds. Add the onions and garlic and sauté until the onions soften, about 3 minutes. Add the bell peppers and poblano peppers. Continue sautéing for 3 minutes. Add the frozen corn kernels and sauté for another 5 minutes. Stir in the cayenne and remove the pan from the heat.

❯ Lower the oven temperature to 200 degrees after you remove the sweet potatoes. Cool the sweet potatoes and scoop out the flesh into a large bowl. Mash the sweet potatoes with just enough vegetable stock to loosen. The mixture should not be smooth.

❯ Combine the sautéed vegetables with the mashed sweet potatoes. Taste for spice and adjust as needed. Lay out 8 tortillas. Spread the sweet potato mixture over the surface of each one and gently press the remaining 8 tortillas on the top.

❯ Warm a 9- or 10-inch skillet on medium heat. Place a quesadilla into the skillet and let it crispen, 1 to 2 minutes. Flip and repeat with the remaining 7 quesadillas. Keep the quesadillas covered and warm in the oven before serving. At serving time, cut each round into 6 triangles. Serve with Lime Zest Crema on the side.

Makes 48 pieces.

*If you have a mortar and pestle, buy whole coriander and grind it with a mortar and pestle right before cooking.

**Gigi says to make it hotter!

This is an easy way to create your own Mexican-style crema. You culture the heavy cream in a method similar to crème fraîche. It is quite good, lush yet delicate, spread over a quesadilla triangle.

LIME ZEST CRÈMA

1 cup heavy cream

1 tablespoon buttermilk

Zest of 1 lime

1 teaspoon fresh lime juice

○ Pour the heavy cream into a nonreactive bowl. Stir in the buttermilk, cover, and let the mixture sit out at room temperature for a couple of hours. Stir in the zest and lime juice. Over the next hour, stir occasionally. The mixture will really thicken. Pour into a small bowl and serve alongside the quesadillas.

Makes 1 generous cup.

Chock full of shrimp, tomatoes, and "the trinity" (celery, onions, and bell peppers), Jimbo makes his big pot of Creole the traditional way—for the most part. Dry sherry adds compelling depth of flavor to his batch.

JIMBO'S CREOLE FOR A CROWD

2 cups (4 sticks) salted butter, divided

3 large yellow onions, chopped

1/4 cup extra-virgin olive oil

1/2 bottle dry sherry

3 teaspoons sea salt, divided

2 teaspoons freshly ground black pepper, divided

2 bunches celery, chopped

4 large green bell peppers, chopped

1 bulb garlic (8 to 10 cloves), minced

1/4 cup cornstarch

3/4 cup water

2 (12-ounce) bottles chili sauce (such as Heinz)

3 (28-ounce) cans peeled and crushed tomatoes

1 teaspoon cayenne pepper

2 tablespoons firmly packed brown sugar

3 tablespoons local honey

3 pounds medium-size (31 to 40 count) shrimp, peeled and deveined

1 teaspoon granulated garlic

Hot cooked rice for serving

❯ In a large pot or Dutch oven over medium heat, melt 3 sticks (1 1/2 cups) butter. Add the onions and sauté until translucent, about 4 to 5 minutes. Add the olive oil, dry sherry, 1 teaspoon salt, and 1/2 teaspoon black pepper. Add the chopped celery, bell peppers, and garlic and continue sautéing for 15 to 20 minutes.

❯ Mix about 1/4 cup of cornstarch with 3/4 cup of cold water and stir into the vegetables. Reduce the heat to low.

❯ In a large bowl combine the chili sauce and crushed tomatoes. Stir in 1 teaspoon salt, 1/2 teaspoon black pepper, and cayenne. Add the brown sugar and honey. Pour the tomato mixture into the pot. Let this all warm thoroughly, stirring occasionally. Cover and turn the heat off. You want the celery, onions, and peppers to retain some crunch. Let the pot sit, covered, at least 4 hours, stirring occasionally.

❯ Before serving, season the shrimp with the remaining 1 teaspoon salt, 1 teaspoon black pepper, and 1 teaspoon granulated garlic. Heat a large skillet over medium-high heat. Melt the remaining 1/2 cup (1 stick) butter. Sauté the shrimp in batches for about 2 minutes a batch—the shrimp will begin turning pink.

❯ Add to the warm pot of Creole. Stir well. The shrimp will continue cooking in the Creole.

❯ Serve with rice on the side.

Makes 15 servings.

Each summer Wouter works in Santa Fe, New Mexico, and brings home a giant burlap bag filled with Hatch chili peppers to share with lucky friends. I roast, peel, and then freeze the peppers in small packages—ready to cook into stews and soups to warm body and soul. Coupled with a savory spice rub, the pork cooks up sumptuous and caramel sweet-hot.

SANTA FE PORK STEW

1 tablespoon chili powder

1 tablespoon cumin

1 tablespoon Hungarian paprika

1 tablespoon ground coriander

1 tablespoon kosher salt

2 teaspoons coarse black pepper

2 teaspoons granulated garlic

3 pounds boneless pork loin, cut into cubes

4 tablespoons olive oil

1 large onion, diced

3 carrots, sliced

3 celery stalks, sliced

4 cloves garlic, minced

4 Hatch chili peppers (or other peppers, such as poblanos or Anaheims)

1/4 cup all-purpose flour

1 cup water

6 ounces beer

1 cup tomato puree

1 (15-ounce) can red beans, drained and rinsed

2 cups frozen corn kernels

Hot cooked rice for serving

◉ In a large bowl combine the chili powder, cumin, paprika, coriander, salt, pepper, and garlic. Place the pork loin cubes in the bowl and toss to combine with the spice rub.

◉ Warm the olive oil on medium heat in a Dutch oven and add the onion, carrots, celery, garlic, and chili peppers. Cook for 2 to 3 minutes, until the onions begin to soften. Add the meat, a few pieces at a time, and brown on all sides. Add the flour and stir well, coating the browned meat and vegetables. Add the water and beer. Stir in the tomato puree.

◉ Cover and reduce the heat to low. Simmer until the meat is tender, about 2 hours.

◉ Add the beans and corn. Cook, uncovered, for another 20 to 30 minutes. Taste for seasonings and adjust. Serve over rice.

Makes 12 to 15 servings.

A harmony of winter white vegetables, oven-roasted to release their natural sugars.

WINTER WHITES: BABY YUKON POTATOES, HAKUREI TURNIPS, CAULIFLOWER, AND ONION (VEGAN)

2 pounds small Yukon Gold potatoes, washed

1 bunch Hakurei turnips, washed*

3 to 4 tablespoons olive oil

1/2 teaspoon sea salt

1/4 teaspoon white pepper

Several sprigs fresh thyme

1 head cauliflower, washed and cut into florets

3 medium white onions, peeled and cut into chunky pieces

◉ Preheat the oven to 375 degrees.

◉ Place the potatoes and turnips on a baking sheet and lightly coat them with olive oil.** Season with salt, white pepper, and the leaves from several sprigs of fresh thyme.

◉ On a separate baking sheet, place the cauliflower florets and onion pieces. Toss in olive oil and sprinkle with salt and pepper and the leaves from a few sprigs of fresh thyme.

◉ Roast the potatoes and turnips for 40 minutes. Roast the cauliflower and onions for 30 minutes. Check on each tray about halfway through the cooking time and rotate the trays. Test for doneness. Toss all the vegetables together and serve in a large casserole dish.

Makes 15 servings.

*Hakurei turnips are so inherently sweet they are sometimes called salad turnips. Yes, you could eat them raw. In this dish, they burst with sweetness. If you are unable to locate Hakurei turnips, you may substitute young turnips. Peel and pare them into pieces about the size of a golf ball.

**If the potatoes are small, you can roast the turnips and potatoes together. But it is also fine to roast them on separate sheet pans and then combine after cooking.

There are cornbread recipes, and there are cornbread *recipes. This one absolutely sings. Based on her daddy's, and then her sister's, beloved skillet-made bread, Maggie's own recipe developed over time. It's more about method, she says, but using stone-ground cornmeal and whole buttermilk are just as important. And a hot, seasoned cast-iron skillet is a must. What emerges is a rich "corny" bread, an almost melting soft interior encased in a ridiculously toothsome crust. Hoo-wee. As Maggie likes to say, "It's all about the crust."*

MAGGIE'S BEST SKILLET BUTTERMILK CORNBREAD

2 cups stone-ground cornmeal

2/3 cup unbleached all-purpose flour

2 teaspoons salt

2 teaspoons sugar

1 teaspoon baking soda

1/2 cup vegetable oil

2 large eggs, at room temperature

3 cups whole buttermilk, at room temperature

❥ Preheat the oven to 425 degrees. Place a 9-inch cast-iron skillet into the cold oven to heat.

❥ In a large bowl combine the cornmeal, flour, salt, sugar, and baking soda with a whisk or wooden spoon until there are no lumps and the mixture is well blended. When the oven has reached temperature, remove the skillet. Pour the vegetable oil into the skillet, and return it to the oven so the oil will get hot.

❥ Make a well in the cornmeal mixture. Add the eggs and lightly beat. Pour in the buttermilk. Stir well until all the ingredients are combined, but do not overbeat. The batter will be somewhat lumpy.

❥ Remove the skillet from the oven. Pour half of the oil into the batter and whisk until well combined. Pour the batter into the skillet. The heat of the remaining oil will sizzle around the edges. Place the skillet in the center of the oven and bake for 35 minutes. Turn the cornbread immediately out onto parchment or butcher paper.

❥ Maggie likes to slice the round in half and prop each half on its side, claiming that this better preserves the toothsome crust.

Makes 8 to 10 servings.

This dessert is creamy-dreamy smooth with surprising tartness. Serve the graham crumbs on the side for crunch.

KEY LIME ICE CREAM WITH GRAHAM CRACKER CRUMB TOPPING

3 cups heavy cream

12 large egg yolks

2 (14-ounce) cans sweetened condensed milk

1 cup key lime juice (such as Nellie and Joe's)

Graham Cracker Crumb Topping (recipe follows)

❯ Pour the heavy cream into a large saucepan over medium heat and bring to a simmer. Look for little bubbles to form on the sides of the pan. Place the egg yolks in a large bowl and lightly beat. Pour the hot cream in a slow stream into the yolks while steadily beating. Reduce the heat to low and return the mixture to the saucepan. Stir constantly with a whisk until the custard thickens slightly. Do not let the mixture boil or the eggs will curdle.

❯ Remove the pan from the heat and pour the hot custard through a strainer into a large bowl. Allow the custard to cool slightly. Whisk in the sweetened condensed milk and key lime juice. Cover and refrigerate until well chilled. Overnight is best.

❯ Pour the mixture into an ice-cream freezer and churn the mixture according to the manufacturer's directions. When finished, the ice cream will be soft but ready to eat. For firmer ice cream, place the mixture in the freezer for 2 hours after churning. Serve with Graham Cracker Crumb Topping.

Makes 2 quarts.

GRAHAM CRACKER CRUMB TOPPING

22 graham crackers

1/2 teaspoon ground cinnamon

❯ Break the crackers into smaller pieces and place into a food processor fitted with a chopping blade. Pulse until the crackers are thoroughly broken down into crumbs. Stir in the cinnamon. Pour the mixture into a small bowl with a spoon to serve alongside the ice cream. Guests can spoon on however much they like.

Makes 1 1/2 cups graham cracker crumb topping.

This flourless confectionery is almost like baked chocolate mousse—with a kick. Serve with a dollop of cinnamon whipped cream.

FLOURLESS CHOCOLATE CAYENNE CAKE WITH CINNAMON WHIPPED CREAM

10 tablespoons butter, softened and divided

2 tablespoons cocoa

8 ounces bittersweet chocolate (70% or more), chopped

2 teaspoons vanilla

6 large eggs, separated

2/3 cup sugar

1/4 to 1/2 teaspoon cayenne pepper

Pinch of salt

Cinnamon Whipped Cream (recipe follows)

● Preheat the oven to 350 degrees. Line the bottom of a 9-inch springform pan with parchment paper and coat the bottom and sides with 1 to 2 tablespoons softened butter. Dust with cocoa powder.

● Melt the remaining 8 to 9 tablespoons butter and chocolate in a heavy-duty saucepan over low heat, occasionally stirring with a wooden spoon. When the chocolate and butter are melted and combined, stir in the vanilla. Remove the pan and cool.

● In a medium bowl beat the egg whites with an electric mixer until stiff but not dry. Set aside.

● In a large bowl beat egg yolks, sugar, cayenne, and salt with an electric mixer until it becomes light, lemon-colored, and somewhat thickened. Beat in the chocolate mixture.

● Fold a few spoonfuls of egg whites into the chocolate mixture to lighten it, and then gently fold the remaining whites throughout the mixture. Do not overmix—it's okay if traces of white show. Pour the mixture into the prepared pan.

● Bake on the middle rack of the oven for 35 to 40 minutes, until cake tester inserted comes out clean. Set the pan on a baking rack to cool for 15 minutes before removing the cake. Serve the cake slightly warm with Cinnamon Whipped Cream.

Makes 8 to 10 servings.

CINNAMON WHIPPED CREAM

1 cup heavy cream

1/4 cup confectioners' sugar

1 teaspoon ground cinnamon

1/2 teaspoon vanilla extract

● Pour the heavy cream into a chilled medium bowl. Add the sugar, cinnamon, and vanilla and beat until soft peaks form. Cover and refrigerate until ready to serve.

Good Fortunes

ONE DECEMBER, MY DAUGHTER AND I WERE SHOPPING AT A LOCAL MARKET THAT SPECIALIZED IN Russian and Eastern European goods. Her husband is of Croatian descent, and we thought we might find some treats, in particular his favorite ajvar, to put in his Christmas stocking. Sometimes called "Serbian Salsa," *ajvar* is a spicy vegetable spread made with roasted red bell peppers and eggplant.

We had fun perusing the small store, its shelves filled with intriguing and, due to the Cyrillic packaging, some perplexing items. Pierogies, caviar, farmer's cheese, dried fish, brined cucumbers, and Russian DVDs were among the identifiable products. We found the desired ajvar, and some chocolates in the shape of babushka nesting dolls. Pleased with our finds, we stepped up to the register.

Lined up across one end of the checkout counter stood an odd assortment of animal figurines, stylized reptiles. Some looked fierce, like a T-Rex; some more benign, almost comical, like Barney.

"What are these for?" I asked the store owner.

"Dinosaur," he replied in a thick accent. "You know, for special year Japanese celebration."

My mind spun a film reel of Godzilla movies. I nodded and paid. My daughter and I left the market, both feeling a little bewildered.

As we drove home, the light flipped on. *Those weren't dinosaurs; they were dragons. And the coming celebration is Chinese New Year. The year of the dragon!*

We laughed at the collision of languages and cultures. The Russian telling the Americans about a Far East tradition. Things can really get tripped up in translation.

Ultimately, it points to a universal desire for health and prosperity in the year to come. No self-respecting Southerner would start the year off without a bowl of black-eyed peas. We all have our notions of what will ensure good luck.

"In China," my daughter said, "to be born under the sign of the dragon is supposed to be the luckiest of all."

A few weeks later the dragon raised its head again. When I told Gigi about our funny experience with the Russian storekeeper, she said, "Serendipity!" She'd been considering a Chinese New Year theme for our February potluck.

Chinese New Year is based on the lunar calendar. It always falls on the second new moon after the winter solstice. That date changes each year, anywhere from January 19 to February 20. Gigi decided that it fell close enough to our Third Thursday, and furthermore, she already knew what she wanted to make.

"Potluck fortune cookies!"

"And how do you intend to do that?"

"I have it all figured out. I'll make pizzelles. You'll write the fortunes."

Ah, those Italian waffle cookies. Thin, crisp wafers, they can be scented with lemon or anise. Gigi owned a pizzelle maker, a special kind of waffle iron that imprints a snowflake-like design onto the cookie. Hot off the press, pizzelles have a certain degree of flexibility. Cooks can wrap them around dowels to make cannoli shells, so the pizzelles could be folded over easily enough to enclose our strips of fortune-telling paper.

Funny thing, the fortune cookie isn't Chinese at all. There are competing legends, but most concur that it was created in San Francisco at the turn of the last century, its recipe modeled on a Japanese cookie. Further, it is noted that this staple of Chinese-American restaurants got its introduction by a Japanese man.

Our February menu is an homage to the colliding and melding of cultures and traditions. It speaks to the melting-pot makeup of our country. You'll find exciting flavor profiles from around the globe, as widespread as India, Mexico, Persia, and Morocco. Some are authentic recipes from a land, but many are inspired "collisions," starting with Gigi's Chinese-Italian-American potluck fortune cookie.

FEBRUARY: GOOD FORTUNES

Gigi's Chinese-Italian-American Fortune Cookies (Pizzelles)

Silky Butternut Squash Bisque

Wendy's Zesty Napa Slaw

Indian Potato and Onion Curry

Cara Cara Cashew Chicken

Brined Pork Tenderloin with Plum Sauce

Jeweled Jasmine Rice

Moroccan Vegetable Tagine with Saffron Couscous

Pickled Vegetables (Escabeche)

Glazed Kiwi Tart with Orange-Scented Pastry Cream

Garam Masala Kitchen Sink Cookies

Let your imagination go when making up the fortunes. For fun, we've listed some of our potluck fortunes below.

GIGI'S CHINESE-ITALIAN-AMERICAN FORTUNE COOKIES (PIZZELLES)

3 large eggs, at room temperature

3/4 cup sugar

1/2 cup (1 stick) butter, melted and cooled

1 teaspoon vanilla extract

1/2 teaspoon anise extract

Zest of 1 lemon

1 3/4 cups all-purpose flour

2 teaspoons baking powder

❯ In a large bowl beat the eggs and sugar. Stir in the cooled melted butter, vanilla and anise extracts, and lemon zest. In a medium bowl sift the flour and baking powder together. Add the flour mixture to the egg mixture. The batter will be stiff enough to be dropped from a spoon.

❯ Heat a pizzelle waffle iron and brush the grates with oil or butter. Drop a tablespoon of batter onto the center circle of the iron and bake for about 30 seconds or until steam no longer emerges from the iron. Test your iron. Carefully remove the pizzelle and fold it over or roll it into a tube. When cool, tuck your strip of paper with the fortune inside.

Makes 24 pizzelles.

POTLUCK FORTUNES

- Your garden is your nest egg.
- Pick your battles like you pick your tomatoes.
- Applaud (Kiss or Praise) the hand that feeds you.
- A hard freeze makes the kale sweeter.
- There's buried treasure in your compost pile.
- Don't straddle the fence between this and that.
- Be surprised, and then be spurred into action.

- The growing season will be long and prosperous.
- Beware of beetles.
- Grow community.
- Honor thy farmer.
- Cultivate goodwill.
- Best tomatoes ever—this summer.
- The fortune you seek is in the next cookie.
- Shake up conventional kitchen wisdom.

As cooks, we rely on vanilla for sweets, but it can be wonderful in savory applications too. Here, it adds a sumptuous depth of flavor to the soup. If you can find Mexican vanilla, Teresa recommends using it. This soup was inspired by a dish she had in the Yucatán.

SILKY BUTTERNUT SQUASH BISQUE

2 butternut squashes, peeled, seeded, and cut into chunks

4 garlic cloves, peeled

2 medium onions, cut into quarters

6 carrots, peeled and cut into 2-inch pieces

2 to 3 tablespoons olive oil

1 tablespoon cumin

1 teaspoon salt

1/2 teaspoon black pepper

6 tablespoons butter

2 quarts vegetable or chicken stock

2 cups coconut milk

2 cups plain Greek yogurt

4 tablespoons pure Mexican vanilla extract (or scrape 1 vanilla bean)

Pomegranate seeds (optional)

❯ Preheat the oven to 400 degrees. Line a baking sheet with parchment paper.

❯ Place the squash, garlic, onions, and carrots in a large bowl. Add the olive oil, cumin, salt, and pepper. Toss well to coat the vegetables and spread them out on the baking sheet. Bake for 25 minutes, until the vegetables have softened.

❯ In a large pot over medium heat, melt the butter. Add the roasted vegetables and stock. Cover and reduce heat to low. Simmer for 30 minutes. Remove the pot from the heat and use an immersion blender to puree the mixture until smooth and silky. Continue pureeing as you add the coconut milk and Greek yogurt. Finally, stir in the vanilla. Gently rewarm the soup and serve. Garnish with pomegranate seeds, if desired.

Makes more than 1 gallon.

Napa, daikon radish, green onions, and a creamy sesame dressing give this slaw a tasty Asian twist.

WENDY'S ZESTY NAPA SLAW

7 cups shredded Napa cabbage

1 cup shredded red cabbage

1 cup chopped daikon radish

1 cup chopped green onions

1 cup chopped fresh cilantro

1 cup frozen green peas, thawed

3/4 cup mayonnaise (such as Hellman's)

3 tablespoons rice wine vinegar

3 tablespoons sesame seeds

1 tablespoon soy sauce

1/2 teaspoon sesame oil

1/4 teaspoon cayenne pepper

1/4 cup slivered almonds, toasted

◗ In a large bowl toss the shredded Napa and red cabbages. Add the daikon radish, green onions, cilantro, and peas and gently toss to combine.

◗ In a small bowl whisk the mayonnaise with the vinegar, sesame seeds, soy sauce, sesame oil, and cayenne until well combined. Pour over slaw mixture and toss well. Top with toasted slivered almonds and chill for 1 hour.

Makes 15 servings.

We must give Jay's mom, Prasanna, credit for this recipe, an authentic south Indian curry dish. If you cannot find urad dal, otherwise known as urad or black gram, it's okay to leave it out. The curry is still delicious without it.

INDIAN POTATO AND ONION CURRY

5 medium boiling potatoes (such as Yukon Gold)

1 teaspoon turmeric powder

2 teaspoons salt

4 tablespoons canola oil

1 1/2 teaspoons mustard seeds

1 1/2 teaspoons urad dal (optional)

2 to 3 dry red chilies, minced

2 medium yellow onions, thinly sliced

1 teaspoon cumin powder

1/2 teaspoon cayenne pepper

2 teaspoons fresh lemon juice

○ Peel the potatoes and cut them into 3/4-inch cubes. Rinse the potatoes and place them in a 3-quart saucepan over medium-high heat. Add enough water to cover the potatoes. Stir in the turmeric and salt.

○ Cover and bring the water to a boil to cook the potatoes. While the potatoes boil, set a strainer over a large bowl. When the potatoes can be easily pierced with a fork (check after 10 minutes), carefully drain the potatoes in the strainer, saving the cooking water.

○ In a large skillet over medium heat, add the oil. When the oil is hot, add the mustard seeds. When they begin to pop, then stir in the urad dal and the minced dry chilies. (Aromatics can be heady.)

○ Add the onions to the oil and allow them to cook until they are transparent. Add the cumin, cayenne, and the cooked potatoes. Mix well. Add more salt and 1/4 teaspoon more of turmeric if needed.

○ Mash part of the potatoes and if very dry add a little of the leftover water. Finish by folding in the lemon juice.

Makes 10 to 12 servings.

NOTE: If you want to make this into more of a stew, add back more water.

Allison's gift of marmalade, made from Cara Cara oranges (see page 157 for the recipe), inspired this delectable take on Orange Cashew Chicken.

CARA CARA CASHEW CHICKEN

5 tablespoons peanut oil, divided

1 tablespoon sesame oil

2 pounds boneless chicken breast, cut into bite-size pieces

2 medium onions, diced

4 cloves garlic, minced

6 carrots, cut diagonally into $1/2$-inch pieces

4 ribs celery, sliced diagonally into $1/2$-inch pieces

2 cups sugar snap peas

$1/2$ cup orange marmalade

$1/2$ cup chicken stock

$1/4$ cup soy sauce

$1/4$ cup sherry

1 tablespoon cornstarch

1 tablespoon grated fresh ginger

$1/4$ teaspoon red pepper flakes

1 cup cashew halves

1 bunch scallions, chopped, for garnish

1 bunch fresh cilantro, chopped, for garnish

❂ Pour 3 tablespoons of the peanut oil and the sesame oil into a large skillet or Dutch oven over medium-high heat. When the oils are heated but not smoking, add the chicken and fry until the pieces are nicely browned, about 5 minutes.

❂ Remove the chicken from the skillet and set aside in a bowl. Reduce the heat to medium.

❂ Add the remaining 2 tablespoons peanut oil to the cooking vessel and heat. Add the onions and cook until translucent, about 2 minutes. Add the garlic and cook for 30 seconds.

❂ Continue stir-frying each vegetable, beginning with carrots. Cook them for 2 minutes, then add the celery. Stir-fry for 2 minutes, then add the sugar snap peas. Stir-fry for a minute. Remove from heat while you make the sauce.

❂ In a saucepan over medium heat, add the orange marmalade, chicken stock, and soy sauce. Stir well. Pour the sherry into a small bowl and whisk in the cornstarch, ginger, and red pepper flakes. Pour the sherry mixture into the pan. Stir and cook until bubbling.

❂ Add the cooked chicken back to the pan with the stir-fried vegetables. Stir in the cashews. Pour the heated orange marmalade sauce over the chicken and vegetables, folding to coat everything well. Garnish with chopped scallions and cilantro.

Makes 8 to 10 servings.

When the pork bathes overnight in Mark's savory-sweet brine, it becomes infused with herbaceous fruit flavors and retains its juiciness on the grill or in the oven. Post-grilling or roasting, paint the plum sauce onto the meat and let it rest before carving. Serve the extra sauce in a bowl on the side.

BRINED PORK TENDERLOIN WITH PLUM SAUCE

THE BRINE

3 quarts (12 cups) water

3/4 cup kosher salt

1/2 cup firmly packed brown sugar

4 garlic cloves, sliced

1 quart apple cider

3 bay leaves

2 sprigs fresh rosemary

1 teaspoon whole black peppercorns

1 teaspoon red pepper flakes

2 (1-pound) pork tenderloins

❯ Place 4 cups of the water into a 2-quart saucepan over medium heat. Add the salt, brown sugar, and garlic, stirring until dissolved. Pour the mixture into a large nonreactive pan. Add the remaining 8 cups water, apple cider, bay leaves, rosemary, peppercorns, and red pepper flakes. Allow the mixture to cool to room temperature. This should take under 5 minutes. When the liquid is cool, place the pork into the brine. Cover and refrigerate for 12 to 24 hours.

This tangy sauce can be made up ahead of time and kept in the refrigerator. It will keep for six months.

PLUM SAUCE

4 cups fresh plums, washed, pitted, and chopped

3/4 cup raw sugar (such as turbinado or demerara)

1/4 cup balsamic vinegar

1 1/2 teaspoons Dijon mustard

1 1/2 teaspoons fresh ginger, grated

1 1/2 teaspoons ground allspice

continued next page

❯ In a heavy pot over medium-low heat, add the plums, sugar, balsamic vinegar, mustard, ginger, allspice, onion, bell pepper, garlic, jalapeño, and salt. Stir to combine. As the plums warm and release their juices, stir well. Cover and simmer for 1 hour, stirring the mixture periodically. Over time, the plums, onions, and bell pepper bits will soften and meld into a thick sauce.

1/4 cup finely chopped onion

1/4 cup finely chopped red bell pepper

1 garlic clove, minced

1 jalapeño pepper, finely chopped*

1 teaspoon salt

ASSEMBLY

1 tablespoon vegetable oil

◗ Remove the tenderloins from the brine and pat them dry. Cover them and allow them to come up to room temperature while you prepare the grill. You may also roast the tenderloins in the oven, if you prefer.

ON THE GRILL: Light the coals and allow them to burn to ashen, about 25 to 30 minutes. Spread the coals. Brush the grate with vegetable oil. Place the pork on the grill. Cover and grill for 15 minutes, rotating the tenderloins every 2 minutes.

IN THE OVEN: Preheat the oven to 450 degrees. Warm the oil in a large skillet over medium-high heat and sear the pork tenderloins on all sides. Place the tenderloins on a baking sheet and roast for about 10 minutes.

◗ While the meat is cooking, warm the plum sauce in a saucepan over low heat. Stir occasionally.

◗ Insert a meat thermometer into the thickest part of the tenderloin. When it registers an internal temperature of 140 degrees, remove it from the grill (or oven). The meat will continue to cook as it rests and should reach 145 degrees before serving. Generously coat the tenderloin with the warmed plum sauce. Cut the meat into thin slices and arrange on a platter. Serve with a bowl of extra plum sauce on the side.

Makes 8 to 10 servings.

*Remove the seeds if you want less heat.

For its fragrant aromatics, jasmine rice is always a favorite. When folded with dried fruits, nuts, and turmeric, it really becomes exceptional. One trick to keeping the grains separate and fluffy is to soak and rinse the rice. This also softens the grain, making it require less water to cook.

JEWELED JASMINE RICE

2 tablespoons olive oil

1 onion, diced

2 garlic cloves, minced

1 1/2 teaspoons salt

2 1/2 cups jasmine rice, soaked in a bowl of water for 10 minutes and rinsed

4 cups water

2 tablespoons butter

1/2 cup chopped pistachios

1/2 cup golden raisins

1/2 cup currants

3/4 teaspoon turmeric

❯ Warm the olive oil in a large saucepan over medium heat. Add the onions, garlic, and salt. Sauté until the onions become translucent, about 5 minutes. Add the rinsed jasmine rice and stir to coat the grains with the other ingredients. Pour in the water and stir well. Increase the heat to medium-high and cover.

❯ When the water comes to a boil, reduce the heat to low. Simmer for 5 minutes. Keep covered and remove the pan from the heat. Let the rice sit undisturbed for at least 10 minutes.

❯ Melt the butter in a skillet over medium heat. Stir in the pistachios and cook for about 5 minutes, letting them toast. Stir in the raisins, currants, and turmeric. When all of the ingredients are well combined, remove the pan from the heat. Fluff the cooked rice with a fork. Fold in the sautéed nut mixture and serve.

Makes 10 servings.

Don't be thrown off by the name or the ingredient list. A tagine is a savory stew. The assembly of spices quickly combines to make a remarkable complex stew with rousing aromatics.

MOROCCAN VEGETABLE TAGINE WITH SAFFRON COUSCOUS

THE TAGINE

3 tablespoons olive oil

2 onions, chopped

3 carrots, diced

3 celery stalks, diced

3 red bell peppers, diced

2 jalapeño peppers, finely chopped

4 garlic cloves, minced

1 tablespoon minced fresh ginger

1 tablespoon ground cumin

1 tablespoon ground cinnamon

2 teaspoons ground turmeric

2 teaspoons paprika

2 teaspoons crushed red pepper

1 teaspoon black pepper

1 teaspoon salt

2 (28-ounce) cans diced tomatoes

1 cup vegetable stock (enough to thin stew)

1 lemon

2 (15-ounce) cans garbanzo beans

3/4 cup raisins

1/2 cup green olives, diced

1 tablespoon brown sugar

❯ Place the olive oil in a large saucepan and warm over medium-low heat. Add the onions, carrots, and celery. Cook the vegetables until they start to release their juices into the pan. Do not allow them to brown. Increase the heat to medium and add the bell peppers and jalapeños. Cook for 1 minute. Add the minced garlic and ginger, followed by the cumin, cinnamon, turmeric, paprika, crushed red pepper, black pepper, and salt.

❯ Once the spices become aromatic, add the tomatoes and their juices. Pour in the vegetable stock and stir. Peel the rind from the lemon and cut into thin strips lengthwise. Add the lemon peel, garbanzos, raisins, green olives, and brown sugar. Continue cooking on medium-low heat for 20 to 30 minutes.

SAFFRON COUSCOUS

1 3/4 cups water

1/4 teaspoon salt

Pinch of saffron

1 1/2 cups couscous

Cilantro leaves, for garnish

1 to 2 lemons, cut into wedges, for garnish

In a saucepan over high heat, bring the water to a boil. Add the salt and saffron threads and stir. Stir in the couscous. Cover and remove the pan from the heat. Let it rest for 10 minutes. Fluff the couscous with a fork. It should be light and fluffy, not gummy.

Serve the tagine over the couscous and garnish with cilantro leaves and lemon wedges.

Makes 8 to 10 servings.

This is an easy method to marinate—actually, quickly pickle—vegetables found throughout Mexico in countless variations. You can make it more fiery by adding fresh sliced jalapeños to the batch. In the summer, green beans, zucchinis, and yellow squashes would also be delicious in the brine. These will keep in the refrigerator for up to three months.

PICKLED VEGETABLES (ESCABECHE)

8 ounces small new potatoes, (about golf ball size), washed

1/2 cup olive oil

8 ounces pearl onions, trimmed and peels removed

1 red bell pepper, julienned

6 garlic cloves, sliced in half lengthwise

1 pound carrots, peeled and cut into coins

1 head cauliflower, cut into bite-size florets

8 ounces button mushrooms, cleaned, trimmed, and halved or quartered (depending on size)

4 cups white vinegar

2 cups water

2 to 3 bay leaves

2 sprigs fresh oregano or marjoram

2 to 3 dried whole cayenne peppers

2 teaspoons sea salt

2 teaspoons black peppercorns

❯ Place the new potatoes in a large pot. Cover with water and place over medium-high heat. Bring to a boil and cook until the potatoes are just tender when pierced with a knife. This could take 8 to 10 minutes. Drain and set aside.

❯ Warm the olive oil in a large, deep skillet or pot over medium heat. Add the onions, bell pepper strips, garlic, and carrots. Sauté for 3 minutes. Stir in the cauliflower florets. Sauté for another 3 minutes. Stir in the button mushrooms and par-cooked new potatoes. Reduce the heat to low while you make the pickling solution.

❯ In a large bowl stir together the vinegar, water, bay leaves, oregano, dried peppers, salt, and peppercorns. Pour over the vegetables in the pot.

❯ Increase the heat to medium. Simmer for 8 to 10 minutes. The vegetables will be tender but not mushy. Remove the pot from the heat and allow the vegetables to cool. Remove the bay leaves. Spoon the vegetables into glass jars and pour the brine over them, covering the vegetables but leaving a little head space. Put on lids and refrigerate overnight to allow the flavors to marry.

Makes 12 to 14 cups.

Orange zest paired with vanilla gives a distinctive taste to this pastry cream that might remind you of Creamsicles—in the best possible way.

GLAZED KIWI TART WITH ORANGE-SCENTED PASTRY CREAM

SWEET PASTRY CRUST

6 tablespoons butter, chilled and cut into pieces

2 tablespoons sugar

1 large egg

1 cup all-purpose flour

1 tablespoon ice water

◗ In a food processor fitted with a pastry cutter, pulse together the butter, sugar, egg, flour, and water until it forms a large mass. Form the dough into a ball and wrap in plastic. Let the dough rest in the refrigerator for 1 hour.

◗ Preheat the oven to 350 degrees. Roll out the dough on a lightly floured surface. Cut and place into a 9- or 10-inch tart pan with a removable bottom. Prick the dough with a fork. Line the dough with a piece of parchment paper and fill with pie weights (or dried beans). Place in the oven and "blind-bake" for 15 minutes, until the crust is brown. Place on wire rack to cool.

ORANGE-SCENTED PASTRY CREAM

1 tablespoon butter

1/2 cup sugar

3 tablespoons all-purpose flour

2 cups milk, divided

1 teaspoon vanilla extract

1 1/2 teaspoons orange zest

3 large eggs

◗ In a medium saucepan over low heat, melt the butter and mix in the sugar and flour.

◗ Add 1 cup of the milk and stir constantly. Add the vanilla and orange zest.

◗ In a medium bowl whisk the eggs with the remaining 1 cup of milk until well blended and no streaks of yolk can be seen. Pour the egg mixture into the saucepan and stir well. Cook until thickened. Cool to room temperature, cover, and refrigerate until ready to use.

APRICOT GLAZE

1/2 cup apricot preserves

2 tablespoons sugar

2 tablespoons water

◗ In a small saucepan over medium heat, add the preserves, sugar, and water and stir well. As the mixture gets hot, the sugar dissolves and the preserves melt. In 3 to 4 minutes, the glaze becomes thinner and syrupy. If there are small chunks of fruit in the glaze, you can pour the mixture through a strainer into a small bowl to remove. But if you don't mind pieces of apricot, then leave it as it is.

Makes 8 to 10 servings.

This is the king of kitchen sink cookies. Along with rolled oats, walnuts, and bittersweet chocolate, Joy adds orange extract and garam masala, a heady blend of exotic spices: cinnamon, cardamom, ginger, cumin, nutmeg, coriander, and cloves. It's the best chocolate-chip-oatmeal-walnut-spice cookie you'll ever taste.

GARAM MASALA KITCHEN SINK COOKIES

1 cup (2 sticks) butter, softened

1 cup firmly packed brown sugar

1/2 cup white sugar or coconut palm sugar

2 large eggs

1 tablespoon fresh orange zest

1/2 teaspoon orange extract

1 1/2 cups all-purpose flour

1 teaspoon baking soda

1/2 teaspoon salt

1 1/2 teaspoons garam masala

3 cups old-fashioned rolled oats

2 cups chopped walnuts, toasted

2 cups bittersweet chocolate chips

● Preheat the oven to 350 degrees. Line a baking sheet with parchment paper.

● In a large bowl beat the butter and brown and white sugars until creamy. Add the eggs, orange zest, and orange extract and beat well. In a medium bowl combine the flour, baking soda, salt, and garam masala. Beat the flour mixture into the creamed sugar mixture a little at a time until combined. Fold in the oats, walnuts, and chocolate chips.

● Drop rounded tablespoonsful onto the baking sheet and bake for 12 minutes, or until golden brown.

Makes 5 dozen.

Going Green

IN MARCH, OUR THIRD THURSDAY GATHERING ALIGNS CLOSELY WITH THE FIRST DAY OF SPRING: daylight's tipping point. It always sets me to thinking green. The barren ground begins to show renewed life—most striking when Gigi and I would go to the garden to harvest leeks.

"If there's one thing I can grow, it's leeks," our self-deprecating urban farmer would say. But she soon came to recognize that she'd had a hand in growing many other good things.

As we'd trudge up the hill, shovels in arms, to the sunny patch where those leeks grew tall and fat over winter, we'd get easily sidetracked by a host of plantings emerging from somber earth: mounds of thyme and tarragon, rumpled spinach, proud stands of young chives and spring onions, feathery carrot greens, shoots of sorrel, cilantro, rainbow chard, and big tufts of curly kale. A whole world of new green!

As we explored, Gigi's commentary ran a wide gamut—exhibiting exuberance, wonder, even memory loss: "Look, that sorrel came back. Aha! Those herbs must have reseeded themselves. Can you believe it? That clump of onions is bigger. See how well that chard wintered over? Dang, I forgot that I planted that row of carrots last fall. I better check on those parsnips."

But the upshot was this: Mother Nature was doing what she does best, mostly unattended.

Food activist Michael Pollan writes, "The garden suggests that there might be a place where we can meet nature halfway." I agree. I like to think that the garden extends beyond the physical plot, soil churned and rows planted. It includes the pots of herbs in your windowsill, the pear tree in your backyard, the bag of summer squash and peppers from your local farmer. It includes what we do with that bundle of beets, mess of beans, or carton of eggs. In a land of abundance, there's an ugly two-pronged flip side: hunger and waste. It doesn't make sense that almost 40 percent of food is thrown out while close to 15 percent of our population is food insecure.

We're all in this together, on this wondrous planet. How we care for it mirrors how we care for each other. That gives us numerous simple ways to be Mother Nature's good partner. What does it really mean to go green, or be green? It can start with cultivating some common-sense food habits.

REDUCE WASTE

- Use what you've got. This takes some foresight and meal planning, but creates a smart economy in cooking. It also keeps the pantry fresh and vital.
- Use the whole thing. The greens attached to those beets are delicious too. Try them sautéed with garlic and onion. Scraps of vegetables can cook into a lush broth in under 30 minutes.
- Preserve. Canning, freezing, and dehydrating are all terrific methods when you have food in bulk.
- Compost. If you wind up not using the produce you purchased, don't beat yourself up about it. Place it in the compost bin. In a short time, that withered celery or neglected bunch of chard will transform into nutrient-rich soil.
- Mindfully use water. Pure water is a commodity that we cannot take for granted. Don't keep it idly running; put an aerator on the spigot, and reuse when possible (see our special tip on the next page for washing greens).

COOK SEASONALLY

- Grow your own. It doesn't matter if it's basil flourishing in pots on your patio, bushes of cherry tomatoes volunteering on that scrappy patch of land by the sidewalk, or a full-blown plot in a community garden: everything matters. Everything, great or small, contributes to the whole.
- Plant fruit trees. Or bushes. Or vines. What a joy to walk over to that plum tree or trellis of blackberries and pluck fresh, ripe fruit.
- Buy fresh and local. Support your area farmers, producers, artisans, and entrepreneurs through co-ops, CSA shares, farmers' markets, or local retail outlets. Their labors bring many fruits, literally and figuratively. It forms personal relationships, gives a community character, and keeps money in the local economy. Shake, kiss, and praise the hand that feeds you.

SHARE

The heart of potluck!

Our menu this month shares a compilation of green favorites, inspired by the first of spring and the greenest of green: Saint Patrick's Day.

A GREEN TIP

My friend Tammy of Agri-Girl shares this good green tip. What all greens have in common is the need to be washed. Her method makes wise use of the water:

1. Fill a bucket or large pot with cold water.
2. Separate the greens by the bottom of the stalks.
3. Holding your greens by the root end, plunge them into the water.
4. Swish them around and pump them up and down in the cold water for about a minute. The dirt washes out and then sinks to the bottom of the pot.
5. Remove your greens and dry in a salad spinner.
6. Use the water to hydrate your houseplants or other patio flowers.

"When the world wearies and society ceases to satisfy, there is always the garden."
—Minnie Aumonier

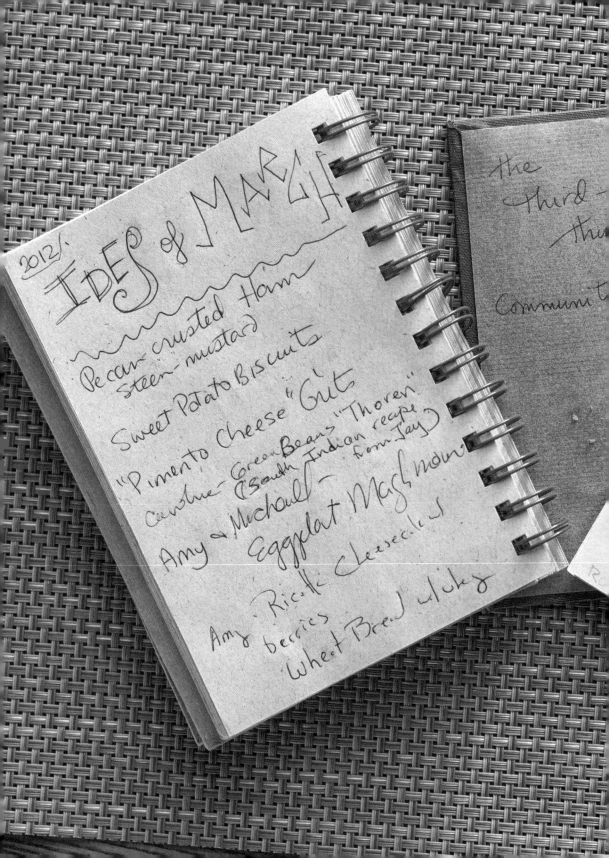

MARCH: GOING GREEN

A Spring Green Tonic

Mustard Greens Salad

Greens, Straw, and Hay

Bacon-Leek Tart in Puff Pastry

Fancy-Pants Shepherd's Pie

Val's Mother-in-Law's Mandarin Chicken and Cabbage Salad

Butternut Squash and Heirloom Bean Chili

Parmesan-Sage Polenta with Spinach and Onions

Luck-o'-the-Irish Ganache-Filled Cupcakes

Mint Chocolate Chip Ice Cream

A tonic, Teresa tells us, is used to help restore and reinvigorate—it promotes general health and well-being. She concocted this delicious tonic with the brilliant color of early spring in mind. It will "get your motor running!"

A SPRING GREEN TONIC

8 cucumbers, peeled and seeded

1 (2-inch) piece fresh ginger

1 1/2 cups raw sugar (such as turbinado or demerara)

1 1/2 cups water

Juice of 6 limes

2 1/2 cups white rum

1 cup melon liqueur (such as Midori)

Seltzer

1 lime, sliced into small wedges, for garnish

❯ Cut the cucumbers into chunks and place in a food processor with a chopping blade. You may have to do this in batches. Process until the cucumbers are pureed with no chunks. Pour the puree into a colander lined with two layers of cheesecloth or a fine sieve sitting over a bowl to catch the cucumber juice. Use a rubber scraper to press the puree through the cheesecloth or sieve to get out most of the liquid. You should have about 3 cups of cucumber juice. Cover the bowl and refrigerate.

❯ Peel the ginger and cut it into thin slices. Place the ginger pieces and raw sugar into a saucepan over medium-high heat. Add the water and bring to a low boil. Cook for about 5 minutes, stirring often. Remove the pan from the heat and allow the syrup to cool. Pour the cooled syrup through a strainer into a small bowl to remove the ginger pieces.

❯ In a large nonreactive pot or bowl, mix the cucumber water, lime juice, ginger syrup, white rum, and liqueur. Stir and pour into serving pitchers or bottles. Chill.

❯ To serve, fill a tall glass with ice. Pour in the tonic until the glass is about two-thirds full. Top with a splash of seltzer water. Garnish with lime.

Makes 2 quarts.

Young mustard greens make a delicious salad base, their raspy tooth softened by the dressing.

MUSTARD GREENS SALAD

2 bundles mustard greens

2 large carrots

2 beets

4 tablespoons boiled cider* (such as Wood's Boiled Cider)

Zest and juice of 4 clementines

4 tablespoons extra-virgin olive oil

1 teaspoon salt

1/2 cup pine nuts, toasted

1/2 cup crumbled feta cheese

❯ Wash the mustard greens in a sink (or large pot) full of cold water to remove any sand or dirt. It's a good idea to wash them three times to remove all the grit. Remove the greens from the water and allow them to dry on a clean dish towel, or use a salad spinner to remove the excess water.

❯ Grate the carrots and beets on a cheese grater with large holes. Place the greens, carrots, and beets in a large bowl.

❯ In a small bowl combine the boiled cider, clementine juice and zest, olive oil, and salt. Whisk together. Pour the dressing over the greens.

❯ Massage the dressing into the salad for about 5 minutes, or until the greens start to break down. Top with toasted pine nuts and feta.

Makes 10 servings.

* For ordering information, check out the Resources (page 318). You can substitute pomegranate molasses, which is available at many global and ethnic markets.

Three types of sautéed greens folded throughout three kinds of pasta equals one stupendous dish.

GREENS, STRAW, AND HAY (VEGAN)

6 to 8 tablespoons olive oil

1 bundle spring onions, chopped (white and green parts)

1 bunch Swiss chard, cleaned and dried (stems chopped and leaves coarsely chopped)

2 teaspoons sea salt

1/2 teaspoon red pepper flakes

1 bunch Red Russian kale, cleaned, dried, and leaves torn from main stem

1 bunch beet greens, cleaned, dried, and leaves torn from main stem

2 cups vegetable stock

1/2 cup golden raisins

1/2 cup pine nuts, toasted

4 ounces linguine

4 ounces spinach fettuccine

4 ounces whole wheat capellini

1 cup grated Parmesan or Romano cheese

❯ Heat a large pot or skillet over medium heat and add the olive oil. Sauté the spring onions and the chopped chard stems for 5 to 7 minutes. Sprinkle with sea salt and red pepper flakes. Stir in the coarsely chopped chard greens, kale, and beet greens and sauté for another 2 minutes. Pour in the vegetable stock and stir well. The greens will collapse. Add the golden raisins and toasted pine nuts. Toss throughout the mixture. Remove from heat.

❯ Bring a 5-quart pot of lightly salted water to a boil. Cook the linguine, fettuccine, and capellini according to package directions so they are all done at the same time. Drain the pasta and reserve 2 cups of the pasta liquid.

❯ Gently toss the pastas with the sautéed greens, ensuring a good distribution of all the elements throughout. If the mixture doesn't seem wet enough, add a little of the reserved pasta water. Serve with a bowl of grated Parmesan or Romano cheese on the side.

Makes 8 to 10 servings.

Cottage cheese and Greek yogurt combine to make a smooth, tangy foundation for this simple appetizer that highlights leeks and crisp bacon.

BACON-LEEK TART IN PUFF PASTRY

1 cup whole milk cottage cheese

1/2 cup plain Greek yogurt, drained

1/2 teaspoon salt

1/2 teaspoon black pepper

2 sheets puff pastry, thawed but still chilled

1 large leek, cleaned well and sliced very thinly (white and light green parts)

12 slices bacon, cooked crisp and broken into pieces

1 cup freshly grated Parmesan cheese

❷ Preheat the oven to 400 degrees. Line 2 baking sheets with parchment paper.

❷ In the bowl of a food processor with a chopping blade or in a blender, add the cottage cheese, yogurt, salt, and pepper, and blend until smooth.

❷ Slightly roll out the pastry sheets on a lightly floured surface with a rolling pin. You will have two 15 x 10-inch rectangles. Place one piece of pastry onto each baking sheet.

❷ Spread the cheese mixture over the surface of each to within 1 inch of the edge all the way around. Sprinkle thin slices of leeks all over, followed by the crumbled bacon. Top with grated Parmesan cheese.

❷ Bake the pastries until they are golden brown and puffy, about 25 minutes. Rotate the pans halfway through baking time. Remove from the oven and let the pastries rest for a few minutes. Cut into small "two-bite" squares to serve. Each sheet makes 30 pieces.

Makes 60 appetizer servings.

NOTE: This recipe can be cut in half if you wish to make a smaller quantity of hors d'oeuvres.

Onions, carrots, and parsnips are oven-roasted to caramel sweetness and folded with tender chunks of beef browned in a cast-iron pot. Whipped potatoes are piped in rosettes over the top. The whole shebang gets baked to a golden puff. Utterly irresistible.

FANCY-PANTS SHEPHERD'S PIE

THE BEEF

5 pounds boneless chuck roast, trimmed and cut into cubes

4 to 5 garlic cloves, minced

1/4 cup plus 1 tablespoon olive oil, divided

4 tablespoons balsamic vinegar

1 1/2 teaspoons kosher salt

1 teaspoon black pepper

A few sprigs of fresh thyme

A couple sprigs of fresh rosemary

2 bay leaves

2 tablespoons flour

● Place the cubed meat in a large bowl. Stir in the minced garlic, 1/4 cup olive oil, and balsamic vinegar. Sprinkle with salt and pepper. Strip the sprigs of thyme and rosemary and stir into the meat. The meat should be well coated. Add the bay leaves and allow the meat to marinate for at least 4 hours or overnight.

● Heat a Dutch oven or large pot over medium heat. Add the remaining 1 tablespoon olive oil. Add the meat, a few pieces at a time. Do not crowd the pan. Brown the meat on all sides and remove to a clean bowl. Continue the browning process until all the beef is browned. When all the meat is browned, toss it with the flour.

● Return the flour-coated meat to the pot and cook gently, toasting the flour. Stir in enough water to cover the meat and scrape up browned bits from the bottom and sides of the pot. Cover and continue cooking on medium heat for at least 1 hour. The meat should be fork-tender.

ROASTED ROOT VEGETABLES

1 pound carrots, cleaned and sliced on the diagonal into pieces

1 pound parsnips, cleaned and sliced on the diagonal into pieces

2 to 3 medium onions, sliced lengthwise into 1/2-inch strips

Olive oil

Salt to taste

Black pepper to taste

1 bundle fresh parsley leaves, chopped

A few fresh celery leaves

● Preheat the oven to 400 degrees.

● Spread the carrots, parsnips, and onions out on a baking sheet and lightly coat with olive oil. Season with sea salt and black pepper. Roast the vegetables for 20 minutes, until pieces are softened and caramelized. Remove from the oven and reduce the heat to 350 degrees.

● When the beef is tender, add the vegetables to the pot. Stir in the chopped parsley and celery leaves. Taste for seasoning and add additional salt and pepper if needed.

continued next page

WHIPPED CHIVE POTATOES

4 pounds Russet potatoes, washed, peeled, and quartered

1/2 cup (1 stick) butter, cut into pieces

Salt to taste

Black pepper to taste

1 bundle fresh chives, chopped

1 cup milk

Paprika

◉ Place the potatoes into a large pot of lightly salted water and bring to a boil over high heat. Reduce to low and cook until the potatoes are tender when pierced with a knife tip. This could take 15 to 20 minutes.

◉ Pour the cooked potatoes into a colander. Drain well and return to the pot. Place the pot over low heat and toss the potatoes in the pot to cook off any remaining water.

◉ Place the warm potatoes into a large bowl. Using an electric mixer, beat the potatoes until the lumps are broken down. Beat in the butter. Season to taste with salt and black pepper. Beat in the chives. Slowly add the milk, continuing to whip the potatoes until they become creamy and somewhat fluffy.

◉ Preheat the oven to 350 degrees. Spoon the whipped potatoes into a large pastry bag fitted with a star tip. Pipe the potatoes in rosettes all over the top of the beef stew, filling the pot generously. Sprinkle the top of the potatoes with paprika and bake for 30 minutes, until the stew is bubbly and the potato topping is puffed and golden.

Makes 16 to 20 servings.

This is one of those recipes that got its start trying to replicate a dish eaten at a restaurant. Val's mother-in-law would get this favorite at a Chinese restaurant in New Jersey and sought to make it on her own. Over the years, her recipe has been endlessly fiddled with and tweaked. While Val thinks it likely bears little resemblance to the restaurant creation, it is nonetheless a delicious and healthful salad. And possibly better than the original!

VAL'S MOTHER-IN-LAW'S MANDARIN CHICKEN AND CABBAGE SALAD

1 1/2 pounds boneless chicken breasts

Ginger-Soy Dressing (recipe follows)

1 head green cabbage, shredded

1 cup sliced almonds, toasted

1/4 (or more) cup sesame seeds, toasted

3 to 4 green onions, chopped

1 (3-ounce) package ramen noodles, broken into small pieces

1 cup mandarin orange sections, cut into small pieces

1 cup mandarin orange sections for garnish

❯ Preheat the oven to 375 degrees.

❯ Place chicken breasts onto a baking sheet and brush them with 3 to 4 tablespoons of Ginger-Soy Dressing. Bake for 25 minutes or until thoroughly cooked. Remove from the oven and allow the chicken to cool. Slice the chicken into thin pieces or shred, if you prefer.

❯ In a large bowl place the shredded cabbage, toasted almonds, sesame seeds, green onions, and ramen noodles. Add the sliced chicken, chopped orange pieces, and the remaining Ginger-Soy Dressing. Toss well. Garnish the salad with 1 cup orange sections. Chill and serve.

Makes 8 servings.

GINGER-SOY DRESSING

3 garlic cloves (or more), minced

2 heaping tablespoons minced fresh ginger root

1/3 cup rice vinegar

1/4 cup low-sodium soy sauce

2 tablespoons local honey

1/2 cup sesame oil

1/4 cup canola oil

❯ Place minced garlic and minced ginger into a medium bowl. Add rice vinegar, soy sauce, and honey. Whisk until well combined. Measure sesame oil and canola oil into a liquid measuring cup. While constantly whisking, slowly pour the sesame-canola oil blend into the ginger-soy mixture until the dressing is emulsified.

Makes 1 1/2 cups.

A potluck favorite, this vegetarian chili has a robust meaty quality that appeals to omnivores and vegans alike. We served it with cornbread, but it is also delicious ladled over hot cooked rice.

BUTTERNUT SQUASH AND HEIRLOOM BEAN CHILI (VEGAN)

3 cups chopped (large dice) butternut squash (I used 2 small)

1 large or 2 medium poblano peppers, halved, stemmed, and seeded

5 tablespoons olive oil, divided

Salt to taste

Black pepper to taste

1 medium onion, chopped

2 banana peppers, chopped

2 garlic cloves, minced

1 heaping cup of dry beans (such as kidney or black beans or heirloom beans from Rancho Gordo)

1 jalapeño pepper, thinly sliced

2 teaspoons ground allspice

1 teaspoon ground cumin

1/4 teaspoon cayenne pepper

1 1/2 cups sour cream (optional)

5 to 6 chopped green onions (optional)

❂ Preheat the oven to 425 degrees.

❂ Spread the diced butternut squash and halved poblano peppers on a baking sheet. Coat with 3 tablespoons olive oil, sprinkle with salt and pepper, and roast for about 20 minutes. Peel, chop, and set the peppers aside. Place the roasted squash into a medium bowl. Cover and refrigerate.

❂ In a large saucepan over medium heat, warm the remaining 2 tablespoons of olive oil. Add the onions, banana peppers, and garlic. Season with salt and black pepper, and cook until the onions are translucent.

❂ Add the dry beans to the pan and stir until they are coated with the olive oil and onion mixture. Pour in enough water to cover the beans by at least 2 inches. Add the roasted poblano pieces and the jalapeño slices.

❂ Increase the heat to medium-high and bring to a boil. Cover and reduce heat to medium-low. Simmer until the beans are tender, at least 2 hours, adding more liquid as necessary. When the beans are soupy and yield tender flesh, remove the roasted butternut squash from the refrigerator and add it to the pot. Season with allspice, cumin, and cayenne.

❂ Taste for salt and peppery heat. Warm the mixture thoroughly and serve. Dollop with sour cream and garnish with green onions, if you like.

Makes 10 servings.

If you've never worked with polenta, don't be daunted. It is essentially coarse cornmeal and readily cooks into a delicious, creamy mass.

PARMESAN-SAGE POLENTA WITH SPINACH AND ONIONS

POLENTA

6 cups water

1 tablespoon finely chopped fresh sage leaves

1 1/2 teaspoons sea salt

1 1/2 cups polenta*

2 teaspoons olive oil

1 cup grated Parmesan cheese

SPINACH-ONION LAYER

2 to 3 tablespoons olive oil

1 medium onion, chopped

2 cloves garlic, chopped

Salt to taste

Red pepper flakes to taste

1 large bundle spinach, cleaned, stemmed, and leaves coarsely chopped

1/2 cup vegetable broth

● Place the water, sage leaves, and salt into a large pot over medium-high heat and bring to a boil. Slowly stir in the polenta. Reduce the heat to low and continue to stir the mixture as the polenta incorporates into the liquid. After it is incorporated and somewhat thickened (12 to 15 minutes), cover the pot and let it finish cooking. Every 5 minutes or so, stir it and then re-cover. Cook the polenta for a total of 30 minutes, then stir in the olive oil and Parmesan. Remove the pan from the heat.

● Warm the olive oil in a skillet over medium heat. Add the onions and garlic and cook for 2 to 3 minutes. Season with salt and a dash of red pepper flakes. Stir in the spinach and cook until the leaves wilt. Stir in the vegetable broth. Remove the skillet from the heat and allow to slightly cool.

ASSEMBLY

Preheat the oven to 350 degrees. Brush a 9 x 13-inch casserole dish with olive oil.

Pour half of the polenta mixture into the dish. Spread the spinach-onion mixture over the polenta. Top with the remaining polenta. Bake for 25 to 30 minutes.

Makes 10 to 12 servings.

*If unavailable, use 1 1/2 cups regular cornmeal and cook for about 12 minutes.

Each member of this Irish trio—Guinness, Jameson, and Baileys—plays a major role in making these filled cupcakes worthy of a St. Pat's fete. Wow!

LUCK-O'-THE-IRISH GANACHE-FILLED CUPCAKES (ADAPTED FROM *SMITTEN KITCHEN*)

CUPCAKES

1 cup stout beer (such as Guinness)

1 cup (2 sticks) butter

1 cup unsweetened cocoa

2 cups all-purpose flour

2 cups sugar

1 1/2 teaspoons baking soda

1 teaspoon salt

2 large eggs, at room temperature

3/4 cup sour cream

❯ Preheat the oven to 350 degrees. Line 24 muffin tins with paper liners.

❯ In a heavy saucepan over medium heat, bring the beer and butter to a simmer. Add the cocoa and whisk until the mixture is smooth. Remove from heat and allow the mixture to cool slightly.

❯ In a large bowl whisk the flour, sugar, baking soda, and salt together. With an electric mixer, in another bowl beat the eggs and sour cream. Add the beer–chocolate mixture to the egg mixture and beat just until combined. Add the flour mixture and beat for a minute on slow speed. Using a rubber spatula, fold the batter until completely combined.

❯ Divide the batter among the cupcake liners, filling them two-thirds to three-fourths full. Bake them until a tester inserted into the center comes out clean, rotating them once front to back if your oven bakes unevenly, about 17 to 20 minutes. Remove the cupcakes from the pan and cool completely on a rack.

GANACHE FILLING

8 ounces bittersweet chocolate, finely chopped

2/3 cup heavy cream

2 tablespoons butter, softened

1 to 2 teaspoons Irish whiskey (such as Jameson)

❯ Place the chocolate into a heatproof bowl. Pour the cream into a saucepan over medium heat. Bring it to just under a boil and pour it over the chocolate. Let it sit for 1 minute and then stir until smooth. Add the butter and whiskey and stir until combined. Let the ganache cool until thick but still soft enough to be piped.

❯ Meanwhile, cut plugs out of the center of the cooled cupcake tops (a 1-inch round cookie cutter works). Go down about halfway into the cupcake. Spoon the ganache into a piping bag with a wide tip and fill the holes to the top.

continued next page

IRISH CREAM ICING

1 cup (2 sticks) butter, softened

1 (8-ounce) package cream cheese, softened

1 tablespoon instant coffee

1 tablespoon vanilla extract

6 tablespoons Irish cream liqueur (such as Baileys)

4 cups confectioners' sugar

1/4 cup cocoa to dust over the cupcake tops (optional)

❂ In a large bowl cream the butter and cream cheese together using an electric mixer or a hand mixer until light and fluffy. Place the instant coffee, vanilla, and Irish cream liqueur together in a small bowl and stir together. Beat this into the cream cheese–butter mixture. Beat in the confectioners' sugar, 1/4 cup at a time. The icing will be smooth and creamy.

❂ Using a pastry bag with a star tip, pipe the icing onto the tops of the cupcakes. You may also use a spatula and simply ice the cupcakes, if you prefer. Dust with cocoa and serve.

Makes 24 cupcakes.

TIP: If the chocolate is not sufficiently melted, place it over a double boiler to gently melt.

(I used a grapefruit spoon to carefully remove each center.)

Fresh mint infused into the milk makes this ice cream really special. You won't get the same green color often associated with the store-bought kind, but the mint flavor is much more vibrant.

MINT CHOCOLATE CHIP ICE CREAM

6 cups whole milk

3 cups fresh mint leaves, washed and coarsely chopped

2 cups sugar

12 large egg yolks

1 quart (4 cups) heavy cream

1 tablespoon vanilla extract

12 ounces bittersweet or semisweet chocolate chips

❯ Pour the milk into a large saucepan over medium heat. Stir in the mint leaves and sugar. Heat until the sugar is dissolved. Remove the pan from the heat and let the mixture sit for at least 30 minutes. Strain the liquid through a sieve over a bowl, pressing the mint leaves with the back of a wooden spoon to extract all the flavor. Discard the mint leaves. Return the "minted" milk to the saucepan and heat over low.

❯ In a medium bowl beat the egg yolks. Pour in some of the warmed milk and beat well to temper the eggs. Pour the tempered egg mixture into the milk, stirring constantly. Be sure to scrape the bottom and sides of the pan with a wooden spoon or a spatula. As the mixture thickens, it will coat the spoon or spatula. After the mixture is thickened, pour it through a fine strainer or sieve into a large bowl. Whisk in the cream and vanilla until well combined and allow to cool. You can speed up the cooling process by placing the bowl over an icy bath. When cool, cover and refrigerate to chill the mixture thoroughly (overnight is best).

❯ Churn the custard in your ice-cream maker following the manufacturer's directions. Add the chocolate chips during the last 5 minutes of churning.

Makes 1 gallon.

NOTE: To make 2 quarts, follow the method using this quantity of ingredients: 3 cups whole milk, 1 1/2 cups fresh mint leaves, 1 cup sugar, 6 large egg yolks, 2 cups heavy cream, 1 1/2 teaspoons vanilla extract, and 6 ounces bittersweet chocolate.

Pasta Party

"FLOUR, EGGS, AND SALT," PAULETTE SAID, KNEADING THE DOUGH WITH VIGOR. "THAT'S IT."

"That's amazing," I said. Gigi and I peered over the work island, watching as this petite woman pressed, tucked, thwacked, and rolled the clumpy mass. What a workout! In ten minutes, she had transformed three basic ingredients into a shiny, elastic sphere.

"Now we're gonna let it rest," Paulette said, sealing the dough in plastic wrap. "Thirty minutes, room temperature." She set the dough aside and proceeded to clamp the stainless-steel hand-cranked pasta machine onto the counter. Soon, we would be rolling her handiwork into impossibly long, thin strips of fettuccini. Fresh pasta! I pulled out a large pot and filled it with water, and marveled at our good fortune to have an Italian chef in our group.

Italian-American by birth, Paulette grew up in Brooklyn, New York, and her parents are first-generation immigrants from Sicily. Joyous, their apartment was food and family central. Imagine a household where you, your mom, dad, sister, cousins, aunts, and uncles all gathered around the kitchen table every Sunday, everyone laughing and chattering, in Italian, in English, hands in constant motion, gesticulating wildly, passing bowls of spaghetti and grated Pecorino, swiping hunks of bread through a pork-and-meatball-packed red sauce.

Paulette built on her heritage of good food through her culinary studies, focusing her research and practice on the regional cuisines of Italy. She traveled throughout the country to get firsthand experience. She took classes, dined at rustic inns, shopped at local markets, cooked alongside nonnas and chefs, immersing herself in the rich culture and cuisine of an area. (Paulette confesses that some of her best Italian language lessons came from studying Italian cookbooks.)

Homemade pasta is universal throughout Italy, but how it is cut, shaped, sauced, or stuffed varies from province to province.

When Gigi and I asked Paulette to be our guest chef and teach us to make pasta, she readily agreed. "We'll make fettuccine Alfredo," she said, "the real Roman way."

That real way, we learned, bears little resemblance to the heavy cream–laden clumps that we stopped eating a long time ago. The original Alfredo, Paulette informed, was created in Rome by chef and restaurateur Alfredo di Lelio in 1914 and possesses no cream.

Instead, ribbons of fresh pasta are coated in a silken sauce made from softened butter, grated Parmigiano-Reggiano, and pasta water, artfully tossed on a warm platter. And served immediately.

That's it.

And it's that sheer simplicity that makes the Alfredo so seductive and lush—yet light. The real Alfredo is a revelation to eat.

It also makes a terrific foundation for a potluck dinner. It's hard to imagine anything that wouldn't be good with it. I figured that while we had Paulette and her pasta machine with us, it was a prime opportunity to roll out some fresh linguine to serve with my meatballs in red sauce. To honor her family tradition.

Here's a little-told fact: the preparation for potluck is as much fun as the actual feast. Sometimes more so. We formed and kneaded two more dough balls. We took turns pushing the pieces through the machine, rolling it in successive runs—each time a wee bit thinner—until great pliable swaths, like fine cloth, were ready to be cut into fabulous strands.

Paulette planned to cook the pasta just minutes before serving time. The immediacy of the dish is part of its appeal. As guests entered the kitchen, they all became enthralled with the idea of the real-deal Alfredo. Serendipity: some came bearing antipasti. Liz had baked "frico," crisp little cheese cookies made of shredded Parmesan. Joy brought a jar of her strawberry-balsamic syrup, which she spooned over a log of chèvre and served with crackers. Folks noshed and stood by to watch the show.

Paulette took a copious amount of soft Kerrygold butter and, using the back of a wooden spoon, spread it over the bottom of a wide, flat bowl. She had her mound of grated cheese at hand, the pepper grinder standing nearby. The big pot of salted water had reached a rolling boil. She was ready.

She gathered up the fettuccini like long tresses of hair and lowered the bundle into the water. Moments later, I was helping her scoop out the pasta and gingerly maneuver it into the butter-lined bowl.

The final step? It's art in motion. I thought about Paulette and the Sundays spent with family in that Brooklyn kitchen. Clutching wooden spoons double-fisted, Paulette began to toss and twirl, spoon and swirl—coating all those delicate strands. A shower of grated cheese, and then it's . . .

Mangia! Mangia!

APRIL: **PASTA PARTY**

John Egerton's Sweet Mint Iced Tea

Pecorino-Parmesan Crisps

Kale Caesar

Goat Cheese with Joy's Balsamic-Strawberry Syrup

Chilled Avocado Soup and Fixin's

Real Roman Fettuccini Alfredo

Italian Meatballs in Hearty Italian Tomato Sauce

Provençale Chicken in a Pot

Frizzled Leek Focaccia

Victoria Sponge Cake Filled with Strawberries

Local Strawberry Ice Cream

John knew how a garden bed of mint can take over like kudzu, but he kept his somewhat corralled during its long growing season by using it liberally in this thirst-slaking tea. "It ages well in the fridge," John would say, "but on hot days, it disappears fast."

JOHN EGERTON'S SWEET MINT ICED TEA

1 cup sugar

15 to 20 stems fresh mint, rinsed and trimmed

4 family-size tea bags

1 (12-ounce) can frozen limeade, thawed*

◔ Fill a large pot with 2 quarts of water and bring it to a boil over high heat. Stir in the sugar and plunge in the big batch of mint. Mash it with a wooden spoon to release its flavor. Then add the tea bags.

◔ When the water returns to a boil, cover and reduce the heat to low. Simmer for 10 minutes. Remove the pot from the heat and allow the brew to cool. Empty the thawed limeade into a gallon jug and pour in the cooled mint tea. Shake well. Top off the gallon with fresh water and shake again.

Makes 1 gallon.

*You can substitute lemonade if you prefer.

Otherwise known as frico, these savory, lacy crisps are so simple to prepare, it's almost not a recipe. But their salty, cheesy crunch makes a welcome appetizer, ideal with a glass of wine.

PECORINO-PARMESAN CRISPS

1 cup grated Parmigiano-Reggiano cheese

1 cup grated Pecorino-Romano cheese

1/4 teaspoon black pepper

2 pinches cayenne pepper

Lemon zest (optional)

Chopped sage leaves (optional)

Minced rosemary leaves (optional)

❯ Preheat the oven to 375 degrees. Line a baking sheet with parchment paper.

❯ In a medium bowl toss the cheeses with black pepper and cayenne. Place flattened tablespoonsful onto the baking sheet. Sprinkle the tops with lemon zest, sage leaves, or rosemary leaves. Bake for about 10 minutes, until the cheeses are bubbling and the edges are browned. Place the baking sheet on a rack to cool before removing the crisps from the parchment paper.

Makes 24 crisps.

Replacing the traditional romaine lettuce with kale was genius on Caroline's part.

KALE CAESAR

2 large garlic cloves

2 anchovy filets

2 tablespoons fresh lemon juice

2 tablespoons mayonnaise

1 teaspoon Dijon mustard

1 tablespoon red wine vinegar

1/4 teaspoon salt

1/4 teaspoon freshly ground black pepper

1/2 cup olive oil

8 cups Tuscan kale, stalks removed, cleaned, dried, and cut into bite-size pieces

1/2 cup freshly grated Parmesan cheese

2 cups croutons

◗ Using a blender on high speed, puree the garlic, anchovies, lemon juice, mayonnaise, mustard, red wine vinegar, salt, and pepper until smooth. With the motor running, add the oil in a slow stream, blending until emulsified.

◗ In a large bowl toss the kale with the dressing. Sprinkle with the cheese and croutons and toss well.

Makes 10 to 12 servings.

Allowing the berries to macerate overnight extracts more juice, which makes this more of a syrup than a jam. Joy served it spooned over a log of mild goat cheese as an hors d'oeuvre, but we imagine that this would also be incredible over pancakes or French toast.

GOAT CHEESE WITH JOY'S BALSAMIC-STRAWBERRY SYRUP

BALSAMIC-STRAWBERRY SYRUP

8 cups fresh strawberries

6 cups sugar

1/2 cup balsamic vinegar

○ Wash the strawberries and hull. Put in a large glass bowl and crush slightly, using the back of a large spoon. Stir in the sugar, cover the bowl with a dishcloth, and let sit overnight in the refrigerator. The next day, pour the berry and sugar mixture into a saucepan over medium heat and bring to a boil. Reduce the heat to low and simmer for 1 hour. Add the balsamic vinegar for the last 10 minutes of cooking.

○ Spoon into sterilized jars* and process in a hot water bath for 10 minutes.

Makes 10 half-pint jars.

ASSEMBLY

1 (11-ounce) log of goat cheese or 1 (8-ounce) block of cream cheese

1 half-pint jar Joy's Balsamic-Strawberry Syrup

1 box water crackers

○ Place goat cheese log onto a serving plate. Generously spoon the syrup over the log. Serve with water crackers.

Makes 10 to 12 servings.

*For directions on sterilizing jars, see Step 3 in our Canning Tips on page 49.

Rhonda's creamy cool soup provided appetizing sips before the meal. Alongside her tureen she placed separate bowls of diced tomatoes, diced red onion, diced serrano peppers, and chopped fresh cilantro for each person to embellish his or her cup.

CHILLED AVOCADO SOUP AND FIXIN'S

2 tablespoons olive oil

2 garlic cloves, chopped

1 bunch green onions, trimmed, green and white parts chopped

1/2 teaspoon cumin

1/4 teaspoon cayenne pepper

1/2 cup fresh lime juice

6 cups chicken stock

6 to 8 ripe avocados

2 cups buttermilk

2 teaspoons salt

4 serrano chilies, finely chopped

1 red onion, finely diced

2 firm ripe tomatoes, diced

1 bunch fresh cilantro, leaves picked and chopped

❷ Warm the olive oil in a large pot over medium heat. Add the garlic and green onions. Season with cumin and cayenne, and sauté until the green onions are soft, about 3 minutes. Add the lime juice and chicken stock. Stir well and remove the pot from the heat.

❷ Slice the avocados in half. Remove the pits and scoop out the flesh into the seasoned broth. Using an immersion blender, puree the avocados into the broth.* Continue blending until all the pieces of avocado, green onions, and garlic have become pureed. Whisk in the buttermilk and salt. Taste for seasonings and adjust as needed. Chill well (about 2 hours) before serving.

❷ Serve the soup in a large tureen or bowl with a ladle. Small-handled punch cups make ideal individual serving pieces, perfect for sipping the soup—and require no spoon. Set out four small serving bowls filled with the chilies, onions, tomatoes, and cilantro. Allow guests to garnish their soup as desired.

Makes 3 quarts.

*If you don't have an immersion blender, you can puree the avocados in a food processor fitted with a chopping blade or in a blender. Cut the avocados into 1-inch chunks. Place them into the food processor bowl fitted with a chopping blade or blender along with the green onions and garlic. Add some of the buttermilk (about a cup) to facilitate the pureeing. Whisk the puree into the broth, along with the remaining buttermilk.

This is the real deal—the "Vere," as the Romans say. The original Alfredo is a true revelation. You'll never want a heavy, cream-laden version again. With such basic ingredients, it's important to use the best you can find. Farm-fresh eggs, with their deep orange-gold yolks, make the pasta exceptional.

REAL ROMAN FETTUCCINI ALFREDO

PASTA

2 cups unbleached all-purpose flour (such as King Arthur)

1/4 teaspoon sea salt

3 large eggs, lightly beaten

❍ Mix the flour and salt in a large bowl. Make a well in the mound and add the eggs. Using a fork, mix the flour into the eggs, until all the flour is mixed in and the dough comes together. Gather and knead the dough on a lightly floured surface for 10 minutes. It will become smooth and a little shiny. If it's too sticky, add a little flour—if it's too dry, add a little water. Wrap the dough tightly and let it sit at room temperature for 30 minutes to rest.

❍ Cut the dough into 4 pieces and rewrap the remaining pieces until it's time to use. Take the first piece, slightly flatten it, and run it through the pasta machine roller on the first setting. Fold the piece over on itself and run it through the machine on the same setting. Repeat.

❍ Then move the setting to 2 and run it through. Continue this process until you reach the next to the last setting. If the dough gets sticky while you are working with it, dust it in flour. Cut the long strip in half and run it through the fettuccine cutter. Separate and drop the cut noodles onto a floured baking sheet. Toss in flour so they won't stick. Repeat with your other pieces of dough until you have stretched, rolled, and cut it all into lovely fettuccine.

❍ Bring a 6-quart pot of lightly salted water to a rolling boil over high heat. Add the fettuccini and cook for 3 minutes. Drain the noodles, reserving 1 cup of the pasta water for the sauce.

continued next page

ASSEMBLY

3/4 cup (1 1/2 sticks) butter (such as Kerrygold Irish Cream Butter), softened

Fresh fettuccini

2 1/2 cups grated Parmigiano-Reggiano cheese or in combination with Pecorino-Romano cheese, divided

1 cup reserved pasta water

Sea salt to taste

1/2 cup chopped fresh flat-leaf parsley (optional)

A few grindings of black pepper

◉ Spread the softened butter on the bottom of a large platter or bowl. Lay the cooked fettuccini on top of the butter. Sprinkle 1 cup grated cheese over the pasta and vigorously but gently toss to coat the noodles. Add a little of the pasta water as you toss. You won't need the whole cup, perhaps half.

◉ The noodles will glisten with the simple emulsion of butter, cheese, and pasta water. Taste for salt and season accordingly. Add another 1/2 cup cheese. Toss well and serve immediately. Garnish with a little chopped flat-leaf parsley, if you like. Pass the pepper grinder and a bowl of the remaining 1 cup grated cheese!

Makes 8 servings.

High school tested, Sicilian-American approved. Mark and I teach this recipe in our Cooks Rule cooking camps for teens, and Paulette hailed it at potluck as "Sunday worthy." The meatballs gently brown on a sheet pan in the oven before taking the plunge into the pot of savory red sauce.

ITALIAN MEATBALLS IN HEARTY ITALIAN TOMATO SAUCE

2 pounds lean ground beef

1/2 pound sweet Italian sausage, casing removed

5 to 6 slices French or Italian bread, torn into small pieces

4 garlic cloves, minced

1 medium onion, finely chopped

4 tablespoons dried Italian herbs (or 4 tablespoons fresh basil, 2 tablespoons fresh oregano, 4 teaspoons fresh thyme, and 2 teaspoons fresh flat-leaf parsley, finely chopped)

2 teaspoons salt

1 teaspoon black pepper

2 tablespoons Worcestershire sauce

3/4 cup grated Parmesan cheese

2 large eggs, lightly beaten

Hearty Italian Tomato Sauce (recipe follows)

● Preheat the oven to 350 degrees.

● Break up the ground beef and sausage into a large bowl. Add the bread pieces, garlic, onions, Italian herbs, salt, pepper, Worcestershire, Parmesan, and the beaten eggs. Vigorously mix all the ingredients together by hand—almost like kneading bread dough—until all the herbs and bread pieces are well mixed throughout the meat. The mixture will get a little fluffy and shiny when it is mixed well. Shape into balls about the size of a golf ball (or smaller, if desired). Place the meatballs on a baking sheet.

● Bake for 20 minutes or until done. Drain any excess grease and place the cooked meatballs into the Hearty Italian Tomato Sauce.

Makes 48 meatballs.

continued next page

A wintertime variation: place a sprig or two of fresh rosemary into the sauce as it simmers.

HEARTY ITALIAN TOMATO SAUCE

6 tablespoons olive oil

2 onions, finely chopped

5 to 6 garlic cloves, minced

2 (28-ounce) cans tomatoes in juice, coarsely chopped, juice reserved

1 (6-ounce) can tomato paste

1 to 2 bay leaves

2 tablespoons balsamic vinegar

2 teaspoons salt

1 teaspoon black pepper

2 tablespoons dried basil

4 teaspoons dried oregano

◉ In a 3- to 4-quart saucepan over medium heat, warm the olive oil. Add the chopped onions and sauté until soft and translucent, about 7 minutes. Then add the garlic and cook for another minute or so, stirring constantly. Add the coarsely chopped tomatoes and their juice, the tomato paste, bay leaves, balsamic vinegar, salt, pepper, basil, and oregano. Stir well until the mixture begins to boil. Reduce the heat to low and simmer for 1 hour, stirring occasionally. Add the cooked meatballs and continue simmering. Remove the bay leaves. Taste and adjust for seasoning.

Makes 10 to 12 servings.

The coarse grain mustard pesto acts as a vehicle for holding the herbs and garlic in place while adding nice piquancy to the chicken. It also contributes thickening powers to the sauce. The beans break down and add more body to the sauce too. You can serve the chicken whole, carved at the table, with the savory brown sauce on the side. For potluck, I carved the chicken and returned the slices to bathe in the sauce before serving.

PROVENÇALE CHICKEN IN A POT

1 batch Coarse Grain Mustard Pesto (recipe follows)

1 whole roasting chicken

1 tablespoon olive oil

2 onions, chopped

3 stalks celery, chopped

3 to 4 carrots, cut into 1/2-inch pieces

2 sprigs fresh rosemary

2 cups red wine

2 cups water

2 cups cooked white or cranberry beans

◉ Preheat the oven to 350 degrees.

◉ Spread a nice dollop of the Coarse Grain Mustard Pesto underneath the skin of the chicken breast and liberally coat the remainder all over the outside of the chicken. Truss the chicken with kitchen twine.* Heat a Dutch oven over medium, add the olive oil and the chicken, and brown on all sides, starting with the breast side down. This process should take about 15 minutes.

◉ Remove the browned chicken to a plate or platter and add the onions, celery, and carrots to the pot.

◉ Sauté the veggies for 5 to 7 minutes. Add the rosemary sprigs and pour in the red wine.

◉ Pour in 2 cups of water. Stir in the beans, return the chicken to the pot, and place uncovered in the oven. Roast for 1 hour, periodically basting the bird.

◉ Serve either as a whole roasted chicken, with its savory brown vegetable sauce on the side, or carve up all the meat and return the meat to the Dutch oven to soak up juices. Serve over crusty bread or potatoes.

Makes 6 to 8 servings.

*See sidebar about trussing on page 8.

continued next page

COARSE GRAIN MUSTARD PESTO

2 tablespoons coarse grain mustard (such as country-style Dijon)

3 garlic cloves

2 tablespoons fresh sage leaves

Leaves stripped from 1 sprig of fresh rosemary

2 tablespoons olive oil

Salt to taste

Black pepper to taste

○ Place the mustard, garlic, sage, rosemary, olive oil, salt, and pepper in a food processor fitted with a chopping blade. Pulse until the garlic and herbs are well chopped throughout the mixture. Spoon into a jar, cover, and refrigerate until ready to use. Keeps at least one week.

Makes 1/2 cup.

Needing only one primary rise, this Italian yeasted flatbread is a breeze to make. We like the look and taste of leeks baked onto its dimpled top. Cut into squares and serve with our savory Sun-dried Tomato and Artichoke Tapenade (next page).

FRIZZLED LEEK FOCACCIA

1 $2/3$ cups warm water

1 (.25-ounce) envelope quick-rising yeast

1 teaspoon local honey

2 teaspoons salt

$1/4$ cup plus 5 tablespoons olive oil, divided

5 cups all-purpose flour, divided

1 large leek, cleaned well and thinly sliced

Coarse sea salt or finishing salt to taste

Sun-dried Tomato and Artichoke Tapenade (recipe follows)

◗ In the bowl of an electric mixer fitted with a dough hook, stir together warm water, yeast, and honey. Cover and allow to bloom, 5 to 10 minutes or until foamy.

◗ Add the salt, $1/4$ cup olive oil, and 4 $1/2$ cups of flour (more can be added as needed).

◗ Mix until dough starts to come together and begins to climb up the dough hook. This could take 8 minutes. Let the dough mix for 2 more minutes, adding flour a tablespoon at a time if the dough is too sticky. Then turn it out onto a floured board. With floured hands, knead the dough for 1 minute or until a smooth ball forms.

◗ Coat the bottom of a 15 x 10-inch baking pan with 3 tablespoons olive oil. Place the dough ball in the pan and press it into an even rectangle shape. Cover with a kitchen towel and keep in a warm place for 1 to 1 $1/2$ hours to rise.

◗ Place a skillet over medium heat. Add the remaining 2 tablespoons olive oil and sauté the leeks until softened. Remove from the heat and allow to cool a bit.

◗ Preheat the oven to 425 degrees.

◗ With your finger, gently make indentations 1 inch apart all over the dough. Spread the leeks over the top, dust with salt flakes, and drizzle with a little olive oil. Cover again while you wait for the oven to heat. Bake the dough for 20 to 25 minutes. (Keep an eye on it toward the end—all ovens are different.) Remove from the oven and place on a rack to cool. Cut into squares and serve with Sun-dried Tomato and Artichoke Tapenade.

Makes 24 servings (cut into 2 1/2 x 2 1/2-inch squares).

SUN-DRIED TOMATO AND ARTICHOKE TAPENADE

1 can quartered artichoke hearts, drained

2 cloves garlic, in their skins

3/4 cup sun-dried tomatoes packed in oil, drained with oil reserved

1/2 teaspoon oregano

1/2 teaspoon thyme

1 tablespoon white balsamic vinegar

1/4 teaspoon salt

◉ Preheat the oven to 375 degrees.

◉ Place the artichoke hearts and garlic cloves on a small baking sheet and brush with oil reserved from the sun-dried tomatoes. Roast for 15 minutes, until artichoke hearts get bronzed and garlic cloves are softened and pop out of their skins.

◉ Place the sun-dried tomatoes, oregano, thyme, vinegar, and salt in the bowl of a food processor fitted with a chopping blade. Gently pulse for 30 seconds to break up the tomatoes. Add the roasted artichokes, garlic, and residual oil from the baking sheet. Pulse until the mixture is finely chopped, but still retains texture.

Makes 1 1/4 cups.

Towering! Teresa says this cake sounds fancy and looks fancy, but couldn't be easier to make. Originally named in honor of Queen Victoria, who relished a slice with afternoon tea, a traditional sponge cake features a layer of raspberry jam sandwiched with whipped cream. Teresa showcases a trove of sweet local strawberries in her version.

VICTORIA SPONGE CAKE FILLED WITH STRAWBERRIES

1 cup (2 sticks) butter, plus 1 to 2 tablespoons, softened, divided

1 cup sugar

4 large eggs

1 3/4 cup self-rising flour

1 pinch of salt

2 tablespoons warm water

2 1/2 cups heavy cream

3/4 cup confectioners' sugar, divided

2 teaspoons vanilla extract

3 cups fresh strawberries, rinsed, hulled, and sliced

❯ Preheat the oven to 350 degrees. Grease two 8-inch cake pans with 1 to 2 tablespoons butter and line the bottom of each with a circle of wax paper.

❯ Using a hand mixer, cream together 1 cup of the butter and the sugar in a large bowl until well mixed. Add the eggs, one at a time, beating well after each addition. Sift the flour and salt over the creamed mixture. Add the warm water and beat until well mixed. The batter should be thick, light, and creamy.

❯ Divide the cake mixture evenly between the cake pans. Bake 18 to 20 minutes, until tester inserted into the middle comes out clean. Turn the cake layers out onto cooling racks until completely cool.

❯ Place heavy cream into a chilled medium bowl. Add 1/2 cup confectioners' sugar and the vanilla. Whip the cream until soft peaks form.

❯ Using a serrated knife, split each cake horizontally. Place one layer on a cake stand or cake plate and cover with a third of the sweetened whipped cream. Top with 1 cup of sliced strawberries. Add the second cake layer and press down slightly. Repeat the process: spread with whipped cream, add berries, and then add the third layer. Spread with remaining whipped cream and top with remaining berries.

❯ Place the fourth cake layer on top of the berries, pressing down slightly. Dust the top with the remaining 1/4 cup confectioners' sugar. Place the cake in the refrigerator to chill until ready to serve.

continued next page

◉ This cake is best assembled a couple of hours before serving. To serve, cut into wedges with additional dusting of confectioners' sugar if desired.

Makes 12 to 16 servings.

SELECTING STRAWBERRIES

One of my daughter's favorite books growing up was *Bunnicula*, the tale of a vampire rabbit who sucked the juices out of vegetables, leaving behind ghostly versions of carrots, beets, celery, and such.

I was reminded of that hilarious story when I helped at a strawberry tasting at our farmers' market. We offered market goers samples of commercially grown berries

(trucked in from a state far, far away) and ones that were grown locally in College Grove, Tennessee. As I was quartering the strawberries into bite-size pieces, I couldn't help but marvel at the difference. The local berries were small to medium-size, juicy, and red all the way through. The commercial counterparts were larger, firmer, with somewhat hollowed interiors drained of all color. The mark of the vampire rabbit!

"These," I told my fellow strawberry-tasting volunteer, "are Bunnicula Berries!"

Our local little heart-shaped strawberries were easy winners in the tasting. Poor Bunniculas! Based on just the visual, some people opted not to try them. Others noted with surprise that they were sweeter than the locals, but definitely not strawberry-er.

Local strawberry time in Tennessee can begin in late April and lasts just a few weeks. When you buy local berries, it's best to eat them or cook with them within days; they are perfectly ripe when picked.

I treat strawberries the same as tomatoes—no refrigeration (unless absolutely necessary!). It would be a shame to let them go to waste because they languished on the counter a day or two too long. But considering how delicious they are, that isn't too likely.

Strawberries love a splash of balsamic vinegar.

LOCAL STRAWBERRY ICE CREAM

2 quarts fresh strawberries, washed, hulled, and chopped

4 cups sugar, divided

1/4 cup white balsamic vinegar

2 quarts whole milk

1 vanilla bean

2 quarts heavy cream

1 teaspoon sea salt

Place the chopped strawberries in a large bowl. Stir in 3 cups sugar and the white balsamic vinegar. Cover and refrigerate for 4 hours or overnight to allow the berries to macerate.

Pour the milk into a large saucepan over medium heat. Split the vanilla bean in half and add it to the pan. Bring the milk to the scalding point, bubbles forming around the edge of the pan. Remove the pan from the heat.

In a large bowl whisk together the heavy cream, the remaining 1 cup sugar, and salt until the sugar and salt are dissolved. Remove the vanilla bean from the milk. Whisking constantly, pour the milk into the cream mixture. Stir in the macerated strawberries. Cover and refrigerate until well chilled, about 1 hour.

Churn in an ice-cream maker following the manufacturer's directions. Freeze until serving time.

Makes 6 quarts.

Berry Happy Birthdays

WHEN YOU HAVE A GROUP AS LARGE AND FLUID AS OURS, ANY GIVEN THIRD THURSDAY COULD ALSO BE A potlucker's birthday. I learned this early on: the first time I held potluck at my home, it fell on my birthday. Although I wanted to keep that a secret—this was about celebrating good food, not my birth—a few clever ones found out and surprised me with a gorgeous ice-cream cake. Having birthday toasts and cheer at Third Thursday was great. By its nature, potluck is a ready-made party.

When Gigi's special Zero birthday aligned with potluck, she decided to make the most of it. Planning months ahead, she called me with a request. At the time, I was in a whirl, preparing for my daughter's wedding.

"I know that you're *really* busy," she said, "and it's still a *long* way away, but I discovered that our April potluck happens to be on my fiftieth birthday." She continued, "I love white wedding cake. Since I don't think that I'll ever get married, would you make me a white wedding cake for my fiftieth?"

Without hesitation, I agreed. As time drew near, I checked back with her about the cake. "White cake, white icing. Don't you want something else as a filling? Strawberry? Lemon?"

> ## "All the world is a birthday cake, so take a piece, but not too much."
> —George Harrison

She was emphatic. "No, just vanilla. White. White. White. Give this sugar junkie her fix."

"Okay," I said. But it stuck in my mind that the cake needed something else *defining*. This was her Big Five-0 birthday. I would just have to be patient and see what might inspire me. In the meantime, I would research recipes and develop the *ne plus ultra* of white cakes.

By the morning of that April potluck, I had baked soft white layers, nuanced with almond and vanilla. I had whipped up a batch of cream cheese buttercream. With no sparks of insight,

I was resigned to making the all-white confection.

When it came time to assemble the layers, I found a very large ripe mango that had been forgotten in my produce bin. And, in a flash, I saw it: mango puree. A seductive filling for this white wedding cake. A glisten of sunny yellow-orange glaze, a line of tropical tang running alongside vanilla cream.

After a quick peel, chop, and turn on the stovetop, the mango cooked into a brilliant sauce. Once it cooled, I spread it between the cream-iced layers. So beautiful. I dotted and pooled the luminous glaze onto the cake in decorative whirls and thought, *That bolt of inspiration sure took its time getting here.* No matter, as the defining ingredient to Gigi's special birthday cake, it was well worth the wait. In looks and taste, it was hailed by all as the ultimate.

Our sugar junkie friend agreed. We'll hold off making that all-white cake for another time. Who's to say she'll never get married? To say never just limits the possibilities.

Another sweet convergence of birthday and potluck occurred when one week before a potluck, Gigi's friends from California, Dave and Sabino, gave her a call. Vintage clothing buyers on the return loop of a cross-country buying trip, they had planned a one-day stopover in Nashville to scout out some shops.

They also wanted to take Gigi to dinner, but she responded, "I can't. It's Third Thursday. Come to potluck instead!"

The idea appealed to Dave.

"It's Sabino's birthday," he confided, once his friend was out of earshot. "He wants to ignore it. No way! Can we get him a cake?"

New potluck plans were set in motion.

Each potluck has its own distinct and unpredictable feeling. The confluence of people, their contributions of food and drink, and the weather combine to create a mood. We've seen that swing from low-key gatherings to upbeat celebrations, mellow to boisterous, and all points in between.

There must have been something in the air on this particular evening. Late spring, it was warm and sunny. Skies crystalline and not a speck of humidity. It compelled people, all around town, to get out into the world and be in this day. Everywhere, people were out walking, cycling, working in their yards, visiting with neighbors.

As I got ready for the potluck, I wanted to bring the outside in and swung open both front and back doors. Honeysuckled air moved through the house. At 6:30 p.m., so did droves of guests. That beneficent day called up so many potluckers—a dozen more than our norm.

Folks congregated in the kitchen and spilled out onto the back patio. The house hummed with chatter and laughter. Jimbo jammed on the piano. With her young son in arms, Cassi navigated the crowd speaking to everyone, this being her last potluck before moving to Minnesota. She wasn't the only person in transition: both Jenn and Declan would soon be leaving for graduate school; they too wanted to celebrate their final time. Dave and Sabino fit right in, engaging all in lively conversation. In the lead-up to dinner, Cathey passed trays of her Raspberry Mojitos, ruby-jeweled glasses garnished with mint.

Her cocktail was pretty . . . and potent. Maybe the mojitos fostered the high spirits. I think it was that rare air of the day, and the mojitos gave it an extra nudge. Regardless of the causes, this potluck was nothing short of euphoric.

Its apex came at dessert time. Gigi set the candles ablaze while our group of forty, clamoring around the table, belted out "Happy Birthday" to Sabino, wishing this man we'd just met, who was touched and beaming and somewhat overwhelmed, birthday cheer.

A birthday celebrated with strangers could be the best birthday of all.

Blanched Chilled Asparagus with Green Goddess Aioli

MAY: BERRY HAPPY BIRTHDAYS

Cathey's Euphoric Raspberry Mojitos

Cilantro Lemonade

Pressed Tuna Nicoise Finger Sandwiches (Pan Bagnat)

Clever Zucchini Cakes with Citrus Remoulade

Braised Brisket of Beef

Rhonda's Farro with Vegetables and Toasted Sesame Sweet Garlic Dressing

Spring Greens with Crispy Herbed Goat Cheese
Croquettes and Shallot-Honey Vinaigrette

Texas Rice Casserole

Crab Macaroni and Cheese

Blanched Chilled Asparagus with Green Goddess Aioli

"Mango-Tango" White Butter Cake

Mexican Chocolate Ice Cream

You've been warned! Tart, refreshing, and a wee bit dangerous.

CATHEY'S EUPHORIC RASPBERRY MOJITOS

1 1/2 cups sugar

1 1/2 cups water

10 limes, divided

4 cups (2 pints) raspberries, rinsed and dried, divided

1 bunch fresh mint leaves (about 32 leaves), divided

2 1/2 cups (20 ounces) white rum

1/2 cup (4 ounces) raspberry liqueur (such as Chambord)

2 liters lime seltzer

◗ Place the sugar and water into a saucepan over medium heat. Stir and heat until the sugar is dissolved. Cool.

◗ Juice 8 limes into a large bowl. Add 3 cups raspberries and 24 torn mint leaves and muddle to release their juices and oils. If you don't have a muddler, a flat-bottomed tool used to crush vegetables, fruits, and herbs, you may use a wooden spoon or pestle instead. Stir in the cooled simple syrup, rum, and raspberry liqueur. Cover and refrigerate.

◗ Fill a tall pitcher with ice. Pour 1 1/2 cups of the muddled mixture into the pitcher. Top with the seltzer and stir. Slice the remaining 2 limes. Garnish with lime slices, the rest of the fresh raspberries, and the remaining mint.

Makes about 1 gallon.

Cilantro pairs well with citrus, imparting a fresh, herbal grassy note to this lemonade.

CILANTRO LEMONADE

CILANTRO SIMPLE SYRUP

2 cups water

1 1/2 cups sugar

1 lemon, zested and sliced

1 cup coarsely chopped cilantro

◗ Pour the water into a saucepan and stir in the sugar. Add the zest. Bring to a boil over high heat. Remove the pan from the heat and stir in the cilantro. Toss in 3 thin slices of lemon. Let cool for a couple of hours. Strain, discarding zest, cilantro, and lemon slices. Pour into a container, cover, and refrigerate. This will keep at least one week.

Makes 2 1/2 cups.

TO SERVE BY THE PITCHER

Ice

Juice of 6 lemons

1 1/2 cups Cilantro Simple Syrup

1 liter sparkling water (such as Pellegrino)

1 lemon, sliced, for garnish

A few sprigs fresh cilantro for garnish

◗ Fill a 2-quart pitcher with ice. Pour in the fresh-squeezed lemon juice and simple syrup.

◗ Top with sparkling water. Garnish with lemon slices and cilantro sprigs and serve.

Makes 8 to 12 servings.

TO SERVE BY THE GLASS

2 tablespoons Cilantro Simple Syrup

Juice of 1/2 lemon

Ice

Sparkling water (such as Pellegrino)

Lemon slice for garnish

Sprig of fresh cilantro for garnish

◗ Pour the simple syrup into a tall glass. Squeeze in the lemon juice. Add the ice. Pour in the sparkling water and stir. Garnish with lemon slice and cilantro sprig. Sip and enjoy.

Essential to this Provençale-style pressed sandwich is tuna packed in olive oil, pesto, and very good bread. All the "relishes"—red onion, capers, cornichons, pepperoncinis, black olives—can vary somewhat, Whitney tells us, depending on your taste and, she confesses, what's in the fridge at the moment. After pressing, the loaf can be cut into delectable appetizer slices. A sunny taste of the South . . . of France!

PRESSED TUNA NICOISE FINGER SANDWICHES (PAN BAGNAT)

3 (4.5-ounce) cans tuna packed in olive oil

3 tablespoons fresh lemon juice

2 to 3 tablespoons capers, chopped

1 tablespoon minced cornichons

1 tablespoon minced pepperoncini

1/3 cup chopped black olives

3 tablespoons chopped red onion

1 1/2 tablespoons olive oil

1 1/2 tablespoons white balsamic vinegar

3 tablespoons chopped fresh flat-leaf parsley

1 1/2 teaspoons finely chopped fresh rosemary

1 loaf French or Ciabatta bread, cut in half horizontally

1/2 cup pesto

◉ Preheat the oven to 375 degrees.

◉ In a medium bowl break up the tuna with a fork. Add lemon juice, capers, cornichons, pepperoncini, olives, onion, olive oil, balsamic vinegar, parsley, and rosemary and mix well. Scoop out a bit of the soft interiors of each half of the bread. Place the halves onto a baking sheet and lightly toast the bread, about 6 to 8 minutes.

◉ Remove from the oven and allow to cool for 5 minutes. Spread the pesto onto the inside of each half. Fill the cavity of one side with the tuna mixture. Top with the other half and wrap tightly with plastic wrap.

◉ Place a baking sheet on top of the sandwich and place weights on top of the sheet to press the sandwich. Refrigerate. This allows the flavors to marry and soak into the bread. Press the sandwich for at least 1 hour—although you could leave it longer, even refrigerated overnight, with delicious results. Unwrap and cut the filled loaf into 1-inch-wide slices and serve.

Makes 12 to 16 finger sandwiches.

Clever, not only because it's a great way to use the abundance of zucchinis, but also because these truly mimic crab cakes in taste.

CLEVER ZUCCHINI CAKES WITH CITRUS REMOULADE

4 cups coarsely grated zucchini (2 to 3 zucchinis, depending on size)

Salt to taste

2 cups fresh bread crumbs*

2 large eggs

4 green onions, thinly sliced (white and green parts)

1/2 cup small-diced red bell pepper

1 tablespoon Old Bay seasoning

2 teaspoons Dijon mustard

2 tablespoons mayonnaise

Juice of 1 lemon

1/4 to 1/2 teaspoon red pepper flakes

1/4 cup vegetable oil

1 teaspoon butter

Citrus Remoulade (recipe follows)

◗ Place the grated zucchini in a colander, sprinkle lightly with salt, and allow to stand for 30 minutes, draining. Squeeze the zucchini to remove additional liquid—it should be fairly dry. Place the zucchini in a large bowl and add the bread crumbs, eggs, onions, bell peppers, Old Bay, mustard, mayonnaise, lemon juice, and red pepper flakes and mix well.

◗ Form the mixture into 16 patties the size of crab cakes.**

◗ Place the oil and butter in a skillet over medium heat and cook the patties on both sides, browning well, about 3 to 4 minutes per side. Drain the cakes on paper towels. Serve warm with a bowl of Citrus Remoulade on the side.

Makes 16 crab cakes.

*I used a baguette.

**You can make these smaller, about half that size, for 32 appetizer cakes—good for potluck!

CITRUS REMOULADE

1 garlic clove

1 large egg, at room temperature

1/2 teaspoon Dijon mustard

1/2 teaspoon lemon zest

1/2 teaspoon orange zest

1 teaspoon fresh lemon juice

1 teaspoon orange juice

1/2 teaspoon salt

1 cup olive oil

◗ In the bowl of a food processor fitted with a chopping blade, add the garlic, egg, mustard, lemon and orange zest, lemon and orange juice, and salt. Process for 1 minute to break down the garlic into the other ingredients. Then, with the motor running, slowly pour the olive oil into the bowl. The mixture will become thick, like mayonnaise. Keeps refrigerated for 3 days.

Makes 1 generous cup.

The surprise ingredient—ginger ale—helps tenderize the meat while adding zing to the braising juices.

BRAISED BRISKET OF BEEF

2 tablespoons olive oil

6 pounds beef brisket, trimmed of excess fat

Kosher salt to taste

Cracked black pepper to taste

Paprika to taste

3 to 4 yellow onions, sliced and divided

1/2 cup red wine

1/2 cup ginger ale

1/2 cup chili sauce

3 to 4 garlic cloves, minced

❯ Heat a Dutch oven over medium. Add the olive oil. Liberally rub the trimmed brisket with salt, black pepper, and paprika. Brown the brisket on both sides, cooking about 5 to 6 minutes per side, and remove. Add half of the sliced onions to the Dutch oven and sauté for 5 minutes. Lay the brisket on top of the bed of onions. Pour the red wine and ginger ale over the brisket. Spread the chili sauce over the top of the brisket and sprinkle with the minced garlic and the remaining sliced onions. Cover and turn the heat down to the lowest setting.

❯ After 3 hours, remove the lid and flip over the brisket. Cover and cook for 2 more hours.

❯ The meat will feel very tender when pierced with a fork. When done, remove the brisket from the Dutch oven and allow the meat to rest for 15 minutes before slicing. Slice the brisket thinly, across the grain, and lay out on a serving platter. Smother with the hot oniony gravy and serve.

Makes 15 to 20 servings.

Farro is a protein-rich grain long popular in Italy but now finding favor on this side of the Atlantic. If you can't locate it, wheat berries make a fine substitute.

RHONDA'S FARRO WITH VEGETABLES AND TOASTED SESAME SWEET GARLIC DRESSING (VEGAN)

FARRO AND VEGETABLES

6 cups water

Salt to taste

1 cup farro, rinsed

1 tablespoon canola oil

8 kale leaves, washed, stemmed, and chopped

Pinch of red pepper flakes

1/2 pound carrots, cut on the bias

1 large yellow bell pepper, cut into julienne strips

1/2 pound sugar snap peas, strung and cut on the bias into threes

Toasted Sesame-Sweet Garlic Dressing (recipe follows)

5-ounce package arugula

> Fill a large pot with the water and place over high heat. When the water begins to boil, add a large handful of salt. Stir and add the farro. Cook, uncovered, for approximately 25 minutes. Drain into a large bowl.

> Warm the oil in a skillet over medium heat. Add the kale and cook until it collapses, about 2 minutes. Season with salt and red pepper flakes. Add the carrots and continue to cook—stir-fry style—for another 3 minutes. Add the yellow pepper strips and cook for 3 minutes, and finally add the sugar snaps, which will cook in about 1 minute. The kale will be tender and the other vegetables will be crisp-tender.

> Fold the vegetables into the cooked farro, along with the Toasted Sesame-Sweet Garlic Dressing. Reserve a little dressing to enliven the salad later or dollop on top when you serve it. Delicious warm, room temperature, or chilled over a bed of fresh arugula.

Makes 8 to 10 servings.

TOASTED SESAME-SWEET GARLIC DRESSING

11 tablespoons canola oil, divided

3 garlic cloves, thinly sliced

1/2 teaspoon mustard seeds

4 tablespoons cider vinegar

1 tablespoon sugar

1/4 teaspoon salt

1 green onion, coarsely chopped

1 tablespoon toasted sesame oil

Pinch of red pepper flakes (optional)

> Place a small skillet over medium heat. Add 1 tablespoon canola oil. Then add the garlic and mustard seeds. Sauté about 2 minutes, just enough to "sweat" the garlic. It will become softened and sweeter. Do not let it brown. Remove from heat.

> Place cider vinegar, sugar, salt, green onions, and garlic–mustard seed mix into a food processor fitted with a chopping blade. Pulse together, then process, slowly pouring in the remaining 10 tablespoons of canola oil, followed by the 1 tablespoon of toasted sesame oil.* The dressing will emulsify nicely.

Makes 1 cup.

*If you want a little peppery heat, add a pinch of red pepper flakes while adding the toasted sesame oil.

Panko crumbs seasoned with fresh thyme encase the creamy cheese discs with toothsome crunch. Serve warm over a bed of spring lettuces and arugula and drizzle with Shallot-Honey Vinaigrette.

SPRING GREENS WITH CRISPY HERBED GOAT CHEESE CROQUETTES AND SHALLOT-HONEY VINAIGRETTE

HERBED COAT CHEESE CROQUETTES

1 pound plain goat cheese or chèvre log

1/2 cup all-purpose flour

1 large egg

1/2 cup panko crumbs

1/4 teaspoon salt

1/4 teaspoon black pepper

2 tablespoons fresh thyme leaves

Olive oil or canola oil blend for frying

◉ Cut the chèvre log into 16 pieces. Form each into a disk shape. Place the flour into one shallow bowl and the egg beaten with a little water into another shallow bowl. In a third shallow bowl, mix the panko with salt, pepper, and fresh thyme leaves.

◉ Dust each disk in flour, then dip each one into the egg wash, and finally dip into the seasoned panko, pressing the crumbs lightly onto the goat cheese.* Place the panko-coated disks onto a baking sheet until ready to fry.

◉ Heat a large skillet over medium heat and coat the bottom with oil. Add the goat cheese disks and cook until brown, about 3 minutes. Turn and brown on the other side.

Makes 16 croquettes.

*Use one hand to dip into the flour, egg, and panko, and use the other hand to press the panko.

SHALLOT-HONEY VINAIGRETTE

1/4 cup diced shallots

2 tablespoons local honey

1/4 cup white balsamic vinegar

1/4 teaspoon salt

1/4 teaspoon black pepper

1/2 cup extra-virgin olive oil

1/2 cup canola oil

◉ Place the shallots, honey, balsamic vinegar, salt, and pepper into a blender or food processor fitted with a chopping blade and pulse until smooth. Slowly drizzle in the olive and canola oils. The vinaigrette will become a smooth, thick emulsion. Pour into a jar and refrigerate until you are ready to assemble the salad.

ASSEMBLY

1 pound spring lettuce mix, washed and spun dry

◉ Place the spring lettuces onto a large serving platter. Arrange the warm goat cheese croquettes over the top. Drizzle with Shallot-Honey Vinaigrette and serve.

Makes 12 servings.

Folded with sour cream and Monterey Jack cheese, this ultra-rich casserole has an undercurrent of mild, tingly heat from green chilies.

TEXAS RICE CASSEROLE

1 1/2 cups long-grain white rice

1 1/2 cups sour cream

1 bundle green onions, chopped

1 1/2 teaspoons salt

2 (4-ounce) cans chopped green chilies

1 pound shredded Monterey Jack cheese, divided

● Preheat the oven to 350 degrees. Butter a 9 x 13-inch casserole dish.

● Cook the rice according to the package directions. Fluff the rice and allow to cool. Stir the sour cream, green onions, salt, chilies, and half of the cheese into the rice. Pour the mixture into the casserole dish. Top with the remaining cheese. Bake for 25 to 30 minutes, until browned and bubbly.

Makes 10 servings.

Lee's first contribution to Third Thursday won our hearts and stomachs. If mac 'n' cheese is the ultimate childhood comfort food, then this crab mac must be the adult version.

CRAB MACARONI AND CHEESE

1 pound penne pasta

2 tablespoons vegetable oil

1 small onion, chopped

1 garlic clove, minced

$1/2$ cup (1 stick) butter, divided

$1/3$ cup all-purpose flour

3 cups milk

12 ounces Gruyere cheese, shredded

8 ounces extra-sharp Cheddar cheese, shredded

$1/2$ teaspoon salt

$1/2$ teaspoon white pepper

$1/4$ teaspoon ground nutmeg

1 to 2 tablespoons sherry

1 pound lump crabmeat

1 ounce grated Pecorino-Romano cheese

$1/2$ cup panko crumbs

❷ Preheat the oven to 350 degrees.

❷ Cook the pasta according to the package directions and drain well. Meanwhile, warm the oil in a large saucepan over medium heat. Add the onions and garlic, and cook until translucent, about 3 minutes. Stir in 6 tablespoons butter. Slowly add the flour and continue stirring. Add the milk, 1 cup at a time, stirring constantly. As the sauce begins to thicken, remove the pan from the heat.

❷ Stir in the Gruyere and extra-sharp Cheddar cheeses, salt, white pepper, nutmeg, and sherry. Fold in the crabmeat, then the pasta. Spoon the mixture into a 9 x 13-inch casserole dish.

❷ Place the remaining 2 tablespoons butter into a medium bowl and melt in the microwave. Mix in the Pecorino-Romano and panko. Sprinkle the panko mixture over the top of the casserole. Bake uncovered for 30 minutes, until the casserole is browned and bubby.

Makes 10 servings.

Lush green spears dressed with this fresh, herbal Green Goddess–inspired sauce bring the best of spring to the table.

BLANCHED CHILLED ASPARAGUS WITH GREEN GODDESS AIOLI

2 bundles young asparagus, washed and woody ends trimmed

3 heads Boston or Bibb lettuce, washed, spun dry, and torn into bite-size pieces

2 green onions, sliced

4 radishes, thinly sliced

Green Goddess Aioli (recipe follows)

◉ Fill a pot or large skillet with water and bring to a boil over high heat. Plunge the asparagus spears into the boiling water and blanch for 2 minutes. Do not overcrowd—you should do this in batches. While the asparagus blanches, fill a large bowl with ice and water. Remove the asparagus from the pot and immediately plunge into the water bath to stop the cooking process and set the bright green color. After 1 minute, remove the asparagus from the bath and pat dry.

◉ Lay out a bed of lettuce leaves onto a large platter. Arrange the asparagus spears, green onions, and radishes in layers. Dollop the Green Goddess Aioli over the spears or serve in a bowl on the side.

Makes 8 to 10 servings.

GREEN GODDESS AIOLI

3 sprigs fresh tarragon

1 bunch fresh parsley

1 bundle fresh chives

2 tablespoons fresh lemon juice

1 tablespoon lemon zest

1 tablespoon white balsamic vinegar

1 teaspoon salt

1 large egg, at room temperature

1 cup extra-virgin olive oil

◉ Strip the leaves off of sprigs of tarragon and pinch off clusters of parsley. Coarsely chop together with the chives. Place all the herbs into the bowl of a food processor fitted with a chopping blade. Add the lemon juice and zest, balsamic vinegar, and salt. Pulse gently for 15 seconds. Add the egg and continue pulsing. With the motor running, pour in the olive oil very slowly. The aioli will become a creamy green, almost as thick as mayonnaise. Taste for salt. Spoon into a bowl. Cover and refrigerate until serving time. This will keep for 3 to 5 days.

Makes 1 1/2 cups.

A real beauty, this cake, worthy of a wedding or significant birthday. Tangy yogurt, vanilla, and almond extract add nuanced taste to the batter.

"MANGO-TANGO" WHITE BUTTER CAKE

THE CAKE (ADAPTED FROM *KING ARTHUR FLOUR*)

5 1/2 cups unbleached cake flour

3 1/3 cups superfine sugar*

2 tablespoons baking powder

1 1/2 teaspoons salt

1 1/2 cups (3 sticks) butter, softened

8 large egg whites

2 whole large eggs

1 cup nonfat Greek yogurt

1 cup heavy cream

4 teaspoons vanilla extract

2 teaspoons almond extract

❯ Preheat the oven to 350 degrees. Grease two 10-inch cake pans and line with parchment paper.

❯ Place the flour into the bowl of an electric mixer. Mix on low speed to aerate. Add the sugar, baking powder, and salt to the flour and mix well. Beat in the butter, then the egg whites, then the whole eggs, scraping the sides well between each addition to build the cake's structure. Continue the process, adding the yogurt, then the heavy cream, then the vanilla and almond extracts.

❯ Pour the batter into the prepared cake pans and bake for 40 to 45 minutes, until a tester inserted in the center of the cake comes out clean. Remove the cake pans from the oven and place on a wire rack to cool in their pans for 12 to 15 minutes. Invert the cakes and remove the pans, allowing the cakes to become completely cool.

❯ You may make the cakes ahead of time; wrap tightly in plastic when cooled, and place into the freezer. The layers will split in half more easily.

Makes one 4-layer cake.

NOTE: Cut the recipe in half to make two 8-inch or 9-inch rounds or one 9 x 13-inch sheet cake.

*If using regular sugar, put it in the food processor fitted with a chopping blade and process for 2 minutes to make the crystals finer.

WHITE ICING

2 cups (4 sticks) butter, softened

2 (8-ounce) packages cream cheese, softened

2 tablespoons vanilla extract (or more to taste)

2 1/2 cups confectioners' sugar

❯ Using an electric mixer, cream the butter in a large bowl. Slowly add pieces of soft cream cheese, creaming it into the butter until smooth. Mix in the vanilla, then the confectioners' sugar. Taste for sweetness and vanilla. This should make enough to ice the 4-layer 10-inch round cake.

continued next page

MANGO FILLING AND GLAZE

1 large, very ripe mango

1 cup water

1 1/2 cups confectioners' sugar

Juice of 1 lemon

◉ Peel the ripe mango and cut into pieces, placing them and the juices into a saucepan over medium heat. Add the water and confectioners' sugar. Stir well and bring to a simmer. Cook until the mango pulp becomes dissolved and incorporated into the liquid. Add the lemon juice. Simmer until somewhat thick and glazy. Remove the pan from the heat, pour the glaze into a bowl, and allow to cool.

ASSEMBLY

◉ Split the cooled cake layers in half. If you have a lazy Susan or a rotating cake stand, place the layer on it. Hold a long serrated bread knife stationary at the midpoint of the cake's side and slowly turn the stand, scoring the perimeter of the cake. Finish slicing through the cake using a gently sawing action horizontally through the layer, with the score as your guide.

◉ Ice the first layer with a thin coating over its top. Spoon some of the mango glaze over the icing and spread to the sides—but leave a 1/2-inch edge. Place the next layer on top and repeat. After you have all four layers filled and stacked, ice the top and sides of the cake.

◉ Using a pastry bag with a star tip, pipe simple border work around the top of the cake, if you like, as well as any other bordering, such as at the cake's base. Spread a layer of mango glaze over the top.

Makes 24 servings.

Sparked with cinnamon and cayenne, this creamy chocolate treat was divine on its own, and a tantalizing complement to the Mango-Tango White Butter Cake.

MEXICAN CHOCOLATE ICE CREAM

6 cups 2% milk

3 cups heavy cream

6 ounces unsweetened chocolate, coarsely chopped

1/2 cup coffee liqueur (such as Kahlua) (optional)

1 1/2 tablespoons vanilla bean paste*

2 cinnamon sticks

1 1/2 cups cocoa

6 large eggs

3 cups sugar

1/2 teaspoon salt

1/2 teaspoon cayenne pepper

❯ Warm the milk and cream in a large saucepan over medium heat. Stir in the chopped unsweetened chocolate, coffee liqueur, vanilla bean paste, cinnamon sticks, and cocoa. Stir well to dissolve the cocoa. Continue stirring and cook until the chocolate is melted and little bubbles form along the edge of the mixture in the pan. Do not let this come to a boil. Remove the pan from the heat and let the cinnamon steep into the mixture. Remove the cinnamon sticks.

❯ In a large bowl beat the eggs and sugar together until well combined. Beat in the salt and cayenne. Slowly pour 1 cup of the hot chocolate mixture into the eggs, whisking constantly. Pour the tempered egg mixture into the large saucepan. Return the pan to medium heat and stir, stir, stir until the mixture begins to thicken. Do not let this come to a boil or the eggs will curdle. Pour the cooked mixture through a strainer into a large bowl.

❯ Cover and refrigerate for a few hours or overnight to chill.** When thoroughly chilled, churn according to the ice-cream maker's directions. Freeze until ready to serve.

Makes 1 gallon.

NOTE: To make 2 quarts follow the recipe using the quantities: 3 cups 2% milk, 1 1/2 cups heavy cream, 3 ounces unsweetened chocolate, 1/4 cup coffee liqueur, 2 teaspoons vanilla paste or extract, 1 cinnamon stick, 3/4 cup cocoa, 3 eggs, 1 1/2 cups sugar, 1/4 teaspoon salt, and 1/4 teaspoon cayenne.

*You can scrape 3 whole vanilla beans instead, or use 1 1/2 tablespoons vanilla extract.

**You can speed this up by first placing the large bowl into an ice-filled container on your kitchen counter. As the outer edges and bottom chill, stir the mixture. Just be sure to chill thoroughly before churning.

The Big Garden Gathering

A METAL SCULPTURE WITH COLORED PLEXIGLAS DISKS TOWERING OVER A MASS OF FLOWERS FIRST grabbed my attention. Driving down an unremarkable stretch of Wedgewood Avenue near the fairgrounds, I made a hasty U-turn to get another look. A once scrappy lot had been transformed, seemingly overnight, into a vibrant green oasis. With art! Curious, I pulled into the driveway and got out to explore.

Before me were pine bark–covered paths that wound through a garden replete with fruit, flower, and vegetable plantings. There was a meditative labyrinth, a spiral of stones lined with perennials in bloom. A concrete bench had been placed beside a fig tree, beckoning a wistful sit. Up the hill, terraced with shade-loving herbs and hostas, a path led to a deck built under and around a great maple tree. On one side, daylilies strained for the sunlight. On the other, a picnic table provided a sheltered place to dine. Cresting the hill was an expanse of wood fencing that enclosed a plowed field.

Alone, I strolled these paths, pausing every few moments to admire the plantings. At every turn, there was something surprising. Ruby stalks of rhubarb. Rosemary, big as hedges. Strawberries trundling out of soil-filled tires embedded in the hillside. I wondered, *Who's behind this effort?*

In the months to come, I befriended Gigi, and learned the answer.

Concerned about sustainability in a world of depleting resources, Gigi had been looking at run-down urban properties to transform into a working farm. When she found two side-by-side homes for sale, with backyards that stretched out like open fields, she caught the vision. *I can farm here.*

She purchased both. Soon after, she bought the tract below that fronted Wedgewood Avenue. At almost two contiguous acres, Wedgewood Urban Gardens was born.

It was an ambitious undertaking whose plan was conceived in an hour and took many seasons to unfold. During the first year, she created an accessible garden for the community on the lower tract. Landscaped with fruit trees and perennial herbs, its style melded permaculture and art with areas devoted to seasonal veggies. In 2008, she expanded to the upper acreage, planting half of it that year and its entirety the following.

By mid-2010, the garden, from top to bottom, was an Eden. There were vast rows of tomatoes, beets, fennel, beans, and kale, all flourishing. Asparagus beds produced a thicket of

luscious spears. Yellow crooknecks and zucchinis competed for ground space while other heirloom squashes made crazy loops over the fence. Her crop of American black raspberries, which had somehow escaped the birds' notice, was spectacular in yield.

After gathering in our homes for a year, it was time for Third Thursday to come to the garden.

Unlike our homebound potlucks, this grand venue would require more planning. I put on my catering hat and met Gigi under the great maple tree to talk logistics and menu.

"We'll set up the buffet on the deck," Gigi said, pointing to the stretch of railing facing the lower garden, "and a beverage station in the gazebo."

I agreed. "This will be big. We'll need another table by the buffet for plates and flatware."

Providing enough seating was another consideration. Already there were two long picnic tables with benches. Gigi had three round tables in her basement and a smattering of folding chairs. "One more picnic table should do the trick," she said. "I'll hire my carpenter Barron to build it."

Garden assistants Stacy and Austin had a punch list, areas to weed and mulch. And there was the movie screen to assemble. Gigi had two poles anchored at the base of a grassy slope where a screen would be stretched for outdoor viewing. She planned to show a segment from the *Planet Earth* series.

We determined sunset time for our date was a few minutes after 8 p.m. and decided where to string twinkle lights and place candle pillars. Then, to the heart of the matter: the food.

The raspberry surplus played the lead in forming our menu. I envisioned a stacked salad—layers of roasted beets, lettuces, berries, and goat cheese, napped in tangy black raspberry vinaigrette. Those jammy bramble fruits would play nicely off the earthy sweetness of the beets.

Gigi elevated the game, suggesting grilled chicken with a black raspberry barbecue sauce. Ingenious! It was proof again of why we made a good team. "I can't execute like you," she said, "but I have good ideas." And we had berries galore to make 'em all.

For this third Thursday of June, the meteorologists had forecast an erratic day: sunny with a threat of scattered showers and isolated thunderstorms developing in the afternoon. "Scattered and isolated" leaves a lot of room for doubt, but the morning was so sun-filled that we couldn't help but feel optimistic. We hauled our crates of china and glassware up to the deck. We draped the buffet tables and set up the beverage stations.

At noon, ominous clouds hovered over the garden. "Rogues!" I said, looking out at blue sky just blocks away. We scrambled to put the china and glassware into the back of Gigi's SUV just as they rumbled. Lightning flashed, followed by ten minutes of heavy downpour. An hour later there was no evidence of rain at all.

I began grilling the chicken in mid-afternoon, figuring it could take over an hour to cook the fifteen pounds of boneless breasts and thighs that were marinating in my fridge. I'd brush the pieces with my black raspberry barbecue sauce as they came off the grill.

The afternoon heated up, but we didn't mind. Being in the garden, we were content and engaged in our tasks. Time and the cares of everyday living seemed to fall away. Austin mowed the grassy slope. Stacy weeded and mulched. Gigi strung lights across the fencing while I presided over the barbecue.

At 5 p.m., the skies darkened again. Only these weren't isolated "rogue" rain clouds. They enveloped the city in gloom. And then began spitting rain.

"Here we go again!" Gigi shouted.

We rolled up the tablecloths and threw plastic tarps over baskets of silverware. Winds whipped up as the rain became hard and steady. We raced around, tipping chairs and benches on their sides. Once more, Gigi and I hoisted the crates of dinner plates and glassware into the back of her car, now the catering mobile.

The promise of our garden fete was becoming rain-soaked. My thoughts, as I rushed home to prepare for our fallback plan: *Keystone Kops Caterers . . .*

And, *Please, storm, don't last.*

Gigi sent out e-mails, even posted on her Facebook page: "If it's not raining at 6:30, come to the garden. Otherwise, go to Nancy's."

A little while later, Rick, our unofficial radar monitor, sent us a text: "Checked 3 reports. System moving out. All clear."

I loaded up my salad, barbecued chicken, and stack of towels and sped back to the garden.

Shortly after six, the front had moved on, forming a distant gray line as the sun boldly shone. Fleecy clouds stretched across the sky, now brilliant blue. What could have been a muggy evening—another summer night in Nashville—was replaced by cooler air, washed clean by the storm.

Within the next hour, fifty people arrived at the Wedgewood Urban Gardens. They came laden with salads and casseroles, cakes and tarts, and abundant good cheer. They poured glasses of peach sangria and herbed lemonade. They strolled and sipped and marveled. Some walked the labyrinth. Others ambled through the upper acreage, admiring the tangles of scarlet runner beans, the curious kiwi tree, and the chicken coop, still a work in progress. Children played hide-and-seek between rows of beans and tomatoes.

Meanwhile, the harvest tabletop became hidden under the bounty of beautiful food. I kept shifting plates and bowls to make enough space. As dusk approached, Gigi and I called everyone to the buffet under that grand maple tree. We thanked them for coming out on this now-magical night.

Filled plates in hands, people found their places at the stagger of tables throughout the garden. Some claimed cushy spots on quilts spread upon the grassy slope. Giggly kids chased fireflies in front of the movie screen, their shadows dancing over the film projecting silent, sweeping migrations of animals. The drone of traffic on the nearby highway faded as garden sounds came to the fore: the clicks and chirps of summer insects, the rustle of breezes through the lilies, the murmurs and laughter of our community as we feasted in the comfort of nature's dining room. The evening rotated into nightfall, a Milky Way sky spread over our little pastoral enclave in the city.

————

And what is so rare as a day in June?
Then, if ever, come perfect days;
Then Heaven tries the earth if it be in tune,
And over it softly her warm ear lays:
Whether we look, or whether we listen,
We hear life murmur, or see it glisten;
Every clod feels a stir of might,
An instinct within it that reaches and towers,
And, grasping blindly above it for light,
Climbs to a soul in grass and flowers.

From *The Vision of Sir Launfal*, prelude to pt. I, st. 5
James Russell Lowell, 1848

JUNE: THE BIG GARDEN GATHERING

Summer Peach Sangria

Sun-Dried Tomatoes Orecciette Salad

Watermelon Margarita Wedges

Black Raspberry Barbecue Chicken

Cuban Grilled Corn

Stacked Black Raspberry and Beet Salad

Lemon Cucumber Salad with Lemon and Red Wine Vinaigrette

Summer Crop Circle Salad

Cast-Iron Skillet Roasted Rat-a-Tat Stack

Green Beans and New Potatoes in Mustard Cream

Cherry and Peach Clafoutis

Joy's Petite Shortcakes with Blueberries and Whipped Cream

Rockhill's Rocky Road Ice Cream

Me-Me's Chocolate Sheet Cake

Showing off the colors of summer, white sangrias are as visually appealing as they are refreshing. You can make up the mixture—minus the sparkling water—the night before to allow the fruits to really macerate in the wine.

SUMMER PEACH SANGRIA

4 to 5 ripe peaches, peeled, pitted, and diced

1 pint blackberries, rinsed

Juice of 2 limes

Juice of 2 lemons

1.5 liters dry white wine, chilled

1 cup peach liqueur (such as Mathilde)

Several sprigs of fresh mint

1 liter sparkling water (such as Perrier)

Ice

> Place the peaches and blackberries in a large bowl. Pour in the lemon and lime juice, and then add the white wine and peach liqueur. Gently stir. Add a sprig or two of mint.

> When ready to serve, scoop out 3 cups of the fruity mixture into a quart-size pitcher. Top with sparkling water. Garnish with mint sprigs. Fill your glasses of choice with ice and pour.

Makes 3 quarts.

Whitney makes this sunny, Mediterranean-inspired pasta salad with orecchiette—a pasta whose name means "little ears." Their curved shape naturally captures the flavorful pesto dressing.

SUN-DRIED TOMATOES ORECCHIETTE SALAD

1 pound orecchiette pasta, cooked al dente according to package directions, drained, and cooled

1/2 cup sun-dried tomatoes packed in oil, drained and cut into slivers

1 pint cherry or grape tomatoes, cleaned and cut in half

1/2 pound Fontina cheese, cut into small cubes

1/3 cup pesto

1/4 cup olive oil

3 tablespoons white balsamic vinegar

Juice of 1 lemon

2 garlic cloves, minced

1 tablespoon minced fresh rosemary

1 tablespoon minced fresh thyme

1 tablespoon minced fresh oregano

1 1/2 teaspoons Greek seasoning salt (such as Cavender's or McCormick's)

1/2 teaspoon kosher salt

1 teaspoon freshly ground black pepper

4 cups fresh baby spinach

◔ In a large salad bowl toss the pasta with the sun-dried tomatoes, fresh tomatoes, and cheese. In a small bowl whisk together the pesto, olive oil, balsamic vinegar, lemon juice, garlic, rosemary, thyme, oregano, seasoning salt, salt, and pepper. Pour the pesto mixture over the pasta mixture and toss well to coat. Fold in the fresh spinach right before serving.

Makes 15 servings.

Whitney made these clever appetizers that impart a puckery margarita-style bite. Some of the alcohol vanishes when simmering the tequila-infused simple syrup, but that distinctive taste remains.

WATERMELON MARGARITA WEDGES

1/2 cup good white tequila (such as Tito's or Patron)

1 cup sugar

1/4 cup water

Juice of 2 limes

Seedless ripe watermelon, cut into wedges

Lime slices for garnish

Mint leaves for garnish

Kosher salt for garnish

● In a small saucepan bring the tequila, sugar, and water to a boil over high heat. Reduce the temperature to low and cook until it is reduced to 1 cup. This could take 10 to 12 minutes. Let the syrup cool and stir in the fresh lime juice.

● On a large platter, arrange the watermelon wedges. Pierce the flesh with a fork in several places. Brush or drizzle the cooled syrup over the wedges. Cover and refrigerate, allowing the syrup to soak in for at least 1 hour before serving, or overnight.

● When serving, garnish with lime slices and mint. Serve with a small bowl of kosher salt for sprinkling.

Makes 20 to 24 servings.

You can make this tangy fruit barbecue sauce with whatever raspberries you can find; I had Gigi's outstanding crop of American black raspberries for the sauce. I also marinated and grilled boneless chicken cuts, but you could certainly use an assortment of wings, drumsticks, breasts, and thighs.

BLACK RASPBERRY BARBECUED CHICKEN

1 1/2 cups olive oil

1/4 cup coarse-grain mustard

1 tablespoon granulated garlic

1/3 cup raspberry vinegar

1 teaspoon sea salt

1 teaspoon coarse ground black pepper

6 pounds boneless chicken breasts, washed

6 pounds boneless, skinless chicken thighs, washed

Black Raspberry Barbecue Sauce (recipe follows)

❯ Whisk the oil, mustard, garlic, raspberry vinegar, salt, and pepper together in a large bowl. Dip chicken into the marinade and place pieces into zip-top bags. Seal and refrigerate overnight.

❯ Prepare the grill. A clean and oiled grate prevents sticking. When the coals in a charcoal grill are ashen (which can take 25 to 30 minutes to achieve) or the gas grill is heated to medium-high (375 to 425 degrees), remove the chicken pieces from the marinade and shake the excess marinade off. Lay the chicken pieces out on the grill. Do not crowd them. Cook the boneless chicken thighs approximately 7 minutes per side over direct heat. Depending on the thickness, boneless breasts may take 5 to 6 minutes per side.*

❯ Insert a meat thermometer into the thickest part of the chicken. Remove the chicken from the grill when the internal temperature reaches 160 degrees. The chicken will continue to cook once it is removed from the grill. Once it reaches 165 degrees, it is safe to eat. As you remove the charred pieces from the grill, place them in a long baking pan (like an aluminum roaster or a stainless-steel hotel pan) and brush them with the Black Raspberry Barbecue Sauce.

❯ Cover and keep warm in a 200-degree oven until serving time. If you are making the chicken hours in advance, cover and allow to cool before refrigerating. Gently rewarm the chicken in a 200-degree oven for 30 minutes before serving time.

Makes 36 to 40 servings.

*Depending on the size of your grill, a large batch of chicken like this can take more than an hour to cook.

BLACK RASPBERRY BARBECUE SAUCE

1 tablespoon vegetable oil

1/4 cup diced onion

2 garlic cloves, minced

4 pints raspberries

1 cup firmly packed brown sugar

1/2 cup raspberry vinegar

1/4 cup water

1 tablespoon Worcestershire sauce

2 teaspoons dry mustard

1 1/2 teaspoons ground allspice

1 teaspoon salt

1 teaspoon Sriracha sauce

1 teaspoon red pepper flakes

- Warm the oil in a large saucepan over medium heat. Add the onions and garlic and cook until softened, about 3 minutes. Stir in the raspberries, brown sugar, raspberry vinegar, and water. Cover and reduce the heat to medium-low, stirring occasionally as the raspberries release their juices.

- Stir in the Worcestershire, dry mustard, allspice, salt, Sriracha sauce, and red pepper flakes. Continue simmering, uncovered, stirring occasionally.

- You can strain this sauce if you want it smooth, but we like it somewhat chunky. You can make this ahead of time and store it in jars in the refrigerator. It should keep at least a month.

Makes 8 cups.

This recipe is based on the popular street food found in Mexico and Cuba: corn is chargrilled and slathered with chili-sparked mayo, rolled in Cotija cheese, and spritzed with lime juice. It will give you a new answer to the question, what's the best way to eat summer corn? Break the cobs into halves (or thirds, if they are large) to feed a potluck crowd.

CUBAN GRILLED CORN

12 ears fresh corn on the cob

1 1/2 cups mayonnaise

2 tablespoons chili powder

1 teaspoon cayenne pepper

1/2 teaspoon sea salt

4 limes, divided

1 1/2 cups grated Cotija cheese*

❷ Prepare your grill. If using a gas grill, bring the temperature to 350 degrees.

❷ Peel back the husks and remove the silks. Do not remove the husks. Rinse the corn and loosely pull the husks back over the cobs. Place the corn on a hot grill and cover with lid. Grill for 5 minutes and turn the cobs a quarter rotation. Cover and continue grilling for another 5 minutes. Rotate again and cover and repeat.

❷ Place the mayonnaise, chili powder, cayenne, salt, and the juice from 2 limes in a medium bowl and whisk until well combined.

❷ Remove the corn from the grill. Peel the husks from the corn and discard. Brush each ear with 2 tablespoons of the seasoned mayonnaise and sprinkle each with about 2 tablespoons of the cheese. Cut the 2 remaining limes into wedges and serve with the corn. Squeeze the lime onto the corn right before you bite in.

Makes 12 full-size ears or 24 half-cob servings.

*Substitute grated Parmesan if you can't find Cotija.

Use a clear glass bowl or a pedestal trifle bowl to display the layers of this gorgeous salad. Beets and berries are delicious together; each has a different sort of sweetness.

STACKED BLACK RASPBERRY AND BEET SALAD

1/2 pound mixed salad greens or frisée, divided

6 beets, roasted and sliced, divided

6 ounces goat cheese, sliced and crumbled, divided

2 pints fresh raspberries, divided

Black Raspberry Vinaigrette (recipe follows)

◗ Place half of the salad greens in the bottom of a clear glass bowl. Layer half of the beet slices in a circle on top of the greens. Sprinkle with half of the goat cheese, then with half of the raspberries. Drizzle with the Black Raspberry Vinaigrette. Repeat the stack, finishing with the vinaigrette.

Makes 8 to 10 servings.

A lush vinaigrette for our stacked berry-beet salad that we imagine would be delicious spooned over vanilla ice cream too.

BLACK RASPBERRY VINAIGRETTE

1 cup black or red raspberries

3 tablespoons sugar

3 tablespoons red wine vinegar

4 tablespoons balsamic vinegar

1/4 teaspoon salt

A few grindings fresh black pepper

1 cup extra-virgin olive oil

◗ Place the raspberries and sugar in a saucepan over medium heat. Gently cook, stirring occasionally, until the berries release their juices and the sugar dissolves. Remove the pan from the heat. Allow to cool.

◗ Pour the raspberry mixture into a food processor fitted with a chopping blade. Add the vinegars, salt, and pepper. Pulse together. With the motor running, drizzle in the olive oil until the mixture is thickened and emulsified. Taste and adjust for sweetness, acid, salt, and pepper.

Makes 2 1/2 cups.

Be on the lookout at the farmers' market for these curious round cukes, with their evocative lemon shape and color. They don't taste like lemons, but possess a sweetness that you won't find in your common green cucumber.

LEMON CUCUMBER SALAD WITH LEMON AND RED WINE VINAIGRETTE

8 lemon cucumbers

Lemon and Red Wine Vinaigrette (recipe follows)

1/2 cup ricotta salata, shaved or crumbled*

1/4 cup pine nuts, toasted

⊙ Cut the cucumbers into thin wedges (almost as you would cut a lemon). Arrange the wedges along the length of a platter. Pour the Lemon and Red Wine Vinaigrette over the wedges. Sprinkle the cheese and toasted pine nuts over the top and serve.

Makes 10 to 12 servings.

*You can substitute another dry-salty cheese, such as Cotija, Pecorino-Romano, or mizithra.

LEMON AND RED WINE VINAIGRETTE

1 garlic clove, minced

2 green onions, chopped

2 tablespoons chopped fresh flat-leaf parsley

3 tablespoons fresh lemon juice

1 teaspoon lemon zest

3 tablespoons red wine vinegar

1 teaspoon dry mustard

1/2 teaspoon salt

1/2 teaspoon black pepper

1 cup olive oil

⊙ Place the garlic, green onions, parsley, lemon juice, lemon zest, red wine vinegar, dry mustard, salt, and pepper into a food processor fitted with the chopping blade. Pulse to chop and mix the ingredients for a minute. With the motor running, slowly add the olive oil. The mixture will become emulsified.

Summer fruits and herbs arranged in concentric rings around a mound of bulgur wheat reminded Teresa of crop circles. Her colorful choices bring savory-sweet flavors to the hearty grain.

SUMMER CROP CIRCLE SALAD

2 cups bulgur wheat

2 teaspoons salt

3 cups boiling water

3 peaches, peeled and cut into large dice

1 pint strawberries, washed and hulled

1 bunch green onions, chopped (white and green parts)

1 red bell pepper, finely diced

2 jalapeño peppers, minced

1/4 cup mint, coarsely chopped

1/4 cup cilantro, coarsely chopped

1/4 cup fresh flat-leaf parsley, coarsely chopped

1 cup olive oil

1/3 cup white balsamic vinegar

2 tablespoons local honey

2 teaspoons herbs de Provence

1/2 teaspoon sea salt

1/4 teaspoon black pepper

❯ Place the bulgur wheat and salt into a large bowl. Stir in the boiling water. Seal with plastic wrap and let the mixture sit undisturbed for 20 minutes. Remove the plastic wrap, fluff the bulgur wheat, and allow it to cool. Mound the bulgur in the middle of a large round serving dish.

❯ Arrange radiating circles of ingredients around the bulgur wheat, starting from the outer edge: first peaches, then strawberries, then green onions, then bell pepper, then jalapeños. Sprinkle the mint over the strawberries and peaches, and the cilantro and parsley over the onions and peppers. Cover and refrigerate until serving time.

❯ Place the olive oil, balsamic vinegar, honey, herbs de Provence, salt, and black pepper into a lidded jar. Seal and shake vigorously.

❯ When ready to serve, remove the salad from the refrigerator. Shake and drizzle the dressing over the "crop circles" and serve.

Makes 10 to 12 servings.

There are many good ways to prepare Ratatouille, popular in summer for using all those garden veggies that ripen at the same time. Everyone especially likes the roasting and layering in this unique version.

CAST-IRON SKILLET ROASTED RAT-A-TAT STACK

Olive oil

2 medium-large eggplants

Salt to taste

Black pepper to taste

2 medium-large zucchinis

4 tomatoes,* cored and sliced in half

1 large onion, sliced lengthwise into 1/2-inch strips

4 garlic cloves

2 red bell peppers, cut into halves and seeded

Pinch of red pepper flakes (optional)

A few sprigs fresh basil

❯ Preheat the oven to 425 degrees. Lightly oil 3 baking sheets.

❯ Slice the eggplants into 1/4-inch thick lengthwise slices and lay them out flat on one of the baking sheets. Brush with olive oil and sprinkle with salt and pepper. Slice the zucchinis in similar fashion and lay out on the second baking sheet. Brush with olive oil and season with salt and pepper. Place the tomato halves on the third baking sheet. Add the onion, garlic, and seeded bell pepper halves.

❯ Roast the vegetables until the edges of the eggplants and zucchinis are browned and the skins of the tomatoes and peppers are blistered, 15 to 20 minutes. Check the pans halfway through roasting time and rotate.

❯ Lower the oven temperature to 325 degrees. Remove the skins from the tomatoes, peppers, and garlic. Coarsely chop 2 of the roasted tomato halves with the garlic. Season with some red pepper flakes, if you like.

❯ Brush the bottom of a cast-iron skillet with olive oil and layer half of the roasted vegetables in a circular design in this order: chopped tomatoes with garlic, sliced eggplants, sliced zucchinis, onions, basil leaves, and bell peppers. Repeat the layering with the remaining vegetables in similar fashion. Bake for 20 minutes.

Makes 10 servings.

*Try 2 yellow and 2 red, with a smattering of Roma and cherry tomatoes.

Fresh green beans and new potatoes are delicious tumbled together, especially when drizzled with this piquant mustard sauce.

GREEN BEANS AND NEW POTATOES IN MUSTARD CREAM

1 garlic clove, sliced

1/2 teaspoon salt

2 pounds fresh green beans, ends trimmed and snapped in half

1 tablespoon butter

1 shallot, diced

1 heaping tablespoon all-purpose flour

2 cups half-and-half

2 tablespoons Dijon mustard

1 tablespoon coarse-grain mustard

1/2 teaspoon salt

1/4 teaspoon black pepper

2 pounds small new potatoes

2 to 3 tablespoons chopped fresh tarragon (optional)

❷ Fill a large skillet about two-thirds full of water over medium-high heat. Add the sliced garlic and salt. Bring to a boil.

❷ Plunge the green beans in batches, taking care not to crowd them, into the boiling water. Cook until crisp-tender. Very thin green beans, like haricots verts, will take 2 minutes. Other beans, such as Kentucky Wonders, will take longer, up to 5 minutes. Drain the green beans and place into a large bowl. Set aside.

❷ Dump the water and garlic, and use the same skillet to make the mustard cream. Melt the butter over medium heat. Add the shallots and sauté until translucent, about 2 to 3 minutes. Stir in the flour and stir to create a light roux. Pour in the half-and-half and stir well. While continuing to stir, add the Dijon and coarse-grain mustard. Season with salt and pepper. Simmer and stir, allowing the sauce to thicken. This will take several minutes. Taste for seasoning and adjust as needed.

❷ Cook the new potatoes in a pot of lightly salted boiling water until they are tender when pierced with a knife tip. This could take 7 to 10 minutes, depending on the size of the new potatoes. Drain. Slice the larger potatoes. Toss with the green beans and mound into a serving bowl. Spoon the warm mustard cream over the vegetables. Garnish with chopped fresh tarragon leaves, if you like. Serve at once.

Makes 8 to 10 servings.

A clafoutis is a rustic French dessert that melds custard, cobbler, and cake. It possesses elements of all three, and yet is completely different. Originally it was made with fresh cherries, but it loves all kinds of fruit. Joseph pairs summer peaches and cherries in his version.

CHERRY AND PEACH CLAFOUTIS

1 tablespoon butter, softened

1 1/2 cups pitted sweet cherries (such as Rainers or Bings)

1 1/2 cups sliced peaches (such as Freestones)

4 large eggs

1/2 cup all-purpose flour

1/2 cup sugar

1 cup whole milk

1/2 cup heavy cream

1 1/2 teaspoons vanilla extract

1/2 teaspoon almond extract

1/4 cup confectioners' sugar

❯ Preheat the oven to 350 degrees. Coat the bottom and sides of a 6-cup casserole dish* with softened butter. Place the cherries and peaches in the casserole dish.

❯ Using an electric mixer with a whisk attachment, beat the eggs, flour, and sugar together.

❯ With the motor running, slowly pour in the milk, heavy cream, and vanilla and almond extracts. Beat until the batter is smooth. Pour the batter over the fruits in the casserole dish.

❯ Bake on the middle rack for 1 hour and 15 minutes, until the top is golden and the custardy batter feels set. Spoon the confectioners' sugar into a strainer and tap it over the clafoutis, showering the warm dessert. Serve immediately.

Makes 8 servings.

*You can also use a springform pan.

Gigi and I fell in love with these at a potluck before we even tasted them. Joy's presentation—a basket of petite cream-brushed shortcakes, a Mason jar of gently cooked freshly picked blueberries, and a small bowl of whipped cream—drew us right in.

JOY'S PETITE SHORTCAKES WITH BLUEBERRIES AND WHIPPED CREAM

SHORTCAKES

2 cups all-purpose flour

2 tablespoons sugar, plus additional for biscuit tops

1 tablespoon baking powder

1 teaspoon salt

3/4 to 1 cup heavy cream, plus additional for brushing on biscuit tops

❯ Preheat the oven to 425 degrees. Line a baking sheet with parchment paper.

❯ Sift the flour, sugar, baking powder, and salt into a large bowl. Add the heavy cream to moisten. Turn the dough out onto a lightly floured surface and pat out very gently until about 3/4 inch thick. Cut the dough with a round 2-inch cookie cutter without twisting. Place on the baking sheet, and then brush each biscuit top with cream and sprinkle with sugar. Bake 15 to 18 minutes, until golden brown. Remove and allow to cool on a wire rack. You may store these in an airtight container if you are making these in advance.

BLUEBERRIES IN SYRUP

4 cups fresh blueberries, divided

1/2 cup water

1/2 cup sugar

1 teaspoon fresh lemon juice

1/2 teaspoon lemon zest

Pinch of salt

❯ Place 2 cups of the blueberries, water, and sugar in a medium saucepan over high heat. Bring to a boil, and then reduce the heat to low. Simmer until the blueberries start to split. Remove the pan from the heat and stir in the remaining 2 cups blueberries, lemon juice, lemon zest, and salt. Let cool.

WHIPPED CREAM

1 pint heavy cream

1 teaspoon vanilla extract

2 tablespoons confectioners' sugar

❯ Place the cream into a chilled medium bowl. Add the vanilla and confectioners' sugar. Whip the cream until soft peaks form.

ASSEMBLE

Split the shortcakes in half and top with the blueberry syrup and lightly sweetened whipped cream.

Makes 16 to 20 shortcakes.

Rick adapted David Lebovitz's recipe, lightening it with half-and-half instead of heavy cream and expanding it to create his own rockin' Rocky Road for a crowd. It's rich and full of terrific rocky textures and tastes.

ROCKHILL'S ROCKY ROAD ICE CREAM

8 cups half-and-half, divided

4 cups whole milk

3 cups sugar

1/2 teaspoon kosher salt

20 large egg yolks

1 pound bittersweet chocolate, chopped

1 cup Dutch cocoa

1 cup brewed coffee

1 1/2 cups mini marshmallows

1 1/2 cups slivered almonds

1 1/2 cups semisweet chocolate shavings and chunks

1 1/2 cups unsweetened organic coconut flakes

> Fill a very large bowl with several inches of ice water (mostly ice). Set another, slightly smaller bowl in the bath. Pour in 4 cups of half-and-half.

> Pour the remaining 4 cups of half-and-half, milk, sugar, and salt into a large saucepan over medium-high heat. Stir well, dissolving the sugar, and heat the mixture for about 5 minutes. Remove the pan from the heat when little bubbles form around the edge.

> Beat the egg yolks in a large bowl. Slowly pour in about half of the warm milk mixture while constantly whisking to temper the egg yolks. Pour this back into the large saucepan to finish making the custard.

> Lower the heat to low and return the saucepan to the stovetop. Cook, stirring constantly, scraping the bottom and sides of the pan, about 8 minutes—take care not to let this overcook, boil, or curdle. When the custard is thick enough to coat the back of the spoon, remove the pan from the heat.

> Place the chocolate, cocoa, and coffee in a heavy-duty pot or saucepan over medium-low heat. Melt them together, stirring occasionally, until the mixture is smooth. Remove the pan from the heat. Strain the custard into the bowl of chilled half-and-half as it rests in the icy bath. Whisk in the melted chocolate mixture. Allow the mixture to cool to at least room temperature, stirring over the icy bath.

> Cover and chill thoroughly in the refrigerator. Chill overnight, if you like, and then churn in your ice-cream maker according to the manufacturer's directions. When the ice cream is almost finished churning, fold in the mini marshmallows, almonds,

chocolate chunks and shavings, and coconut flakes. Freeze in an airtight container for a few hours or serve soft immediately.

Makes 1 gallon.

NOTE: To make 2 quarts follow the method, using this quantity of ingredients: 4 cups half-and-half (divided), 2 cups whole milk, 1 1/2 cups sugar, 1/4 teaspoon kosher salt, 10 large egg yolks, 8 ounces bittersweet chocolate, 1/2 cup Dutch cocoa, 1/2 cup brewed coffee, 3/4 cup each: mini marshmallows, slivered almonds, semisweet chocolate shavings, and coconut flakes.

A very old recipe made anew. Joy's grandmother Me-Me authored the original for this lush chocolate sheet cake; Joy updated it with coconut palm sugar, white whole wheat flour, and organic coconut oil. While the cake still retains its homespun goodness, Joy's touches enhance the taste. Me-Me would be proud.

ME-ME'S CHOCOLATE SHEET CAKE

1 cup sugar

1 cup coconut palm sugar*

1 cup all-purpose flour

1 cup white whole wheat flour**

3/4 teaspoon kosher salt

1/2 cup (1 stick) butter

1/2 cup organic coconut oil

4 tablespoons cocoa (such as Pernigotti)

1 cup water

2 large eggs, slightly beaten

1/2 cup buttermilk

1 teaspoon baking soda

1 teaspoon vanilla extract

⊙ Preheat the oven to 375 degrees.

⊙ Mix together the sugars, flours, and salt in large bowl. Place the butter, coconut oil, cocoa, and water in a medium saucepan. Bring to a boil over high heat, and then remove from the heat and let cool slightly. Pour the cocoa mixture over the flour mixture. Mix until well blended. Add the eggs, buttermilk, baking soda, and vanilla and whisk to combine. The batter will be thin.

⊙ Pour the batter into a 9 x 13-inch pan and bake for 30 to 35 minutes. Remove from oven and cool on a wire rack before icing.

CHOCOLATE ICING

6 tablespoons butter

4 tablespoons cocoa, sifted

Pinch of salt

6 tablespoons whipping cream

1 teaspoon vanilla extract

1 1/2 cups confectioners' sugar, sifted

⊙ Melt the butter in a small saucepan over low heat and remove the pan from the heat. Whisk in the cocoa, salt, whipping cream, and vanilla. Whisk in the confectioners' sugar until smooth and pour over the cooled cake.

Makes 12 to 15 servings.

*You may substitute raw sugar, such as turbinado.

**You may use all-purpose flour entirely instead of the white whole wheat flour.

•

Epilogue

IN 2011, AFTER FOUR YEARS OF COMPOSTING, AMENDING, TILLING, SOWING, WEEDING, WATERING, nurturing, and harvesting, Gigi stepped back from her role as an urban farmer. Health reasons prompted the change.

"I learned a lot about farming and a lot about myself," she said. "Such hard work! It's given me enormous respect for farmers. They are my heroes."

But her Wedgewood Urban Gardens continue to cultivate good. Gigi formed a relationship with the Nashville Food Project, which has since been growing fruits and vegetables there for the homeless and underserved in our community.

And potluck? Our Third Thursday gatherings—what we're growing, cooking, eating, advocating—carry on. If you happen to be around, c'mon by.

Index

Contributors

Allison Polidor

Amy Kurland

Brian Duke

Caroline Duley

Caroline Trost

Cathey Grossman

Diane Stopford

Gigi Gaskins

Jay Nair

Jesse Hoeft

Jim Stephens

John Egerton

John Shenk

Joseph Kirkland

Joy Martin

Karen George

Kathleen Cotter

Kim Wright

Kristina Krug

Lee Greenberg

Leisa Hammett

Linda Politte

Liz Shenk

Maggie Stanford

Mark Rubin

Marla Lepore

Nancy Davidson

Nancy Vienneau

Paulette Licitra

Rhonda Hamilton

Rhonda White

Rick Rockhill

Susan Turner

Teresa Blackburn

Val Strain

Wendy Zerface

Whitney Kemp

Resources

C. S. STEEN'S SYRUP MILL, INC.

P.O. Box 339/119 North Main Street
Abbeville, LA 70510
1-800-725-1654
www.steensyrup.com

FALLS MILL

134 Falls Mill Road
Belvidere, TN 37306
931-469-7161
www.fallsmill.com

WOODS CIDER MILL

Willis and Tina Wood
1482 Weathersfield Center Road
Springfield, VT 05156
802-263-5547
www.woodscidermill.com

BENTON'S SMOKY MOUNTAIN COUNTRY HAMS

2603 Highway 411 North
Madisonville, Tennessee 37354
423-442-5003
www.bentonscountryhams2.com

CRUZE DAIRY FARM

3200 Frazier Road
Knoxville, TN 37914
865-363-0631
www.CruzeFarmGirl.com

SWEET GRASS DAIRY

19635 US Highway 19N
Thomasville, GA 31792
229-227-0752
www.sweetgrassdairy.com

KENNY'S FARMHOUSE CHEESES

2033 Thomerson Park Road
Austin, KY 42123
888-571-4029
www.kennyscountrycheese.com

NOBLE SPRINGS DAIRY

Dustin and Justyne Noble
3144 Blazer Road
Franklin, TN 37064
615-481-9546
www.noble-springs.com

BONNIE BLUE FARM

Jim and Gayle Tanner
Waynesboro, TN
931-722-4628
www.bonniebluefarm.com

SEQUATCHIE COVE FARM AND CREAMERY

320 Dixon Cove Road
Sequatchie, TN 37374
423-619-5867
www.sequatchiecovefarm.com

THE PEACH TRUCK/PEARSON FAMILY FARM

Stephen and Jessica Rose
615-249-8856
www.thepeachtruck.com

PEARSON FARM

5575 Zenith Mill Road
Crawford, GA 31030
478-827-0750
www.pearsonfarm.com

THE BLOOMY RIND

Kathleen Cotter
501 Gallatin Avenue
Nashville, TN 37206
615-650-4440
www.thebloomyrind.blogspot.com

About the Author

Nancy Vienneau is a "recovered" caterer turned food writer and activist living in Nashville, Tennessee. She began cooking professionally in 1980. Twenty-five years and ten thousand cream cheese brownies later, she sold her catering company. Now she works in her community, promoting local farmers, urban gardens, healthy affordable cooking, and food security. While Third Thursdays are devoted to potluck, most Fridays you'll find her cooking at Second Harvest Food Bank.

Food is at the heart of her stories and poetry. Her work appears in *Alimentum: The Literature of Food*, *Relish Magazine*, *Nashville Arts Magazine*, her weekly restaurant column for the *Tennessean*, and her globally read blog, *Good Food Matters*.